God in Post-Christianity

SUNY series in Theology and Continental Thought
―――――――
Douglas L. Donkel, editor

God in Post-Christianity
An Elemental Philosophical Theology

Lenart Škof

Cover Credit: "Saltements," from the series *Elartemis#Saltemental* by Maja Bjelica

Published by State University of New York Press, Albany

© 2024 State University of New York

All rights reserved

Printed in the United States of America

No part of this book may be used or reproduced in any manner whatsoever without written permission. No part of this book may be stored in a retrieval system or transmitted in any form or by any means including electronic, electrostatic, magnetic tape, mechanical, photocopying, recording, or otherwise without the prior permission in writing of the publisher.

Links to third-party websites are provided as a convenience and for informational purposes only. They do not constitute an endorsement or an approval of any of the products, services, or opinions of the organization, companies, or individuals. SUNY Press bears no responsibility for the accuracy, legality, or content of a URL, the external website, or for that of subsequent websites.

For information, contact State University of New York Press, Albany, NY
www.sunypress.edu

Library of Congress Cataloging-in-Publication Data

Name: Škof, Lenart, 1972– author.
Title: God in post-Christianity : an elemental philosophical theology / Lenart Škof.
Description: Albany : State University of New York Press, [2024] | Series: SUNY series in theology and continental thought | Includes bibliographical references and index.
Identifiers: LCCN 2024012378 | ISBN 9798855800098 (hardcover : alk. paper) | ISBN 9798855800104 (ebook) | ISBN 9798855800081 (pbk. : alk. paper)
Subjects: LCSH: God (Christianity) | Faith. | Christianity.
Classification: LCC BT103 .S55 2024 | DDC 231—dc23/eng/20240807
LC record available at https://lccn.loc.gov/2024012378

*Dedicated to the Amalricians
and their spiritual heirs*

Contents

List of Illustrations — ix

Acknowledgments — xi

Introduction — 1

Prologue: God in the Breath — 7

Part I: The Past

1 God in Stone — 29

2 God in the Neanderthal — 49

3 God in Matter — 69

Part II: The Future

4 God in Telepathy — 87

5 God in the Future — 113

6 God in the Third Age — 139

Postlude: God in Dualis — 153

Notes	171
Bibliography	219
Index	233
About the Author	249

Illustrations

creatio ex materia	6
little stones	28
covenant of salt	48
respiration of matter	68
telephatic coupling	86
bright matter	112
spell of the water	138
earth-kiss	152
elemental resonance	170

Elartemis#Saltemental
Photos by Maja Bjelica, PhD

The photographic series *Elartemis#Saltemental* is one of the rings of the chain project *Elartemis* in which the author researches the visual worlds of the elements, emotions, and echoing experiences. Images are created out of analog unedited black and white photographs that Maja Bjelica takes randomly and intuitively. The photographs are then digitally reframed and presented in print after a playful mirroring process that brings the eye unimagined realities and sp(l)aces.

The images accompanying Lenart Škof's *God in Post-Christianity: An Elemental Philosophical Theology* are a continuation of the collaboration of both authors' mutual commitment and meeting expressions, as engaged with already in Škof's previous book, *Antigone's Sisters*. The photographer, following Škof's ideas in elemental philosophy, embarks on a journey of discovering the four elements, air, fire, soil, and water, envisioning their creation in the forms of various matters, such as stones, minerals, but mainly salt. Traditional salt-working in Slovenia, the home country of both authors, engages in facilitating the playful collaboration of all the four elements in their specific forms, such as wind, sun, seawater, and clay pools, in order for them to concentrate and crystallize into salt.

The artistic project of *Elartemis#Saltemental* is part of the cross-pollinating activities of the research project *Grain of Salt, Crystallising Cohabitation: Salt-Making as Experiential Environmental Wisdom*, financially supported by the Slovenian Research and Innovation Agency (J6-50196).

Acknowledgments

Many people have influenced the emergence of this book, some of them with their philosophical and theological works, others with their encouragement. This book would not have been written without having before us a group of audacious thinkers, such as Amalric of Bène, Giordano Bruno, Arthur Schopenhauer, and Ludwig Feuerbach. Among contemporary thinkers, I am very much indebted to the philosophical and theological ideas of Luce Irigaray, John D. Caputo, and Catherine Keller. Regarding my own research journey, this book is the concluding part of my trilogy on contemporary philosophy of religion and philosophical theology, with *Breath of Proximity: Intersubjectivity, Ethics and Peace* (Springer, 2015) and *Antigone's Sisters: On the Matrix of Love* (State University of New York Press, 2021) being its first and second parts.

This book also could not have been written without various grants from the Slovenian Research and Innovation Agency (ARIS)—I am especially thankful to ARIS for supporting my work with the "Surviving the Anthropocene through Inventing New Ecological Justice and Biosocial Philosophical Literacy" (2019–2022) grant. I thank my institution, the Science and Research Centre Koper and its Institute for Philosophical and Religious Studies, for all the support for my research in philosophy and theology.

I also wish to thank Dr. Vadim Gershteyn, my former PhD candidate, for his assistance with book editing and for making the index and bibliography. I am indebted to Professor Ana Bajželj for her kind assistance with the topic of telepathy in Jainism. And I am grateful to Dr. Maja Bjelica for her new series of photos, which were specially selected and designed for this book. Finally, I cordially thank State University of New York editors James Peltz and Doug Donkel for their continuing support of my work as well as two anonymous reviewers for their most valuable comments and proposals.

Some chapters and portions of this book were previously published in the following journals or edited volumes:

- "God in the Neanderthal": previously published as "Being in the Heart of the Matter: Reflections on the Cosmic Christ for a New Theology of Nature" in *Studies in Spirituality* 30 (2020): 253–68. Reprinted with permission.

- "God in Matter": previously published as "On Two Unpleasant Gestures: Rethinking Marion's Critique of Nietzsche and Heidegger in *The Idol and Distance*" in *Bogoslovni vestnik* 79, no. 2 (2019), 381–94. Reprinted with permission.

- "God in the Future": a shorter and earlier version of this chapter was published as "The Futurity of God" in *Journal for Cultural and Religious Theory* 21, no. 1 (Winter 2022): 136–57. Reprinted with permission.

- "God in the Third Age": a shorter and earlier version of this chapter was previously published as "The Third Age: Reflections on Our Hidden Material Core" in *Sophia* 59, no. 1 (2020): 83–94. Reprinted with permission.

The chapter "God in Stone" was translated into English by Petra Berlot Kužner.

Lenart Škof, November 2023

Introduction

A Path toward Post-Christianity

What is the meaning of theology today? For centuries, theologians have aimed at two closely interrelated things: first, to detach and keep matter (or, the body) away from spiritual reality (or, the soul), and, second, to delineate and keep firmly the reality or the idea of God (even under the condition of an event of incarnation) under the first condition. The illusion of a masculinely represented God being ontologically totally separated from creation under the *creatio ex nihilo* divine act idea has produced numerous arguments on the existence of God and on the radical ontological separateness between the realities of the divine and of the nondivine, as well. The consequences of these illusory conceptions are broad, long-lasting, and devastating for the entire world of creation: the essentialization of only one part of sexual difference has brought Western theology under the strongest possible masculine domination (ontologically, epistemologically, and, last and not least, institutionally), and philosophy itself has become strongly dependent on these exclusivist narratives. Also, within this *god–human being* dichotomy, the latter was ontologically caught in passivity and the former was merely active in *His* creativity. All of these effects are visible in the current environmental crisis as well as in the long and tragic history of sexual, cultural, and socioeconomic exclusion of the large parts of humanity by the dominant elites and their narratives. Ancient cosmological and sacred correspondences between macrocosmic and microcosmic beings (or realities) were thus abandoned and forgotten, and the elemental flow of natural energies was cut. The ancient magic of the world was lost, and both philosophy and theology became mere servants of this unfortunate antiontological gesture. We can affirm with David Abram that "the human mind came to renounce its sensuous bearings, isolating itself from the other animals and the animate earth."[1] In addition to this, key religious phenomena and experiences, such as prayers, visions of God or other (divine) beings, clairvoyances and prophecies, communication with the dead, and all kinds of miracles, are rarely put in dialogue with either philosophy or even science. To the contrary, they are rather presented as "weird" and inexplicable phenomena, irrational (or transrational) exceptions inhabiting the very margin of Western rational thought—having a possible practical and metaphorical value (for our hope, faith, perhaps love), but not being properly "real" or having any proper ontological value.

As philosophers and theologians, we are thus encouraged to become more humble, and, in this sense, we are still far away from our ancestors, who still knew how to live in harmony with nature and its cycles. The hubris of modern humanity, which aims to exploit every natural feature, conquer every piece of the planet, and destroy—one by one—the habitats of countless beings, is immeasurable. The people of ancient cultures were sensitive to the primitive patterns they discerned during their daily secular and ritual activities. Today, due to insights into our essential elemental entanglement with everything (there is) and that surrounds us, we cannot keep laying claim to an ontological or elemental core of other beings of the world. Just as we cannot keep laying claim to "God"—whom we would always want to create in our own image and measure and with whom we would aspire to form a select metaphysical-spiritual tandem; we cannot lay claim to the layers of life that surrounds us. To be able to unite in this future, postreligious community, people will have to establish a contact within ourselves with elemental layers of being and, thus, in the manner of elemental self-affection in the very core of dwelling, establish ourselves as free beings of nature. As we will see in this book, such an epiphany of elements within Indigenous religions and Jesus's cosmic incarnation on Earth are signs that humanity should strive to achieve, in a completely new way, an independent and autonomous self-fulfillment that can no longer be based on any predetermined hierarchy, ideology, or dependence on some other higher (e.g., metaphysical, theological, religious) authority. To dwell in the so-called third age—the "Age of the Spirit" (or, as understood in the elemental sense, "Age of the Breath"), labeled in this book as "post-Christian," will mean to nurture within ourselves the vital breath or vital life force that will enable us to coexist compassionately with others, connected with the elements (first with minerals as the core of matter, and sacred stones) and equally so with plant and animal beings, and divinities. The third age indicates the path toward a subtle divinization of humanity and thereby liberation of any external pressure or influence. Within the Christian tradition (and other similar religious traditions with their own history and institutions), all of these layers have been accessible to those who were able to see in the aspect of a person of the Holy Spirit/Holy Breath, besides the incarnation of the cosmic Jesus on Earth, also in its subtle and material nature in the form of the *sacredness of breath*; while within Indigenous religions these layers were understood by all those who lived in accordance with the primal forces that are embodied and present in all beings of the world. It is our opinion that all this means to embark on a path toward a future era, in which the *taking-place of the post-Christianity will be in ourselves*.

This book on philosophical and constructive theology is an homage to some of the most audacious (and often solitary or neglected) thinkers in the field of philosophical theology—from Joachim of Fiore[2] and Amalric of Bène to Giordano Bruno and Jakob Böhme in the early era; from Franz von Baader, Arthur Schopenhauer, and Ludwig Feuerbach to Carl Gustav Jung, Raymond Ruyer, Maurice Merleau-Ponty, and Luce Irigaray in the modern era. And in the most recent times, to thinkers such as John D. Caputo and Catherine Keller, including their most recent developments in the so-called quantum theology. They all have in common at the same time a humble and bold rethinking of the ontological and ethical core of Christianity. If there is a way toward post-Christianity (as exemplified in this book), then it is along the paths untrodden by these most original thinkers.[3]

Another aim of this book is to rekindle the spark of synchronicity abandoned and lost in our explorations of the vast and rich spaces of philosophical and religious thought all over the world. The task is not only to engage in various encounters with (as in our case) the Indigenous, pre-Socratic, Judeo-Christian (including its most idiosyncratic developments in Mormonism), Vedic and Hindu, Buddhist, Jain, Slavic, Persian, and Islamic traditions and thinkers, but allows us to go one step further—to gesture into and through the matrix of their common cosmologico-ontological and ethico-theological ground, as it were, the *underground water as a reservoir of our common mnemic themes* (as argued by Raymond Ruyer). As humanity (including our predecessors and other *Homo* species such as the Neanderthal) we were/are sharing one common ground: already in Jung, the theory of synchronicity was put in close proximity to the evolving quantum science of his era. The plentiful potentialities of this encounter, especially if understood in the broader religious field (with Indigenous religious studies included, and telepathy/*panpathy* as new philosophical topics) represent another crucial impetus toward the evolving of post-Christianity in our age.

There is also an idiosyncratic ethical thread visible throughout these encounters. According to Bruno and Merleau-Ponty, there is a bond in this world called *vinculum*: a hidden coordination of being(s) that cannot be found in visible things and is somehow secretly present in the cosmos. As exemplified in this book, this sacred or cosmic *nexus* connects nature, humanity, and God; in this view, incarnated god now becomes cosmic Being (in post-Christianity this is now Christ within the deep incarnation), a sap penetrating the *leaf of Being* (Merleau-Ponty). And, with Feuerbach, Christ now becomes *plasticity*[4]—the supreme being able to reach out as *love* to every single element of creation.

Finally, the post-Christian era that we are hoping for in this book will be able to redefine and ethically restructure the spaces of intersubjectivity and proximity, with compassion and love remaining our highest hopes in this endeavor. In the era of post-Christianity, God (or divinities) are greeted and carefully listened to in spaces between-us. The shell of intimacy, as presented in this book, unseals a possibility of an embodied-elemental encounter of two breaths, joined in love through the *breath-kiss*. And it is in this *ethico-carnal* sense that God truly becomes an organ of Love—the sacrament of intersubjectivity.

~

This book is dedicated to the Amalricians and their spiritual heirs. It is hard to imagine an alternative history of Christianity and accompanying Western thought in which this sect would not have been annihilated but rather preserved and prospered until the present day. The Amalricians believed that God was everywhere, *dwelling* in all things: theirs was the beautiful sentence *Deus, hyle et mens una sola substantia sunt*. Theirs also was a vision of the Third Age with the God-filled universe in which the Holy Spirit held sway and within which humanity might aspire to become truly spiritual beings. Just as the ceremonies of the Old Testament ceased with the advent of Christ, for them the sacraments of the Church ceased to be operative with the coming of the Holy Spirit. Women and men, having the Holy Spirit/Holy Breath incarnated within themselves, were now free and independent. The highest law of their idea of humanity was thus to become breathful-spiritual beings, inhabiting the Earth here and now, respectful to its elemental-material core of all-Being. It is such an antinomian and embodied vision of the world that we are hoping for in this book—a future world where "everything will be as it is now, just a little different."[5]

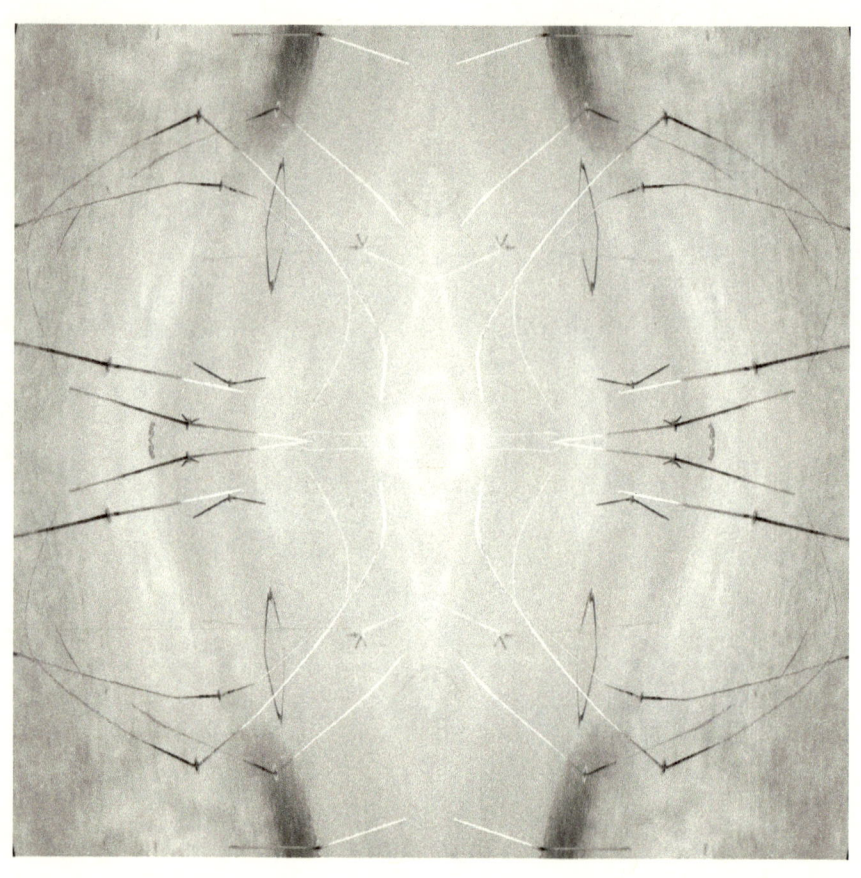

creatio ex materia

Prologue

God in the Breath

With lungs full of space breathes the transparency of god.

—Niko Grafenauer, *Dihindih*[1]

We are living in difficult and demanding times. The impending environmental crisis, with its signs of coming climate-related catastrophes on our planet, requires us to reopen our cosmological, ontological, and theological archives and inquire into Nature's past in order to be able to secure its future. It seems that gods have withdrawn from their presence here into the shades of this world (and its space-time), such that humanity is left alone for the task of its survival. In his *Cross and Cosmos*, John D. Caputo asks about this planetary problem when he writes, "If in Christ all creation, the earth and sun and stars, the cosmos itself, has been reconciled to God, why does creation seem to be rushing headlong into destruction?"[2] How, then, would it be possible to think about the danger of the destruction of life on Earth, and how would it be possible to address the reverse process of an uncreation (or, an undoing of a creation) that humanity is imposing first upon itself, but actually foremost upon nature, and Earth as our planet? To address the current environmental crisis on the earth, and to offer a proper cosmological and theological response, it is thus necessary to rekindle the elemental presence of life in the most distant cosmological past within deep creation, and to call upon gods to help us to recover the primeval cosmological matrix of the earth and of the living, so much needed in these times: to secure our future. As God needed the assistance of humanity during the evils of Auschwitz—this was exemplified by Etty Hillesum in her diary entry from

July 12, 1942: "You cannot help us, but we must help You and defend Your dwelling place inside us to the last"[3]—today, Nature needs to be defended and safeguarded by us and with the help of gods given the danger of the impending environmental and anthropogenic catastrophe. The entirety of creation—as we know it—is endangered. But a preliminary note is needed here: with the development of philosophy and theology, the Western world forsook emotions and sensual perception, the proximity of smell and touch, and, in relation to nature, founded a completely new mode of thought that is characterized by a conceptual and ideological world: a world of unbridled subjectivity based on the dominance of mind over feelings and emotions, of one gender over the other, of man over the animal world, of humanity over nature. Lamentably, the same pattern was adopted by theology, which—quite paradoxically—too frequently banished from its already cold chambers any spirit of elemental materiality that had even the slightest hint of closeness to Jesus: compassion, physical contact, closeness, and bodily proximity were too often considered redundant in favor of grand theological and metaphysical schemata, the meaningless production of theoretical evidence for the existence of God, or, simply, unending prestige wars for the supremacy of one argument or doctrine (or church) over another. The legacies of these processes are visible in humans, societies, and, most notably, in nature. We need a new elemental philosophical theology.

First Breath of Creation

In our search for the elemental core of creation, let us approach our first question now. In reading F. W. J. Schelling's works, Maurice Merleau-Ponty affirms that "this *erste Natur* is the most ancient element, 'an abyss of the past,' which always remains present in us and in all things."[4] The presence and inheritance of Nature, in us, therefore is a cosmological and ontological mystery: a riddle to be solved if we want to find a way to a new elemental sensibility toward earth, and to new creation—now of a thriving future world that our descendants would inhabit. Humans are intrinsically connected to creation and creation breathes, as it were, through us. The creation of a new elemental world and its new *natural eschatology* is a task that we will now need to accomplish by ourselves in an era still to be fully disclosed to humanity. This statement relates to the eschatological schema of the three eras, which we can trace back to the Babylonian Talmud. In it, after a first chaotic age, humanity progresses to the age of the Law of Torah, and, finally, is awaiting a future Messianic age, which is still to come. In the Middle Ages, this thinking was revived by Joachim of Fiore, whose new idea was that history is divided into three ages; now, he argues that after the age of the Father (Old Testament) and the age of the Son (New Testament and Church), we are awaiting the third age: an age of the Spirit (represented in the so-called Third Testament and new Spiritual Church accompanying it) that is still to come, and in which new religious orders would inaugurate a new Spiritual Church here on Earth.[5] The same teaching was then also one of the sources for the heretic medieval sect around Amalric of Bène, and, in its most recent form, it reappeared in G. W. F. Hegel and Schelling, and was finally revived in an idiosyncratic way in Luce Irigaray's teaching of "the age of the Spirit" (also equally, or even more appropriately, called "the age of the Breath"[6]), in which the task of humanity is to become divine spirit, or, in a new material-elemental way, *divine breath* itself. Already for Amalric of Bène, transcendence was hidden in things themselves, and his early theological materialism has thus paved the way toward our era: the era in which any human being could become divine by herself/himself and in which humanity would reunite within a newly acquired sacred alliance with Nature. According to Irigaray, in this new era, following the age of the Father and the age of the Son, humanity would make divine this world—a new world in which (feminine) divine would not be separated from nature anymore, but, quite on the contrary, would transubstantiate it without ruining it. The third age, thus, brings the new idea of the eschatological temporality of nature in which, as our poet announces: *the transparency of god will breathe with lungs full of space*. It is important to notice that, for Irigaray, this age "unites the earliest time and the most future time,"[7] which directly testifies to the temporality we wish to address in this book. This coming of the future Age of Breath will be presented in the sixth chapter of this book. This is why this work is dedicated to the forgotten sect of Amalricians and their spiritual heirs until the present age.

Let us now return to the original question of Nature being the most ancient and abyssal element with its inheritance in us. The presence of Nature, in its cosmological and ontological mystery, will be addressed and presented as a riddle to be solved by humanity if we would like to pave a way toward a new elemental sensibility toward Nature, and its incarnation—our Earth. There is no better starting point for this effort than an ancient hymn from the tenth maṇḍala of the *Ṛgveda*: the Creation hymn ("Nāsadāsīya" or "Bhāvavṛttam"). The opening stanzas 1–3 will be analyzed and interpreted as a testimony of the ancient Vedic cosmogonical and ontological riddles (and its relation to the teachings of the *abyss*), and the concluding stanzas of this hymn will be interpreted as an example of a secret and enigmatic Vedic teaching on the nature of gods.

Vedic poetry is a part of an ancient *triadic* structure of cosmic realms, as it is relationally and ontologically intertwined and interconnected: the macrocosm (or cosmic realm; gods/nature), the microcosm (or the realm of the everyday; humans) and the mesocosm (or the ritual realm; hymns). For the Vedic seers and poets, the ultimate goal was to know these sacred but hidden cosmic correspondences (called *bandhu/*"bond," or *upaniṣad*) between the three realms, which gives them a godlike power in their understanding of the mystery of Nature.[8] This aspiration clearly resonates with teachings from Amalric of Bène's to Irigaray's avenue of thought, and reveals another option of new thinking toward Nature: with the *breath* ("*spirit*") *element* as its vital part. As stated by Joel P. Brereton and Stephanie Jamison, we must be aware that "these homologies are not mere poetic embellishments, imagery for its own sake, but an implicit statement about the way things *really are*, the pervasive underlying connections unifying apparently disparate elements."[9] The Vedic hymn begins with the following three stanzas:

1. The nonexistent did not exist, nor did the existent exist at that time.
   There existed neither the airy space nor heaven beyond.
   What moved back and forth? From where and in whose protection?
   Did water exist, a deep depth?

2. Death did not exist nor deathlessness then.
   There existed no sign of night nor of day.
   That One breathed without wind by its independent will.
   There existed nothing else beyond that.

3. Darkness existed, hidden by darkness, in the beginning.
   All this was a signless ocean.
   What existed as a thing coming into being, concealed by emptiness—that
   One was born by the power of heat.[10]

These verses, without doubt, represent one of the most elaborate ancient teachings on cosmogony and of creation of the world. The interpretation of these three opening stanzas is a difficult task, and we will return to the exposition of their meaning later. But, to try to disclose a meaning for the first stanza, we first wish to propose a dialogic and transreligious exchange with Judeo-Christian creation theology as analyzed by Catherine Keller in her *Face of the Deep*. In search for missing chaos and its mystery, Keller criticizes those theologians who, in their incessant wish "to draw the line at 'God,' say that, whenever the creation starts, it is preceded by absolutely nothing—nothing but the pure and simple presence of God the Creator."[11] In this classical theological conception of creation, the *abyss* is not preserved and nature is disclosed only as the work of this God, the Creator. A theological principle of subordination is established and the ontology of the beginning is suppressed. Instead, with her grammatology of beginning, Keller reinaugurates the *tehom* (Hebr. "the deep," "the abyss") from the second verse of Genesis 1, a too often neglected concept:

> In the beginning when God created the heavens and the earth, the earth was a formless void and darkness covered the face of the deep, while a wind from God swept over the face of the waters. (Genesis, 1.1–2)[12]

Keller retranslates the second verse as follows: "and the earth was tohu vabohu, and darkness was upon the face of tehom and the ruach elohim was vibrating upon the face of the mayim . . ." These two verses of Genesis can, of course, be read in two different ways: first, as a testimony to the priority of God the Lord and monarchical Father over the creation in an ontological and temporal way—hence, *creatio ex nihilo*. But these verses also enable us to invert this logic in which chaos, as Keller affirms, now precedes creation and in which the logic of the abyss is preserved as tehomic alterity; thus *creatio ex profundis*. The consequences of this turn are immense: it enables us to think beyond the dualism of an everlasting God vs. the preceding Nothing and toward an opening of a third way with a release of the cosmogonical difference included in it—a difference that also enables us to address the cosmogonically suppressed feminine aspect of the creation: the goddess of the world. Speaking through the words of Ivone Gebara (who is writing her theology as a lament for the Earth), Keller affirms that "we no longer speak of God as existing before creation" and that "we no longer think of God first and creation later because this sort of gap between atemporality in God and temporality in creation does not make sense to us."[13] But, the most important reading of Gebara's thought comes from Keller in the following sentence: "She offers in the gap a 'con-spiracy,' a 'breathing with' by one who wants a 'new heaven and new earth' to spring from this very ground.' This rhythmic, breathy eschatology lovingly and firmly dislodges God from within the patriarchy of liberation theology and its power—almost in passing."[14] On the grounds of this new theological imagination of God and chaos relocated from their preexisting ontological states, Keller is now undertaking what she names a new *pneumatic conspiracy*: following Rosemary Ruether, a place can now reopen for, as it were, a new Matrix of creation: "God/ess who is primal Matrix, the ground of being-new being, is neither stifling immanence nor rootless transcendence."[15]

Let us now try to explain the hidden cosmogonico-ontological logic behind this *conspiracy of creation*. Before our interpretation of the Vedic cosmogonical hymn, a detour through Schelling's *Philosophical Inquiries into the Nature of Human Freedom* (1809) is warranted. This move to Schelling will enable us to link Keller's reading of the biblical creation myth with the cosmogonical hymn of the *Ṛksaṃhitā*. Following the insights of the leading Schelling scholar Jason Wirth, it can now be stated:

> In the 1809 *Freedom* essay, perhaps Schelling's most daring work and one of the treasures of the nineteenth-century German philosophical tradition, he spoke of a "unity and conspiracy," a *Konspiration*. When something or someone falls out of the conspiracy, they become inflamed with sickness and fever, as "inflamed by an inner heat." Schelling used the Latinate-German *Konspiration*, which stems from *conspiro*, to breathe or blow together. *Spiro*, to breathe, is related to *spiritus* (the German *Geist*), meaning spirit, but also breath. *Geist* is the progression of difference, the A^3, the breathing out of the dark abyss of nature into form and the simultaneous inhaling of this ground, the retraction of things away from themselves. The conspiracy is a simultaneous expiration and inspiration, and each thing of nature is both inspired yet expiring. This is what I call the conspiracy of life, that is, the life beyond and within life and death.[16]

This indeed is an extraordinary observation! In his philosophical works, Schelling elaborates on a mysterious movement within the difference of the Ground (God) itself, as a mark of an enigmatic submersing of the Ground into the abyss (called primal ground/groundless or *Ungrund* by

Schelling)—and, importantly, links this dynamic with the grounding of love itself: "The essence of the basis, or of existence, can only be precedent to all bases, that is, the absolute viewed directly, the groundless. . . . But the groundless divides itself into two equally eternal beginnings only in order that the two which could not be in it as groundless at the same time, or there be one, should become one through love."[17] Now, all these ontological elements (*the abyss, groundless, breath, love*) already appear in our Vedic hymn, which represents a testimony to the earliest ontological questioning on the nature of reality as (non)created—as a cosmogonical riddle as presented in ancient Indo-European thought (in this form, the Creation hymn originates from ca. tenth-century BC). The first verse of the Vedic hymn articulates creation as follows:

The Being did not exist, nor did the Nonbeing exist at that time.

(*nāsad āsīn no sad āsīt tadānīṃ*)

This verse is already a testimony for thought that navigates beyond our ordinary or secure dichotomies of being and nonbeing.[18] In *Face of the Deep*, we have already noticed Keller's intervention toward the third way—operating beyond both an absolute being (God) of the creation and its nihilistic counterpart: nothing; "neither pure origin nor nihilist flux."[19] Derridean *différance* is invoked here, marking the trace of procreation beyond the undifferentiated Origin of a Creator.

In *Nāsadāsīya*, we have a similar cosmogonical milieu: an answer cannot be found within a simple linear temporality of being and nonbeing, but it is a part of a riddle to be resolved by the hymn taken as a whole. The second stance (verses c and d) hints toward an answer by introducing a respiratory element (*ruah elohim*) into creation:

That One breathed without wind by its independent will. There existed nothing else beyond that.

(*ānīd avātaṃ svadhayā tad ekaṃ tasmād dhānyan na paraḥ kiṃ canāsa*)

It is astounding to realize that Vedic poets (being both early natural theologians and early natural philosophers) already knew that the answer to this cosmogonical riddle cannot be searched for without introducing another beginning in which a more primeval mystico-elemental constellation is offered with(in) the One (*tad ekam*, n.) breathing by its own independent will. The One represents a cosmos in its nascent and formless stage, "existing" without any signs of life and death, and without single visible potency—as affirmed in verses a and b of the third stanza:

> Darkness existed, hidden by darkness, in the beginning. All this was a signless ocean.
>
> (*tama āsīt tamasā gūḷham agre 'praketaṃ salilaṃ sarvam ā idam*)

We may, here, remember Keller as she has indicated the abyssal and archaico-elemental constellation with the following words: *and darkness was upon the face of tehom and the ruach elohim was vibrating upon the face of the mayim*. The Vedic One as a possibility of a neutral proto-Being (neither male nor female) is a sign of a bottomless potentiality of a life in the primeval Void/abyss (Sskt. "abhu") with its only sign: breath, which cannot even be imagined as connected to any material substance or denominator, even such as wind ("breathed without wind"). But it is in this *breathing* of the One that we can discern the first subtle movement before any other sign of life could be even anticipated or discriminated: the creation itself *breathes* gently and subtly, and enables the very first germ of life to emanate from this originary respiratory tissue of the evolving cosmogonical matrix. Further, verses c and d of the third stanza further affirm this movement and now—in a fully synchronistic way—indicate the birth of that One *from* warmth:

> What existed as a thing coming into being, concealed by emptiness—that One was born by the power of heat.
>
> (*tuchyenābhv apihitaṃ yad āsīt tapasas tan mahinājāyataikam*)

Here, we have the decisive sequence of creation: as we can see, Vedic poets transform linearity into synchronicity; from the first to the third stanza we are not only facing the linear progression of creation but actually delve more and more into the past. Similar to Keller's deconstructive reading of Genesis 1, also the synchronistic reading of the Vedic cosmogonical hymn slowly uncovers a cosmogonical secret: the One as a proto-Being (beyond any ontological denominator such as existence or nonexistence) emerges from even more primeval cosmogonical matrix—*tapas* or cosmogonical Warmth/Heat/Glow. As exemplified in the first part of the fourth stanza of the Vedic hymn, this primeval Warmth actually is revealed to the Vedic poets as desire/love (*kāma*):

> Then, in the beginning, from desire there evolved thought, which existed as the primal semen.[20]

> (*kāmas tad agre sam avartatādhi manaso retaḥ prathamaṃ yad āsīt*)

This principle of love as a part of creation is decisive now: it enables us to approach and perhaps understand Schelling's most cryptic thoughts from his *Philosophical Inquiries into the Nature of Human Freedom*, where he states: "For not even spirit itself is supreme; it is but spirit, or the breath of love. But love is supreme. It is that which was before there were the depths and before existence (as separate entities), but it was not there as love, rather—how shall we designate it?"[21] For Schelling, love was there even before there were depths (the abyss, cosmogonical Void), but, again, even love cannot be designated as love. Are we facing the cosmogonical dead-end now? To proceed, we must return to the third Vedic stanza: "that One was born by the power of heat" is stated there and let us here focus on the *element of natality* from this verse: that One (n.) was born from the primeval cosmogonical Warmth. That One, breathing before there was any sign of life whatsoever, concealed by emptiness, emerged from the matrix of creation (cosmic egg; nursing element; the matrixiality of creation)—discernible now as a mysterious *khora*, the womb(-heart) of creation, an empty chalice of Being.[22]

Now, the concluding two stanzas of the Creation hymn lead us toward our final question of this part: of a secret and enigmatic Vedic teaching on the nature of gods—a teaching that necessarily accompanies the cosmogonical genesis of Being. Let us listen to the Vedic poet in this sixth stanza:

> Who really knows? Who shall here proclaim it?—from where was it born, from where this creation?
> The gods are on this side of the creation of this (world). So then who does know from where it came to be?

> (*ko addhā veda ka iha pra vocat kuta ājātā kuta iyaṃ visṛṣṭiḥ* |
> *arvāg devā asya visarjanena athā ko veda yata ābabhūva* ||)

The Vedic thinker knows that it is impossible to reveal the cosmogonical secret in words, or to keep it in our minds: as it even precedes—cosmically and ontologically—being and nonbeing, we can only hint at this enigmatic inception of everything from the abyssal M/matrix, both in its discreet breathing and cosmic Warmth (dark energy?).[23] In the seventh and concluding stanza, the Vedic poet winds up his cosmogonical meditation with another, now radically theological gesture of deconstructing all knowledge acquired so far—of creation, gods, and human access to them. Even if there is a possibility of a "God" (Sūrya/Sun?; a cosmic Glow) up there, it is again affirmed that even for this god, inhabiting the farthest heaven, it might still be impossible to oversee or know the abyssal secret of creation:

> This creation—from where it came to be, if it was produced or if not—
> he who is the overseer of this (world) in the furthest heaven, he surely knows. Or if he does not know . . . ?[24]

> (*iyaṃ visṛṣṭir yata ābabhūva yadi vā dadhe yadi vā na | yo asyā-dhyakṣaḥ parame vyomant so aṅga veda yadi vā na veda ||*)

The moment of creation remains unconcealed as the *first Nature* remains hidden. It only can be explained as a moment of a progression of difference—from the abyssal breath-energy to the inception of first discernable being. This is very close to Merleau-Ponty's thinking of nature taken in its barbaric excess and beyond any conceptualization. Patrick Burke knows this precisely, as he succinctly links two of our main themes (abyssal cosmogony and matrixiality) in his analysis of Schelling and Merleau-Ponty:

> The psychoanalysis of nature will reveal the shadow which philosophy must bear, the resistance of the "erste Natur" to consciousness, its barbarous excess, which can never be made amenable to conceptualization but which—carried in gestures of creativity or marginal experiences of surprise, wonder, or horror—breaks through, ignites, and explodes all ontological predication and schematization. In a recollection of Heraclitus, for whom this "erste Natur" is both logos and fire, Merleau-Ponty will call it the primitive element, logos, flesh, mother. Nature is the womb, the vortex, the spiraling matrix which, like the fire of

Heraclitus, contracts into individual entities and expands [*inhales and exhales?*] into styles of Being, into typicality. Merleau-Ponty uses the term "pregnancy" to depict the wild logos of the visible.[25]

As in the Vedic hymn, also in Burke this constellation remains open: apart from its inherent matrixiality, it insists on the subtle plane between logos as divine ground with the creative agency of God included on one side, and dark and barbaric principle of the *Unground* as a principle "older than God" on the other side.[26] This cosmogonical and ontological openness enables us now to address in our second part the plane of matrixiality, a "wild web" of Mary the cosmic Goddess—as poetically revealed in Gerard Manley Hopkins's poem.

Womb-Heart of Creation

As in Merleau-Ponty's concept of Nature as the womb or vortex, we also have approached the theological imagination of Keller, who addresses a new pneumatic conspiracy as a place of the primeval femininity wherein a new Matrix of creation is formed (God/ess as a primal Matrix in Ruether). In our journey toward the past and our search for the first tissue of creation, we have thus discovered that, in order to rekindle the elemental presence of a life in the midst of *the abyss of pre-Being*, as it were, the rhythmic cosmic conspiracy of being and nonbeing was synchronistically posited within the archaic cosmic matrix. But we have also seen that the abyssal breath-energy, as discerned as the first sign of life, still remains enveloped in a mystery: beyond any attempts of conceptualization, and beyond even godlike knowledge ("So then / who does know from where it came to be?" in a verse from the Vedic hymn), this cosmogonical and spiraling matrix still evades any attempt of grasping, naming, or understanding. The cosmogonical constellation therefore remains open: insisting on the subtle plane between the creative agency of God and dark and barbaric principle of the *Unground* as a principle "older than God" on the other side, we now wish to propose a possibility of another beginning, of potentiality of the matrix—as vortex of creation. In this endeavor, again, thought of transreligiously, the poetics of the matrixial-wombing and matrixial-breathing feminine across Christian (via Friedrich Hölderlin) and Buddhist (via Tantras) ways will now help us to uncover a part of its secret. In his insightful elaboration on the maternity and femininity in Hölderlin's late hymns, Jacob Denz traces the problem of maternal address and thus first analyzes one of Immanuel Kant's "most bizarre sentences"[27] from his *Critique of Judgement*:

> Now here the archaeologist of nature is free to let that great family of creatures (for this must one represent it if there is to be a basis for the thoroughly coherent kinship that has been mentioned) originate from the remaining traces of its oldest revolutions in accordance with any mechanism for that is known to or conjectured by him. He can have the maternal womb of the earth, which has just emerged from a condition of chaos (just like a great animal), initially bear creatures of less purposive form, which in turn bear others that are formed more suitably for their place or origin and their relationships to one another, until this birth-mother itself, hardened and ossified, has restricted its offspring to determinate species that will degenerate no further, and the variety will remain as it turned out of the end of the operation of that fruitful formative power.[28]

In this passage, Kant addresses maternal origin as that which gives birth to the animal life on the Earth. Yet maternal origin is not at the same ontological level with life produced from "her" (i.e., cosmic womb/uterus, premother, midwife); as Denz observes, "Kant enlists a disembodied womb or uterus as the figure of a lack of negativity which alone can ground the positive totality of life. But although it is necessarily neither inside nor outside the frame of the family picture of living beings, the womb of the earth that births animal life is itself still *like* one of those beings, specifically a great or large animal."[29] With Kant, therefore, in his idiosyncratic search for the ontological beginning, we are guided toward the abyssal maternal function within Western philosophy (and philosophical theology). Importantly, as this cosmic uterus is disembodied and detached from creation, or *exists* beyond any inside/outside dichotomies (similar to the original Vedic constellation of *the One, breathing* beyond both Being and Nonbeing), it still remains *connected* to the phenomenon of life that it (she?) gives birth to.

Now, in Hölderlin's late and unfinished hymn "To the Madonna," the poet introduces the feminine principle of Madonna (Virgin Mary), which is synchronistically related to the goddess Gaia (as the Mother Earth) and the German goddess of nature, Hertha (and also Antigone and Diotime).

In the hymn, Hölderlin describes Mary as the Queen of the cosmos, and the poem reveals this constellation as follows:

> Yet, heavenly one, yet you
> I'll celebrate and let no one
> Reproach me with
> The beauty of native speech,
> Now that alone
> I go to the field where wild
> The lily grows, fearless
> . . .[30]

Here, the lily is the symbol of Mary and it grows wild and without fear. The wildness of the lily might here (as already observed by Burke on Merleau-Ponty) mark the subtle plane between logos as divine ground and the dark and barbaric, but now feminine principle of the *Unground*, depicting the "wild logos of the visible"—as the principle of matrixiality ("pregnancy"[31]), discretely evolving from the womb of creation. Hölderlin's Madonna is the principle of love: as Mother Goddess, she fulfills the cosmic role that philosophers from Kant to Merleau-Ponty were trying to conceptualize in their attempts to identify the cosmologico-ontological matrix of the world. In his verses on the highest goddess, fulfilling the promise of love, the Madonna is further depicted as follows:

> To the inaccessible
> Primordial vault
> Of the forest,
> the Occident,
> and over mankind
> In place of other deities there reigned
> The all-oblivious, Love.[32]

Reigning over the primordial vault, the Madonna is the cosmic feminine, overarching this world with the promise of love—as expressed in the obscure verse from the hymn "Nichts ists, das Böse / A mere nothing is Evil."[33] The verse affirms the primordiality of the archaic principle of love: the first and foremost potentiality for goodness, an empty chalice of being (*khora*; cf. Vedic hymn). Returning to philosophy now, we may affirm with Denz that

"Kant's own appeal to the womb as a permissible presupposition grounding investigation of the diversity of life suggests that the maternal *function* still haunts thought."[34] Read with the Hölderlin's hymn "Greece," a respiratory element can now be subtly added to this cosmogonical moment, as the hymn states:

> God has put on a garment.
> And his face is withheld from the knowing
> And covers the winds with art.
> And air and time cover[35]

In the center of creation, we can now posit the respiratory matrixial abyssal Ground. If we continue with Hölderlin's legacy, in *Elucidations to Hölderlin's Poetry*, Martin Heidegger names this Ground as he elaborates on the unity of earth and heaven, god and man, and the "center" (abyssal un/ground) in the midst of this cosmic constellation, in his words this is a

> more tender infinite relation . . . The center, so called because it centers, that is, mediates, is neither earth nor heaven, God nor man. The in-finity that is to be thought here is abysmally different from that which is merely without end, which, because of its uniformity, allows no growth. On the other hand, the "more tender relation" of earth and heaven, God and man, can become more in-finite. For what is not one-sided can come more purely to light from the intimacy in which the named four are bound to each other.[36]

So, does the element of *growth* and a *more tender infinite relation* in this passage hint at the possibility of the feminine matrix marking the original plane of "in-finity" in this constellation of Heidegger's?

It is in the poem "The Blessed Virgin Compared to the Air We Breathe" by Gerard Manley Hopkins that we can finally encircle our search for the elemental respiratory *and* matrixial principle of creation as based on Mary as the feminine matrix.[37] This poem from 1883 is a comparison of the Virgin Mary with the physico-elemental atmosphere that sustains our life, but in this poem the air is not used only as a comparison as Mary is intrinsically and thus ontologically linked to this cosmic element. Let us approach the poem first—in the beginning we have the following verses:

> Wild air, world-mothering air,
> Nestling me everywhere,
> . . .
> In every least thing's life;
> This needful, never spent,
> And nursing element;

In these opening words of the poem, Hopkins gives us a respiratory-matrixial constellation in which air is revealed as a nursing element; it is depicted as a "wild air, world-mothering air," and is thus the preeminent of all elements as it never vanishes, sustains all life, and is present in every last thing of this life. This world-mothering element is what reminds us of Mary, whose earthly presence (as being "merely a woman") is transcended by these enigmatic verses about her own divinity:

> Mary Immaculate,
> Merely a woman, yet
> Whose presence, power is
> Great as no goddess's

Here, Mary's womb is the place where God's infinity manifests in a birth of the cosmic Child: a new self, incarnated in the feminine womb ("of her flesh he took flesh"). The originary tissue of this mysterious Marian *wombing motherliness* is now imagined as being like a "wild web, wondrous robe." We have already seen that the creation itself *breathes* gently and subtly—and enables the very first germ of life to emanate from this originary respiratory tissue of the evolving cosmogonical matrix. What, now, is the relation of Mary to all this? In answering this question, we may recall Teilhard de Chardin's Sophiology from his hymn *The Eternal Feminine*, written between 1916 and 1918. For Teilhard, cosmic Mary is "the Pearl of the Cosmos, and the link with the incarnate personal Absolute—the Blessed Virgin Mary, Queen and Mother of all things, the true Demeter."[38] With Teilhard's words from *The Eternal Feminine* hymn: "When the world was born, I came into being. Before the centuries were made, I issued from the hand of God. . . . In me is seen that side of beings by which they are joined as one. . . . I am the eternal Feminine."[39] For Teilhard, the eternal feminine is ontologically still subject to the Lord's creational moment. But this changes within the tradition of Sophiology in which this relation is dissolved into the possibility of another beginning. For John O'Donnell, reading one of the main representatives of this tradition, Sergei Bulgakov, Wisdom-Sophia is now understood in line with the thinking of the abyss as depth of creation, as "the revelation of the depth of the divine being. The Abyss of God's reality is revealed in the divine Wisdom. Hence Wisdom belongs to all three hypostases but is not itself a hypostasis. The Divine wisdom is both uncreated and eternal. It belongs to God's own life."[40] Finally, this thought is even further radicalized by Thomas Merton, for whom Sophia is " 'the dark, nameless *Ousia* [Being]' of God, not one of the Three Divine Persons, but each 'at the same time, are Sophia and manifest her.' "[41] These two extraordinary observations are directly related to what we now can understand as the following constellation on the role of the cosmic matrix in the creation of the world, as depicted by an originary and post-Christian Trinitarian model of the three eras, with the *khora* or womb-heart of Mary *as* incarnated Wisdom-Sophia in the center of the ontological tissue of creation (this constellation represents the task of post-Christianity):

God

Matrix/Womb-heart

Christ   **Holy Breath**

Warm Breath of Creation

In the beginning of this chapter, we proposed a synchronistic reading of ancient Indian and Judeo-Christian cosmologies and creation theologies. By reading ancient ṛgvedic and tehomic creation narratives, we have been invited by the ancient poets toward a new *breathy eschatology*—an elemental setting undoing the *creatio ex nihilo* narratives and their devastating effects on ontology, which became a new one-legged myth, annihilating the abundance of elemental materiality within the creation. This is why Keller had to intervene with her insightful observation as related to Ivone Gebara's eschatology—namely, that she offers "a 'con-spiracy,' a 'breathing with' by one who wants a 'new heaven and new earth' to spring from this very ground."[42] This conspiracy now, beautifully, reveals itself within the Tantric tradition of Tibetan Buddhism: namely the tradition of Ḍākinī as an embodiment of a subtle, yet elemental presence of the vital breath of creation in this world. Within the Tantric tradition, Ḍākinī represents one of the most complex religious symbols, representing the attributes of an enhanced femininity, wisdom, and ultimate reality. Ḍākinī's subtle essence and her power come from the uninterrupted lineage of realization, and her body and mind are the expressions of the highest wisdom available to humans in this world. She thus represents the link of the past with the future; in our terms, she incarnates both creation as well as eschatology.

Being is also labeled as Queen Ḍākinī Secret Wisdom; she is the manifestation of the "mahāsukha Küntusangmo [Samantabhadrī], the all-good queen."[43] As Samantabhadrī (the consort of the Ādi Buddha or primordial and highest buddha according to the Nyingma sect of Tibetan Buddhism), Ḍākinī represents the Mother Buddha—the source of all enlightenment. Queen Ḍākinī is called mother because of her generative powers of "giving birth to all buddhas and tathāgatas,"[44] and she thus also represents the matrixial element in the cosmos. With Ḍākinī as a divine being beyond all dualities or dichotomies (of body and mind, immanence and transcendence, past and future, and also beyond gender[45]), we may remember Keller following Ruether in her naming of the new Matrix of creation as a "God/ess who is primal Matrix, the ground of being-new being, is neither stifling immanence nor rootless transcendence."[46] Now, this Ḍākinī can be synchronistically linked to the Wisdom-Sophia as the revelation of the depth of the divine being itself—now in the immense radiance of pure and unlimited wisdom as a feminine principle of enlightenment, and thus of entire soteriology. For the tradition of Sophiology, as we have already seen, the Abyss of God's reality was revealed precisely in the divine Wisdom that was both uncreated and eternal: this now is the empty place, named as *khora*—the tissue of creation, also represented in a symbol of the womb-heart of Mary, mother of Jesus.

But what is the elemental presence as represented in Ḍākinī? What secret does her warm breath reveal to us? First, Ḍākinī represents unborn, indestructible, and vast space, free of any dualities, conceptualizations, or notions of existence. In the words of Judith Simmer-Brown:

> For ḍākinīs the subtlest quality is pure space combined with the radiating wisdom of Mother Prajñāpāramitā.
>
> From the space of the primordial mind, the Mother Prajñāpāramitā, something occurs, the very vastness of space invites something to occur. . . . This is the dawn of the possibility of appearance, of action, of form arising. It is analogous to the first stirrings that preceded cell division in the swamps, which are thought of in Western culture as the beginning of life.

> Yet, because all insight and understanding arise from this experience, space of the sky is said to be the source of all. For this reason, there is great devotion for the source, which is called mother.[47]

Before there was life—even before the duality of being and nonbeing from the Vedic cosmogonical hymn—there was this pure vastness of space of which secret Ḍākinī is a guardian. The vastness of the primordial space as divinely saturated matrix corresponds to what we will later call quantum or God's field.[48] This space is primordial as it is the basis of all experience—whatever will appear (emotions, sense perceptions, reflections, thoughts) will appear from it. What now first occurs from this vast space is the seed syllable A, the primordial sound of the Sanskrit alphabet and the root of all sounds and of all experience. As a basic element of an oral knowledge, the root syllable is an essence of all transmission of wisdom through a lineage of enlightened ones (buddhas and lamas) in Tibetan Buddhism. The syllable is carried by vital breath, which flows in the subtle or energetic body of Ḍākinī. The subtle elemental presence of the winds or subtle breath (*lung, prāṇa*) in this subtle mind-body is a sign of its concentrated energy. From the first Breath of creation—of the r̥gvedic verse *That One breathed without wind by its independent will / There existed nothing else beyond that*—this hidden presence of the breath in all that lives, now quintessentially manifests in the *warm (mouth) breath* of Ḍākinī. The materiality of the breath is manifested by its moist vapor and its inherent living quality (as movement, freshness, and aliveness): "The warm mouth-breath is also considered damp with saliva, like steam or vapor, indicating its fresh, alive qualities: the experience is always new, and yet there is a continuity. The communication is living instruction, which carries the continuity of lineage."[49] Warm mouth-breath is thus transmitted orally in an intimate communication from the mouth to ear within the space-interval of proximity, in which any syllable and any word is carried out on the primordial breath of creation or the intimate life-breath of all creation: the essence of the world—or *dharmatā*: "The warm breath of the ḍākinīs is the expression of conceptual mind liquefying and wisdom dawning."[50] This is the path of a breathy eschatology now—of a transmission of the breath of love from the distant past and into the future: *the enigma of a first warm breath of creation, mysteriously transformed into the closest proximity of a breath-kiss in loving encounter*—as we are arguing in the postlude.

The Opening of Natural Eschatology

The task of our age is to approach the third era in the history of the humankind: a *spiritual* era enabling us to conceive of a natural eschatology as based on respiratory and matrixial elements of creation. Under this view, the spiritual task of our age consists in disclosing *the matrix of elemental mystical theology*—as revealed from the breath of love and as understood in the abyssal cosmico-ontological key. It is, in our opinion, only from this tissue of the world that the divinization of this world and natural eschatology—as key aspects of any future theology—would be possible to imagine, and, perhaps, to be accomplished in the future. According to Joachim of Fiore, the three stages of history are accomplished in the third and final spiritual era in which this world will be transformed into a terrestrial era in which there would be no war, no worry, and no terror.[51] In times of both environmental crisis and war, this thought is of the greatest importance. This thought would also enable us to embark on a path toward post-Christianity, which is now entirely based on the antinomian and elemental logic of the human being as situated and thus being an *embodied spirit*. The way of this new spiritual-breathful being is a part of the revolutionary era in which a natural conspiracy—a breathing with new earth and new heaven, or with Nature, will disclose a place for the liberating eschatology. It is also an era in which nature will not be alienated from humanity anymore and where humanity itself will also not be alienated from its inherent respiratory-matrixial core.

The matrix (*khora* of creation) as a chalice of being is the first germ of Love. In its abyssal breath-energy, it is the primitive element of creation, *wild logos of everything*, womb of Nature. In our search of the beginning, we were guided toward this abyssal matrixial function both through Christian and Buddhist symbolism: as the cosmic uterus was disembodied and detached from creation, and as it obscurely *existed* beyond any inside/outside dichotomies (similar to the Vedic constellation of *the One, breathing* beyond both Being and Nonbeing), it still remained *connected* to the phenomenon of life that it/she gives birth to. This conspiration of the ground is an announcement of elemental and breathy eschatology: a revelation of natural eschatology that will bring a new era for humanity, and for nature.

Part I
The Past

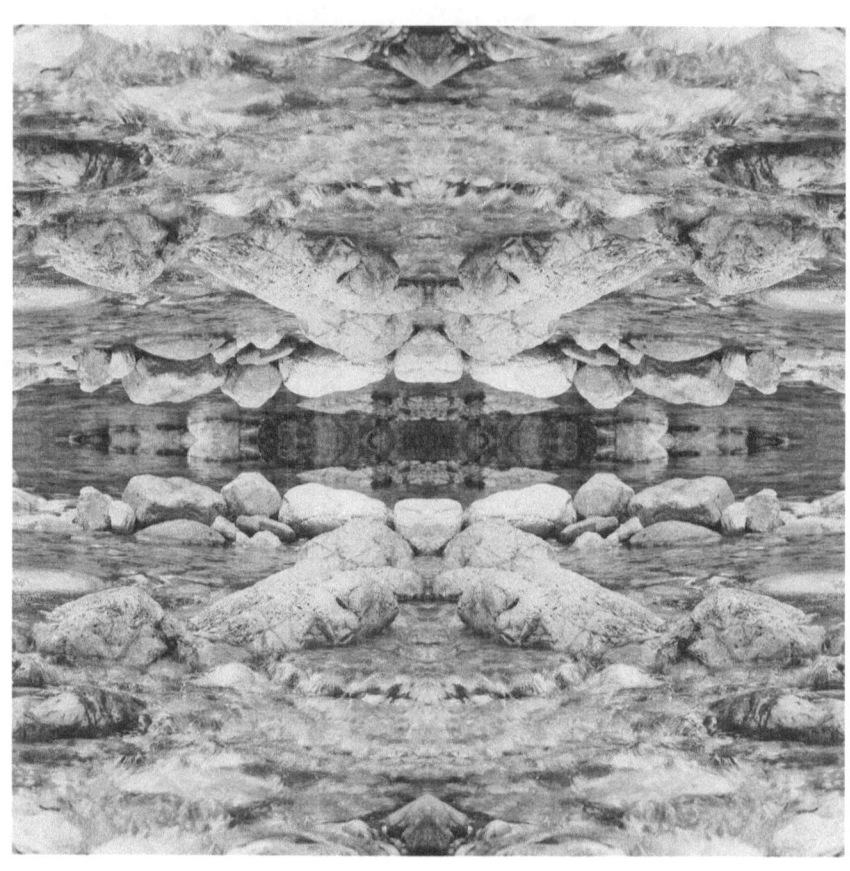

little stones

1

God in Stone

Toward the Reconstruction of Slovenian Elemental Religion

> People felt one with the trees then, regarding them as living beings. Man observed them, listened to them. He saw and heard more than today's man does, as he was still connected to nature; he understood the whispering of the leaves and branches. He was aware of being part of nature himself. The tree was sacred to him. If someone slashed across it, man felt sorry for it as if it were an animal. When he conversed with demons and gods, the tree was his medium.
>
> —France Bevk, *Umirajoči bog Triglav: Zgodovinska povest*[1]

> The point should be obvious: we, human beings, in all our rich diversity, are intimately connected and related to, in fact dependent on, the other living beings, land, air, and water of the earth's biosphere.
>
> —Vine Deloria Jr. and Daniel Wildcat,
> *Power and Place: Indian Education in America*[2]

There are fascinating questions arising in the synchronous study of contemporary philosophical theology, philosophy of religion, and the cosmology of ancient religions, ones that extend to certain key areas of epistemology, ontology, and contemporary environmental ethics. Models of religious and theological experience encountered in this specific constellation range from research into mystical and scientific correspondence between ancient and contemporary or new cosmologies (in humanities and sciences) to the interrogatives of new materialism within the framework of connections between philosophy, theology, and science. Perhaps the most vital part of new materialism in these constellations emerges as the very question of the *elemental* world of dwelling, around which most of our attention in this chapter will revolve, and which, in the concluding part, will be applied to the issue of *entanglement* within the ambit of so-called new quantum theology. In this context, the elemental plane of dwelling is related to the awareness of a connection between beings (plants, animals, humans) and their ontological foundation, which is revealed through the nature of the world that surrounds them—the meaning of the elemental world of dwelling is here linked to the old cosmological matrices of interdependence of dwelling in relation to the ancient "elements" of air, water, fire, and earth. The elemental character of the world of dwelling also embraces the mineral strata of nature (e.g., stones, metals), which are normally understood as inanimate or inorganic forms of nature. Through elemental consciousness, nature unfolds as a space permeated by the omnipresent life force of all living things. In some cultures, this force is expressed through articulations about God; in others as the Supreme Being or life force; and in still others this idea has been closely connected to nature.

In more recent times, humanity has replaced its connectedness to the surrounding or natural world with the ideal of scientific certainty and so-called objective knowledge about man and the world. In order to understand and, even more so, dominate and exploit the planet and its creatures, man has left the latter to their fate of being a standing reserve (Heidegger), while making man the ruler of everything that exists and dwells in this world. The ancient cosmic-mystical correspondences have thus been forgotten and the Earth has become a place of one being asserting its supremacy over all others on the planet. At a time defined and distressed by an ecological crisis of global dimensions, a reflection on the revitalization of the elemental manner of dwelling is truly urgent. Not only were the gods and divine beings of numerous native or Indigenous traditions of the world ousted from the victorious conscience of the Earth's new ruler, the chaos of the human world pulled under its cloak of diabolical supremacy even later gods and their earthly avatars: "Golgotha is a figure of a coming cosmic void (*khora*, the anonymous 'it'), and entropy is the cross on which the universe itself is crucified," states Caputo: nihilistic and post-Christian, regarding the position of theology and god in the modern environmental crisis.[3]

This chapter aims to show that, in the human and social as well as natural and technical sciences (including the breakthrough findings of quantum physics in the early twentieth century), a confrontation between the original elemental cosmological matrices and contemporary theories has traced a space of ontological mystery and at the same time cosmological-quantum *entanglement*,[4] both of which imply the possibility of transitioning to a newly conceived ontology and cosmotheology of man, nature, and God. In this context, we will deal with the extraordinary testimony of the Slovenian Indigenous and pre-Christian religious tradition of Staroverstvo (called "Old Faith" but also known as Naravoverstvo or "Nature Worshippers"[5]), trying to provide it with a modern theological interpretation while abiding by the methods of new cosmology and new materialism. Of course, our designation of this religious tradition as an Indigenous Slovenian religion requires an introductory note. In his chapter titled "Indigenous Lifeways and Knowing of the World," John Grim points out a definition of the notion of Indigenous religion.[6] His understanding relates to the native population of an area that was colonized but has, nevertheless, retained some of its social, cultural, economic, and political institutions; more specifically, it relates to the concept of indigenousness as defined by these communities themselves, with regard to their histories, languages, cultures, beliefs, institutions, and territories as well as the related traditions. Grim defines the concept of indigenousness of a culture as that which refers to "small-scale societies around the planet who share and preserve ways of knowing the world embedded in particular languages, story cycles, kinship systems, world-view dispositions, and integrated relationships with the land on which they live."[7] Later on we will try to outline in what ways this tradition could be understood as an example of Indigenous religion of Slovenia.

In 2015, an extraordinary testimony by Pavel Medvešček-Klančar (1933–2020) about the followers of Slovenian Nature Worshippers from the area of the Soča basin was published in the work *Iz nevidne strani neba* (From the invisible side of the sky).[8] Before Medvešček, testimonies about this tradition from the area of the Slovenian Kras was published by Boris Čok.[9] Both works are based on the originally unwritten, that is, oral tradition of Slovenian pre-Christian religion as it had been preserved through the centuries and passed on from generation to generation. Both books, especially Medvešček's life's work, bring such rich messages and clues that they immediately invite direct comparison with certain key paradigms in the field of the very caesura between the oral and the written, and link to the issue of religious tradition reconstructions as broadly encompassed within the conceptual framework of ethnophilosophy.[10] Much like the efforts of contemporary researchers of autochthonous traditions of African peoples (and, by analogy, all other peoples of the world) that survived the era of colonization and Christianization and managed to preserve the sacred lore of their ancestors, the investigation of the tradition of Staroverstvo also raises some critical questions—among which this book will highlight the importance of this tradition for contemporary philosophical theology and for the elemental and environmentally oriented philosophy of religion. One of the world's greatest experts on the ancient oral traditions of the peoples of the world and the related environmental thought is American cultural ecologist and geophilosopher David Abram. When describing the lore of the Arctic Inuit and Yup'ik peoples in his essay "The Commonwealth of Breath," he approaches their centuries-old tradition and pays homage to it with these words:

> I shudder to speak of matters held so sacred to these oral traditions, and even more so to *write* of these understandings, which were never meant to be written down. . . . I bow to the various peoples indigenous to this region where I dwell, as well as to the animals, plants, and spirits of this parched terrain, asking their permission that I may write, here, of these things. Because these storied knowings, of which I comprehend so little, nonetheless need to be heard once again, and what is common among them needs to be felt, acknowledged, and replenished if life is to flourish.[11]

With this credo of humility and at the same time respect for tradition and life, Abram joins the ranks of those few thinkers—among them Medvešček—whose works reflect their authors' ability to lend an attentive and humble ear and to pass on the sacred traditions of old. They show the respect that had been lacking in an over a millennium-old position of arrogance and contempt from which others viewed these sacred traditions, derogatorily labeling them backward, pagan, pre-Christian, and prescientific. Precisely the changes in contemporary humanistic and scientific movements brought the realization that life on our planet will only thrive if we are able to understand these sacred old traditions in all their complexity and deep interconnectivity with nature and link them to the findings of modern science.

But before taking a closer look at the elements of Slovenian Nature Worshippers as they appear in our philosophical-theological consideration, there is another important point to note: the question whether this lore and the related religion could be considered as the Indigenous religion in the ethnic territory of Slovenia—such was the self-understanding of certain believers from the Soča basin, as inferred from the words of one of them: "Most call it the old faith, but I call it *the first faith* that has survived, albeit in fragments, to this day."[12] Slovenian archaeologist, historian, and ethnologist Andrej Pleterski proposes two important hypotheses in this regard, which are related, respectively, to the narrower, Slavic, and the broader, Indo-European, religions. The first hypothesis relates to Nikolai Mikhailov's observation that "Slovenian mythology is the only Slavic tradition to have preserved so perfectly and thoroughly the so-called 'principal myth' of Slavic mythology," while in the second Pleterski assesses that "of all Indo-Europeans, the Slavs were the ones who led the simplest way of life the longest," and who "at the beginning of the Early Middle Ages were still living in conditions characteristic of the early Neolithic."[13] Pleterski bases his two premises on the preserved archaic structure in the myth of the god Triglav (Three-Headed God), a tale learned from the Slovenian Nature Worshippers and written down by Boris Čok in his book *In the Glow of the Moon*. Within this context, Pleterski thus makes the assumption of a directly preserved archaic (or Indigenous, as we wish to argue) tradition, which displays in its genealogy an *uninterrupted* link that follows the axis of the Slavic mythological and religious traditions while also extending beyond the lore of Slavic Indo-European mythology as far back as the Paleolithic. As we shall see, it is precisely the elemental symbolism of the stone and related elements that manifests the secret connection to modern theology and even science, which we attempt to trace and describe in this chapter. Both observations are important for us for the following reasons: first, they enable the assessment of a new theological reconstruction of the earliest traditions of humanity through their inherent and uninterrupted elemental matrix; second, they acknowledge Staroverstvo as an autochthonous or primordial, and thus—as we wish to contend on a basis of this argumentation—*Indigenous religion* of Slovenian territories and bring it into direct dialogue with the neomaterialist and elemental trend of contemporary post-Christian theology in the making, to which our work belongs.[14]

In his introductory study to the volume *From the Invisible Side of the Sky*, Pleterski defines this tradition as the one cultural code that can help us gain new insight into the understanding of our common civilization, and Medvešček's work as "unprecedented in Slovenia and outside it."[15] Historically, this religion was hardly discussed at all, with its followers keeping it a strict secret, and when it *was* spoken about, it was by Christians, who did not understand it and pejoratively designated it pagan. We should therefore waken at Boris Čok's simple, yet deep and honest realization (emphasized in his *In the Glow of the Moon*) that even as a child he could not embrace the images in the readings from the Bible (e.g., the desert, the strange clothes, unusual customs, remote myths), for they felt alien or nonautochthonous to him at that time. Something completely different was listening to the stories told by his family, which, as he later understood, contained ancient and autochthonous elements of what nowadays can be called Staroverstvo.[16] As we shall see, this not only includes archaic mythological patterns and a variety of divine names, but also testifies to an extraordinary presence of gender distinction—that is, the feminine and masculine poles of the divinity in the very core of this tradition, which was, almost without exception, obscured or suppressed in every major world religion.[17] Our task is to talk with respect about the remarkable value of this uninterrupted cultural history of Slovenia.

A Single God or Multiple Gods: On the Monotheistic Tendency

A fascinating theory to aid in the understanding of the relationships between types of religion (in our case, between the so-called Indigenous religion of Natural Worshippers and Christian monotheism) was put forward by Jan Assmann; it relates to the already forgotten yet epochal writings on primitive (i.e., original) monotheism by Wilhelm Schmidt (1868–1954), which will serve as a selected case of the early treatment of Indigenous religions of the world from the point of view of religious theory. In his lecture on the beginning and development of religion, as well as forms of monotheism and related theories, titled "Monotheism and Cosmotheism," Assmann touches upon some fundamental issues of the relationship between religious studies and theology.[18] It was axiomatic of the dominant religious history of the West that it regarded monotheism as the highest form of religion. This is how evolutionists thought when deriving the development of religion from animism and totemism, and leading it through polytheism to (Christian) monotheism (and some, like August Comte, even through that, further on to a new scientific religion). The trends toward revelation in the development of world religions stand testimony to that, as does, ultimately, the dominant monotheistic-philosophical aspects of thought or worship of oneness in Greece, Persia, and India, which contained a clearly expressed inclination toward "One" as their principle. In this context, Assmann calls attention to three fundamental approaches: the theory of decadence, evolutionism, and the theological method. The latter, however, is not a part of religious studies and is, unlike the former two, based on revelation. Assmann contends that monotheism is neither part of the decadence nor the evolutionist theory. For the so-called decadentists within religious studies, monotheism is the archetype of all religion, as they call it proto-monotheism (*Ur-Monotheismus*): this concept encompasses some primeval/original form of religion that, in their opinion, gradually retrogressed into inferior forms. This theory was argued by French deists as early as the seventeenth century, by Schelling in his *Philosophy of Mythology*, by Max Müller (in the context of later Indian religion vis-à-vis the earlier and, to him, undisputedly "superior" ideal of Vedic religion), and particularly by Wilhelm Schmidt in his monumental *Origin and Growth of Religion*. But, before looking at Schmidt's draft, let us further concentrate on Assmann's work. In this lecture, Assmann rejects the artificially created and essentially evolutionist dichotomy of polytheism vs. monotheism, and with regard to the religion of Ancient Egypt, he prefers to distinguish between two types of monotheism: the cosmological and the political. Assmann also rejects the milder version that would concede to the Egyptian religion the so-called "monotheistic trend within polytheism."[19] In light of this, Assmann argues that the former should be distinguished from the latter as exclusivist in its essential trait: namely, according to him, cosmological monotheism—just like its "successor," political monotheism—speaks about the unity of the world/cosmos/being, but with one important distinction: in the context of cosmological monotheism, this unity means that other gods also still exist or reside in this world. Above them is one god who maintains and preserves them through not always unambiguous relationships. Also in this lecture, Assmann focuses on the case of Egypt and cites Akhenaton's immanentistic cosmotheistic reform theology as a model example of cosmological monotheism, but equally good examples besides Egypt (and Mesopotamia) include ancient Greece and the religions of ancient India. The Vedic religion and its Upanishadic question "How many gods are there?" is an important testimony to cosmological monotheism in the context of Indo-European religions, to which Slovenian Natural Worhippers also belong.[20] In this sense, Assmann's lecture represents a significant religious-theological correction aimed at the very core of the "issue of monotheism."[21]

A theory by Wilhelm Schmidt holds interest for us in that it provides a pioneering analysis of world religions and evidences the transition into the modern theology of religion that was later developed by Wilfred Cantwell

Smith. As a member of the Catholic Church (specifically, of the Societas Verbi Divini congregation), Schmidt pondered world religions according to the principles of theological reflection, but his studies were decisively influenced by the findings of anthropologists and ethnologists who, at the turn of the twentieth century, were just starting to develop a new science, the anthropology of religion (for instance, E. B. Tylor and R. R. Marrett). Thus, Schmidt started taking an interest in the languages of African and Polynesian cultures, and his studies of religious traditions across the globe resulted in his seminal and most comprehensive work, *The Origin and Growth of Religion* (this exceptionally extensive scientific effort was published between 1926 and 1955).[22] Schmidt remained in the priesthood throughout his career and his academic work was closely connected to the Catholic Church. He was preoccupied with the origin of the idea of God, which in different historical periods and in different cultures manifested in various different ways, and tried to integrate the multiple expressions into a single theory using a religious-scientific and empirical method.

Schmidt embarks on his research with the now long-discarded idea and aim of a unified theory of religion. He sought to trace the basis or origin of the religious revelation of God or the Supreme Being,[23] but he was destined to fail in this ambition, as the impossibility of reaching as far back as the prehistorical era (through archaeology) stalled his investigation at a point between the visible or accessible and the invisible or (then yet) inaccessible field in the study of the history and origin of religion. Still, Schmidt's work quietly paves the way for a later current of theology of religion represented by Wilfred Cantwell Smith, and, as such, is a crucial link in the development of modern religious studies.[24] Schmidt's objective was to analyze various peoples (which he called *Naturvolken* or "natural peoples") in order to determine how far back in their history they held a belief in a Supreme Being. He studied peoples of all continents, presenting for each the idea of a Supreme Being in the ways it was expressed in the culture in question: by name, function, place, and quality. In doing so Schmidt sought to illustrate (within the limitations of his time) the similarities between cultures and peoples in imagining and experiencing the idea of God. From a comparison between the ancient cultures of Africa, Asia, and America he extrapolates the existence of an even older, primitive culture (*Urkultur*) and assumed, by analogy, the existence of primitive revelation (*Uroffenbarung*) as understood by people in ancient times. Schmidt's extensive work displayed something not yet seen in his contemporaries: he viewed these ancient peoples—at the time considered "primitive" in the sense of backward, uncivilized—as partners and, therefore, companions in the process of emergence of the divine idea in the world. A case in point is his chapter on the religion of American Indians based on data gathered by A. L. Kroeber, professor of anthropology at UC Berkeley; Schmidt sums up and supports Kroeber's conclusion by stating: "Then, in two monographs, *Indian Myths of South Central California* and *The Religion of the Indians of California*, he showed that, contrary to the animistic and preanimistic theories of the late development of a high god, these very tribes had a clearly developed Supreme Being and an idea of a real creation."[25]

In his work *The Origin and Growth of Religion*, Schmidt focuses on all the mentioned areas in order to prove the existence of primitive monotheism in them. By acknowledging the primitive monotheistic trend in ancient cultures of the world (which we are not going to employ today, of course—replacing it instead by descriptions of the relationships of intertwinement or, to use the jargon of contemporary science, *entanglement* between man, nature, and god/gods), he refutes the theories of animism and evolutionary development of religion. Schmidt claims that "primitive peoples" did not simply believe in a being they associated with the animistic or spiritual principle, and he proceeds to develop a theory of primitive monotheism based on three elements or conditions, which are an expression of the ethnographic nature of his thinking. These are (1) the totality of human needs, (2) unity of time, and (3) unity of space through the idea of God. Only when these conditions are met is it possible to speak of primitive monotheism, Schmidt claims. The totality of human needs implies that such a god (or being or [primal] force) gives meaning to the origin of family, progeny, ethical needs, love, and so forth; unity of time indicates that such a god fills our existence in all times; while unity of space refers to God as governing all space within a specific religious framework. Based on these criteria, Schmidt was able to link the original religions of the world as primitive monotheisms with the major monotheistic systems, interpreting the latter through a lens of continuity, rather than discontinuity and break. Though not foreshadowing that at the time, as his work was not based on the paradigms of religious or theological pluralism, his theories set the scene for both.

Schmidt's line of argument can be understood and employed in two ways: it can either be read through the lens of a monotheist trend and understood as a preceding and inferior stage in the development of a higher religion, or considered—somewhat more discerningly—to be an example of more humble and respectful treatment of the so-called ancient cultures and their religions. In the latter case, this theory allows us a different view of the relationship between models of dominant monotheisms on the one side, and alternative models—so often silenced or ignored in the history of religion—of searching for the meaning of the Supreme Being, God, or Nature, on the other (wherein Assmann's hypothesis of cosmotheism is also very helpful). In light of her work *Beyond Monotheism*, Laurel Schneider would most certainly understand both sides as talk of something that the history of monotheisms has been forgetting since religions, in their new monarchic gesture, started talking about God as a patriarch, an elevated substance completely separate from the world, that is, as something that is not dynamic and no longer possesses an inherent connection to bodies or elements of nature.[26] The same held true for the conception of gender distinction. The shift to the spherical, uncreated, and eternal as principles of perfection of the (masculinized) One and the Unchanging principle with Parmenides marked, in the West, the beginning of a new chapter in metaphysical thinking and philosophical theology in general. Our aspiration is to illustrate the extent of damage thus inflicted on religions that did not fit this matrix, as well as on theology itself, which—alas—all too quickly adopted this same matrix, thereby preventing or restricting its own access to the world of elemental dwelling. In this way, we wish to broadly outline how elemental philosophical theology can bear witness to this gesture of forgetting and forced repression. In Schneider's words, we ourselves can wonder: "When did the stories of God become a story of totality, of a closed system, of One?"[27]

Let us now finally return to the realm of faith of the followers of Slovenian Indigenous religion. In his treatise "Verovanje host v sklopu staroverstva in verovanja starih Slovanov" (The belief of "hoste" in the context of Natural Worshippers in Slovenia and the belief of the ancient Slavs),[28] in addition to the important and already-mentioned aspect of archaism of their mythical story, Pleterski draws attention to the following: both the ancient Slavs and, in the continuity of unbroken tradition all through the end of the twentieth century, the followers of Slovenian "Old Faith" (i.e., Natural Worshippers) after them, believe in a dynamic structure of the divine, which displays inherent structural plurality and clearly acknowledges gender distinction; while in its triadic structure the god Triglav is composed of a Goddess (as the central figure) and next to her gods Kres and Vilež,[29] he also, in this trinity, attaches to the fourfold aspect of the god Svetovid, who has four heads—that is, contains four elements (earth, water, air, fire), the four cardinal points, the four seasons of the year, and the four periods of life. Finally, Triglav and Svetovid, united into a sevenfold divinity, form the multiple oneness of the supreme Slavic god—Dajbog. The supreme goddess of the Natural Worshippers from the Soča basin, on the other hand, was Nikrmana, also known as Velika dobra mati (Good Great Mother) and Velika Baba (Great Old Woman), and Pleterski clearly juxtaposes her typology with that of Dajbog. Like Dajbog, Nikrmana maintains within herself a dynamic and plural dimension of divinity, including gender distinction—for the name does not necessarily imply that as a divinity she is (merely) a woman. Pleterski thus asks a provocative question and, at the same time, answers it himself: "[I]s Nikrmana male, is Dajbog female? . . . The solution is simple. The chief Slavic god, and therewith Nikrmana, should be imagined as an androgynous being."[30] In the continuation of this book we will raise similar questions ourselves. But it is already very clear that the religion of the ancient Slavs, as well as Slovenian Natural Worshippers, allows for broad possibilities of interpretation that reach far beyond the static and artificially created dualities of monotheism vs. polytheism, or the male vs. female aspect in religion, and does not allow the classic and by now dispensed with dichotomies between higher and "earlier/more primitive" (but consequently inferior) models of religious experience. In the spirit of the findings made by Schneider, we could say that ancient Slavic and ancient Slovenian gods and primal forces undisputedly bear witness to the abundance of the dynamic ontological and intersex life force of the divine and the sacred.

To conclude: with the development of philosophy and theology, the Western world forsook emotions and sensory perception, including smell and touch, and in relation to nature founded a completely new mode of thought, characterized by a conceptual and ideational world—a world of unrestrained subjectivity based on the dominance of mind over feelings, of one sex over the other, of man over the animal world, mankind over nature. Lamentably, theology followed suit and—quite paradoxically—too frequently banished from its already cold chambers any spirit of elemental materiality with even the slightest hint of closeness to Jesus; compassion, contact, and physical closeness were too often considered redundant in favor of grand theological and metaphysical schemata, the meaningless production of theoretical evidence of the existence of God or, simply, endless prestige wars for the supremacy of one argument or doctrine (or church) over another.

Elements of Slovenian Indigenous Religion

In his book *Power and Place*, theologian Vine Victor Deloria Jr. (1933–2005, a Standing Rock Sioux), from the Sioux tribe of American Indians, points out the fact that white men scorned the knowledge of American Indians for centuries, regarding their teachings as mere superstition and at the same time believing that "a complex mixture of folklore, religious doctrine, and Greek natural sciences, was the highest intellectual achievement of our species."[31] Only in recent decades has it become evident that American Indian tribes (and, by analogy, other tribes, small-scale societies, and cultures of the world) have been in possession of special and important knowledge about the cosmos and the natural world. The concepts that Deloria puts to the fore are power and place. While the dominant Western tradition in philosophy and science spoke and thought only through the coordinate system of linear space, time, and energy at least up to Henri Bergson or Alfred North Whitehead, Indigenous people have always spoken and thought through the matrix of power/life force and space. But their ideas about the common characteristics of, say, humans and animals, or even about the interconnectedness of the mineral, plant, animal, and human worlds, did not fit into the conceptual framework of tradition nor could this knowledge be framed within the domain of the term "faith." Deloria calls attention to another important dimension that will interest us in this book: "We may grant that the energy described by quantum physics appears to be identical to the mysterious power that almost all tribes accepted as the primary constituent of the universe."[32] The ultimate realization of the philosophical theology of American Indians, as presented by Deloria, that our dwelling is essentially *relational* and connected to other living beings, the land and its elements, opens up ample possibilities of reinterpretation of numerous similar spiritual traditions—of these we shall foreground the philosophical-theological view of the Slovenian Indigenous religion.[33]

The elemental philosophical theology developed in this book is an expression of hidden or (still) mysterious cosmic correspondences between different types of living beings that inhabit and fill the space. As the Nature Worshippers of Slovenia put into the fore stones and their inherent *spiritual materiality*, we shall start with them. In the jargon of modern quantum physics, Catherine Keller describes the ontological status of a stone as follows: "In *Process and Reality*, Whitehead would formulate this radically nonsimple location as his 'ontological principle': 'Everything is positively somewhere in actuality and in potency everywhere.' This potentiality, suggestive of the quantum potential or vacuum, also anticipates the French quantum physicist Bernard d'Espagnat's snapshot of a stone: " 'its 'quantum state' is 'entangled' (this is the technical word) with the state of the whole Universe.' "[34]

Medveščekʼs book, at which we are going to take a closer look now,[35] contains remarkable testimony to the intertwinement or ontological entanglement of everything that exists on Earth. An extraordinary example of such understanding is the testimony by Janez Strgar, who ushered Medveščcek into the sacred realm of his faith. This is what he said about the faith of Toni Javor, the only one, according to Strgar, among his friends who had frequent contacts with the other world:

> On such days he would take time to himself, spend it alone in the mountain or in the woods where he could see, as he put it, beyond the visible, where one could hear echoes and voices from primeval time. . . . Javor also refused to accept the concept of inanimate matter, for to him everything that surrounded him was living matter. . . . They [i.e., his younger contemporaries] find it particularly silly when Javor says he is also friends with trees, water and certain stones. In the end, there follows the teaching that says we should love nature like a mother, for we are part of it. (56)

This passage somehow brings together all that we intend to think about here: the Nature Worshippers were able to cross the linearity of time via their solitary, sometimes even truly ascetic detachment, and enter the so-called timelessness in which they felt the interconnection of all existing things as animate—that is, of the dynamic whole of spiritual matter and the supporting primal force of Nikrmana (The Creatrix) in one of its emanations (it was sighted during the nights when lightning would strike; some saw it in the form of a woman, others as clouds, or also in the form of a bull, a snake, an ibex, or a horse). Nikrmana is an indication that the whole space was revered for the purposes determined by this primal force—this is the clear link connecting the Slovenian Indigenous religion to other Indigenous religions from elsewhere in the world. Based on the tradition and secret teachings passed on to him, Medveščcek is aware that "a stone is not just inanimate matter, but an important element in space and a human's companion that co-creates and ensures human existence" (525). Stones resembling *a snake's head* selected by Nature Worshippers were also worshipped as protectors of seeds, or, in the words of Valentin Hvalica: "The great stone acted as an altar to which people offered the precious seeds on which they depended. In doing so, they also helped the birds, which are a living link between the Earth and the sky" (235).

According to ancient belief, stones symbolized all living nature, and taking into account the previously mentioned credo of quantum physicist Bernard d'Espagnat that the quantum status of a stone is "entangled" with the status of the whole universe, we can derive the conclusion that there existed special knowledge that was for centuries available to Slovenian Nature Worshippers who saw and felt in the consecrated stones an extraordinary power or force—moreover, Valentin Hvalica even says that "when you 'rock' the *green snake head* with some special purpose you may hear the primal time, for the green snake head was born in the sacred river that springs from the heart of the sacred mountain of Triglav, in which our belief is rooted" (236).

Stones were also the composing elements of the *tročan* or triad/trinity, which connected in itself the elements of earth, water, and fire. When building a house, Nature Worshippers selected three stones and laid them so as to form a sacred triangle to express this interconnectedness. Such a *tročan* was believed to protect the house and have a beneficial effect on humans, animals, and plants. It kept the world in balance by way of special cosmic correlation and the knowledge that made that possible was a carefully guarded secret that was passed from father to son, and only in the hour of death. A *tročan* also had an ethical meaning. When Janez Strgar spoke of the *tročan*, he called attention to its cosmic-ethical dimension: "A *tročan* is also something that exists within ourselves, though not inside a single person, it's something which at present exists between you, Tone and me. We cannot be alone, one without the other. Only then does one feel this inner power within oneself" (87–88). In the context of Staroverstvo, this view demonstrates the extraordinary belief (which lies at the foundation of modern environmental ethics) "that in nature, we are all equally important and interdependent" (108). *Tročans* point to a very important characteristic now: namely, that its view of relationships in the world is a matter of *horizontal transcendence*—both at the level of relationships with the macrocosm and at the level of relationships between living beings as parts of nature. Conversely, the classical theology of monotheist religions insisted on vertical or monarchic transcendence, which denied the people (particularly women and children) their full ontological affiliation and did not grant any ontological rights to animals and plants, let alone so-called inanimate nature. As such it was too often intolerant of and violent toward the allegedly pagan religions that exhibited that, including—unfortunately—the Nature Worshippers, which it did not understand. Finally, there is also the blood *tročan* connecting the mother, the father, and the child. This triad also exhibits horizontal genealogy in a special genealogical relationship established between the parents and the children, wherein the child as a part of this triad can now exist as an ontologically equal element of the structure. This is also one of the reasons why the tradition of Staroverstvo prohibits violence against children (as opposed to Christianity, which has supported it for centuries and, lamentably, preserved it to this day).[36]

To recap, we can now say that in the cosmic-theological sense, it is the elemental horizontal ontological connection that enables the understanding of this secret (in the sense of secret cosmic correspondence) connection between the human and nature and its forces—as Valentin Šmončev beautifully described when he said that one should live in such a way as "to equate oneself with all living beings living around us and with us" and that "there is also among us that which we cannot see or understand but which definitely works" (179). At this point we may recall Deloria saying that the energy described by quantum physics appears to be that secret force that ancient peoples and traditions considered to be the main component of the universe. An extraordinary testimony to this mysterious force is provided by Jože Fatorinov, to whom this force was revealed while he was observing a pool in the river. Following a poetic description of the mystical experience he was privy to he writes: "A secret force awoke in me, filling up my body and making it increasingly unrecognizable, different. I felt an amazing power in me. Since then I haven't needed anything else. Everything I need is within arm's reach. But it is up to me to continue to be honest and good and accept all that my friends-uncles do" (192). It is today amazing how highly Nature Worshippers thought of nature. It was the cathedral of their "Church," and the two greatest sanctuaries of Babja jama (cave of old woman) and Padence (an area close to Most na Soči) were only spoken of with deepest reverence. Their insights and teachings about nature are in perfect keeping with the latest insights of environmental humanities and environmental ethics. Perhaps the most compelling testimony on this topic in the entire Medvešček's book is that by his informant Jože Blažev. I shall recap it here by way of introduction to the reflection about the importance of new elemental philosophical theology for the modern debate on the environment. This is what he tells Medvešček in an extraordinary passage related to the devastation of war and arrival of industry in the Soča Valley, a valley so sacred to Nature Worshippers:

> You know what, they destroyed everything. Even the great *tročan*. It was a really large *tročan* formed by [the mountain of] Jelenk, the Jazbenk [chasm] and the Babja jama [cave]. All three were connected to the netherworld, where the great white snake lived. When there was high water next to the cave, it was a sign that

> the snake did not want anyone to come close. It longed for peace and quiet. . . . This vulture [i.e., modern man] is destroying everything and will in the end destroy himself too. That will be a relief for nature, which will be able to recover with the help of Nikrmana. Of course, I won't live to see that day and neither will you. (441)

Nature Worshippers were also called *kačarji* (worshippers of a serpent: *kača* in Slovenian) and one can only imagine the scorn felt for this faith by Christians, who had been instilled by their tradition with hatred for an animal so sacred to them. Their myth of the creation of life says there were once four moons in the sky: the largest was called the procreation moon, and when it cracked, seeds and eggs seeped from its cracks and fell on the Earth. From the first egg hatched a *white snake*, the symbol of Staroverstvo. It settled in Babja jama, making this cave the central Nature Worshippers' sanctuary. All other animals hatched from its eggs there, and all plants sprouted from the seeds. Only then did humanity emerge—from the procreation moon (which had in the meantime become a star), broken in half and fallen onto the Earth, developed the first woman and the first man as the two halves of that moon. This exceptional genealogy suggests a cosmological origin of all living beings, which is inconsistent with the theological and monarchic-monotheistic myth from the Judeo-Christian tradition: "In that day the LORD with his hard and great and strong sword will punish Leviathan the fleeing serpent, Leviathan the twisting serpent, and he will slay the dragon that is in the sea" (Is 27:1). Of course, one should not forget the ancient Indo-European myth about the snake-defeating hero (in the old Indian myth regarding the Vedas, for example, that hero is Indra, who overcomes the cosmic obstacle in the form of snake/dragon called Vritra or the one who kept the waters of the world captive and therewith life; cf. also later Christian versions from the stories about Saint George slaying a dragon), and Pleterski, too, mentions this aspect of the mythical story related to the mytheme of the snake.[37] The Nature Worshippers' myth of the snake thus suggests this is an extremely old subject that does not depart from the elemental world of dwelling (with the elements of water, fire, and air, as well as earth—including the netherworld) and continues to maintain some kind of archaic (pre-Biblical and pre-Christian and preceding later Indo-European corrections toward establishing a new and allegedly higher moral order by killing a primordial mythological snake/dragon) elemental awareness about the world and the life in it. But how do these elemental strata of dwelling manifest? How did the Nature Worshippers link their faith to them?

The world we inhabit is thus divided into the netherworld, the earthly world, and the heavenly world. All three worlds stay in balance through coordinated "cooperation" (or mystic/secret cosmic correspondences) of the beings of nature that have inhabited these worlds—divinities, humans, animals, plants, and rocks/stones. In the sense of horizontal transcendence, an invisible yet sacred connection is preserved among the beings of the world, which is strengthened by the belief that the spirits of the deceased settle as *zduhci* (plural of *zduhec*, meaning "wind spirit") in other beings and remain in contact with us even after death—every Nature Worshipper had their own *zduhec* in some living being through which they maintained this contact with the other or, better, parallel world. This connection is essentially a bond of love, as it contains no elements of violence, hatred, cruelty, or deceit. Through communication with *zduhci*, they traveled into timelessness, in which they were able to establish contact with the memories, suffering, and experiences of their ancestors. It follows that crushing a bug or a butterfly could mean killing the one "who lives in them their second life" (205). Their ethics is in this aspect absolutely comparable with the Jaina ethics of respect and preservation of all living beings, the strictest among the ethics of respect for life.

The Earth that we inhabit has been soaked by blood and pervaded by pain, terror, and suffering for millennia. The Industrial Revolution and unsuspected technological developments transformed it into something readily available for human use and abuse. Man has diverted, restricted, or stopped the waters, polluting them and making many unfit for life; he has tamed the fire and transformed it into an energy of unimagined force, down to its nuclear and destructive power; he has turned the air into a weapon, a medium for poisoning, choking, and killing other living beings, and riddled the earth with remains of weapons, of metal shaped into bullets and missiles. Man has blasted numerous sacred stones and rocks of Nature Worshippers, destroying the old *tročans* that used to preserve the balance of the believers' dwelling in the world, of passages from one season into the other, from life to death and into new life again. Few individuals and even fewer traditions have found the strength to oppose that: the Slovenian Nature Worshippers are undoubtedly a remarkable testimony to that, one that survived till the end of the twentieth century.

From Natural Worshippers to Post-Christianity

What lessons can Christianity learn from this religion? How can this faith help Christianity find its way back to Jesus's teachings about earthly living and closer to the elemental world in which people will, once again, be more connected to other living beings, to the earth and its divinities? And, how can Natural Worshippers help Christianity see the simple truth that the religions of this world—from the ancient to the contemporary—are connected by an invisible yet sacred bond of mutual respect and love: this is the sacred bond of the world that can only be nourished by humility that is shown to every element—however small—of this world.[38]

To transition from here into our concluding reflection, let us refer to an acute observation by Giorgio Agamben in reflecting on the Amalricians and their founder Amalric of Bène: "Amalric interpreted the Apostle's claim that 'God is all in all' as a radical theological development of the Platonic doctrine of the *chora*. God is in every thing as the place in which every thing is, or rather as the determination and the 'topia' of every entity. The transcendent, therefore, is not a supreme entity above all things; rather, *the pure transcendent is the taking-place of every thing*."[39] The Amalricians were those rare Christians who took the hypothesis about God being "everything in everything" very seriously and thereby opened up the possibility of salvation for all beings of this world—even minerals/stones, plants, animals, and of course all humans. Within the framework of the teachings of Slovenian Natural Worshippers, this now means that any entity in its nature already intimates this new "materialistic" theology of salvation and thus contains the *vital breath of creation* in the very core of its being.

Can the Indigenous religion of Slovenian Natural Worshippers, as an expression of *elemental theology* ultimately—with an ontological turn toward the vitalistic or spiritual matter as the heart of nature—open the mysterious portal of nature and thus help Christianity on its own path toward post-Christianity? In his work *The Insistence of God*, Caputo writes the following words about Jesus (note both the mention of stardust—that is, stones, minerals—and the expression "pagan" next to Jesus in the same context):

> Our bodies are the issue of solar, galactic, and cosmic stuff, the offspring of the elements. We are all stardust, made of ancient particles. . . . I treat Jesus as a Judeo-pagan prophet and healer, in tune with the animals and the elements, in whose body the elements dance their cosmic dance, supplying as it does a conduit through which the elements flow, and I treat the elements as a cosmic grace which is channeled by the body of Jesus.[40]

In this exceptional passage, Caputo, invoking Jesus's divine/human or—now—cosmic/natural body, appeals for the deepest respect of intuitions based on ancient elements that have been, as we have seen, either forgotten or "scientified" and classified by "our" philosophies and theologies. Referring also to the work of Irigaray, Caputo mentions by way of a genuine transition to a new elemental theology their cosmo- and theopoetic constellations, now in the sense of "the tandem of sun and eye, air and breath, wind and spirit, sea and life, rock and god. The coupling of the ancient mythic 'elements'—earth and water, fire and air—with the 'gods' is what makes up the divine."[41] This elemental philosophical theology has now come the closest to original cosmic constellations of being, where "rock/stone" and "god/God" can be conceived in the same sentence and in the closest connection or tandem. This thought is now that quantum moment in theology that could, in the way of "telepathic coupling,"[42] as Keller would put it, connect the seemingly as distant things as the bare and ostensibly dead matter of a stone on the one side, and the once highest and infinitely ontologically privileged spiritual essence of God on the other. It is precisely the live materiality of stone, now in its full elemental presence and cosmic entanglement, that can connect the most ancient and, as we can see, continuous traditions of religion dating from the Paleolithic era—to which Slovenian Natural Worshippers also belong—with theological models of a future time as are also expected in the context of new post-Christianity or, now in a common framework, in a future postreligious era, which is just being revealed to us through a post-anthropocentric consciousness.

covenant of salt

2

God in the Neanderthal

Somebody asked me: Do you have a soul?

I told him I do. I said I believed in its eternity and its beauty. But he asked me further: Does an animal have a soul? And I replied that it does. And he went on: Does a tree have a soul? And again I said that it does. Then he got angry and in his anger asked me: a stone too? And when I replied that it does, he turned his back on me.

How strange people are sometimes! When I say that the universe and universal soul are like sky and sea, reflecting each other, they believe it. But when I tell them that every phenomenon has its shine in the universal shimmering of the soul, they don't see it, and sometimes it is in fact true that a stone has a more beautiful soul than people.

—Srečko Kosovel, "Cosmic Life"[1]

The Word (*Logos*) spread himself everywhere, above and below and in the depth and in the breadth: above, in creation; below, in the incarnation; in the depth, in hell; in breadth, in the world. Everything is filled with the knowledge of God.

—Athanasius, *De Incarnatione*[2]

Prologue

This introductory passage from one of the most beautiful prose poems written by Srečko Kosovel reveals to us a profoundly deep, yet simple theological message that spans from mineral to stone, from plant to tree, from microorganism to any other living being, and, finally, from the various representatives of our common *Homo* species[3] to the present posthumanistic (cybernetic) human being living in the era of the death of God, and perhaps also Man. Accompanied by Athanasius's reflection on deep incarnation, this could form the core of new materialism as a part of contemporary environmental theology and Christology. What is shared in these passages is a presence of a *score*, as it were, of various cosmic markers of *a* life throughout creation. What we are getting at in this chapter is to indicate hidden, yet strong, presences of Christ in this vitalistic cosmic constellation. Contemporary discourses on posthumanism and postanthropocentrism, with related notions of vitalistic materialism, need to be accompanied by environmental thoughts on a vitalistic theologico-ontological relationality within nature.[4]

It is in this vein that, in 2017, a video became viral showing a polar bear dying from starvation due to the climate change impact on its lifeworld. Apart from imminent concerns, as well as critical remarks and reactions of the environmentalists, ethicists, and others concerned with broader environmental thought and climate change, this video also reveals to us a more hidden theological message. In an iconic image of an animal, being almost lifeless, with its once magnificent life force waning and with its once strong movements now slowly diminishing toward an imminent death, we are observing the decline of a once perfect being of nature. When the American environmentalist and naturalist John Muir came across a dead bear in Yosemite Valley, he bitterly complained about all those who, in their beliefs and theological views, had no room in heaven for such a noble creature—and we may add for any living creature. In the current environmental crisis, affecting so many of nature's species, and leading many of them toward extinction, it is vital to acknowledge the ethical and theological value of deep intuition, which is fully in line with contemporary views on deep incarnation within environmental or, broadly, contemporary theology. Furthermore, and to come full circle now, in his inspirational book on the cosmic Christ, titled *Christ's Power and Earth Wisdom*, Slovenian artist and writer Marko Pogačnik writes that "Jesus has offered humanity the key, and with its help we can reunite ourselves both with the macrocosmic dimension of the divine and with the elemental worlds of our earthly world."[5]

If we follow the idiosyncratic philosophico-religious lineage, reaching from Ludwig Feuerbach to Irigaray, then for us today it is necessary that we seek help in nature both for our survival (in the future era of the post-Anthropocene) and for our becoming (in the posthumanist post-Christian era). By reflecting also upon theological ideas as present in later works of another great thinker of nature, Maurice Merleau-Ponty, we can affirm that for him, the incarnation of Christ becomes present in the world in the form of vinculum of god(s), human beings, and earthly creatures, which—fully in line with his phenomenology of the flesh—feed into theological ideas of the cosmic Christ; as taken from early Church Fathers to Pierre Teilhard de Chardin and to recent deep incarnation theologies (to be elaborated upon later in this chapter). Thus, in this process of simultaneous expanding of Christ's presence into this world, as well as of debordering or breaking down the barriers between naturalism, humanism, and theism, divinities and earthly creatures are seen as passing into one another, which reveals to us a new possibility of environmental philosophy and environmental theology alike. Being therefore becomes incarnated in the *heart of the matter*, with the sacredness of every living being testifying to a newly revealed ontology of matter. In this chapter, we therefore argue for an environmental theology that is able to think deeper into both Christ's presence in the world as well as into the ability of theology itself to attune to the most profound elemental-material layers of this world—to the ancient elements (water, air, earth, fire), minerals and stones (as in the case of Slovenian Natural Worshippers), the rest of both inanimate and animate life-worlds, and, last but not least, of deep historical layers of our common history—that is, beyond the theological exclusivity of *Homo sapiens*.

Nature Revealed *as* God: Ludwig Feuerbach and the Religious Turn

Ludwig Feuerbach (1804–1872) was perhaps one of the most misunderstood thinkers of the nineteenth century. According to Karl Marx, in his famous *Theses on Feuerbach* from 1845, Feuerbach's greatest mistake as a philosopher was to limit his philosophy (and theology, we may add) of sensitivity only to "sensuous contemplation," and thus "he does not grasp the significance of 'revolutionary,' of 'practical-critical,' activity."[6] Feuerbach is considered to be a transitional philosopher to whom many authors ascribe significance for the later development of certain philosophical topics such as criticism of religion, materialism, sensibility, and so forth, but who nevertheless remains a thinker to whom the Western tradition did not wish to award a place of honor along with other philosophical giants of the West. But in the twenty-first century we can equally regard Feuerbach as an early predecessor of a contemporary theological thought of post-Christianity.

Jeffrey W. Robbins rightly asserts that Feuerbach stands to Friedrich Schleiermacher (from whom he took his central notions of dependency, or *Abhängigkeit*) as Hegel does to Kant.[7] However, Feuerbach's thought contains so many important and key elements for the development of philosophy of religion and postmodern materialistic theology that his position can neither be confined to the framework of the critical culmination of critical German idealism nor to any naïve or schematic form of criticism of religion from the positivistic or materialistic tendencies of the late nineteenth and early twentieth century. Precisely because Feuerbach is not acknowledged as one of the classic thinkers of German philosophy in connection with the tradition from Kant to Hegel and Schelling, and also because he did not participate in the later mainstream within the criticism of religion from Marx to Sigmund Freud on one side, or Søren Kierkegaard, Friedrich Nietzsche, and John Dewey on the other side, it is that much more important to emphasize Feuerbach's participation in and influences on those schools of thought.[8] But one of the most important consequences of Feuerbach's original work, in our opinion, could be found in his link to contemporary environmental theology.

Jakob Böhme was one of Feuerbach's most important influences. According to Feuerbach, Böhme is, as it were, "a mystical natural philosopher, a theosophic Vulcanist and Neptunist, for according to him all things had their origin in fire and water."[9] Feuerbach asserts that God is not only a spiritual "but also a material, corporeal, fleshly being,"[10] and it was precisely Böhme who (after the dawn of the pre-Socratics, we may add) was the first to provide a naturalistic context to this kind of theological reflection. Feuerbach, who himself shared great interest in geology and mineralogy, admired Böhme's passages on nature—comprising ancient elements (of the pre-Socratics), minerals, stones, plants, animals, and human beings. As stated by Feuerbach, Böhme "feels the joys of the mineralogist, of the botanist, of the chemist . . . He is enraptured by the splendor of jewels, the tones of metals, the hues and odours of plants, the beauty and gentleness of many animals."[11] Comparing the beauty of creation with the beauty of physical nature, an important step is taken—and let us now look at Bohme's idiosyncratic yet theologically greatly relevant words on precious stones: "Regarding the precious stones, such as the carbuncle, ruby, emerald, epidote, onyx, and the like, which are the very best, these have the very same origin—*the flash of light in love*. For that flesh is born in tenderness, and it is the heart in the centre of the Fountain-spirit, wherefore those stones also are mild, powerful, and lovely."[12] The beauty and ontologico-theological significance of this passage lies in the following conception: if an inanimate nature is now also subtly ontologically linked to the so called "Fountain-spirit" (*Quellgeister*) of all creation, and thus *is* a part of the highest spiritual economy of love—then important consequences follow. Feuerbach was first among Western thinkers to be able to point at these far-reaching theological effects: "In short, heaven is as rich as the earth. Everything that is on this earth is in heaven, all that is in Nature is in God."[13] Both *The Essence of Christianity* (1841) and *The Essence of Religion* (1846) fully attest to this enhanced religious awareness. And, first of all, it is *love* that will be in the forefront of this new awareness—Feuerbach will prepare the ground for this with a series of "anthropological" (but, in fact, they are theological) interventions into the very core of religion and theology. But it would be utterly wrong to attribute to Feuerbach any naïve or even atheist anthropological reduction of the essence of religion (as is done so many times)—something much more important happens in his thought when we are able to listen more carefully to his tender theological words. The chapter "The Mystery of the Incarnation; or, God as Love, as a Being of the Heart" from *The Essence of Christianity* is our first important testimony for this paradigm shift. Incarnation, for Feuerbach, was "a tear of the divine compassion";[14] clearly a material manifestation of the human nature of God. It is, now, love that shall be exalted into the new substance of religion, for Feuerbach, and this is what happens in incarnation—love now becomes a power that is even higher than God itself and it is only in this sense that the Feuerbachian anthropological reduction should in our opinion be understood and explained:

> Not because of his Godhead as such, according to which he is the *subject* in the proposition, God is love, but because of his love, of the *predicate*, is it that he renounced his Godhead; thus love is a higher power and truth than deity. Love conquers God. It was love to which God sacrificed his divine majesty. And what sort of love was that? another sort than ours? than that to which we sacrifice life and fortune? Was it the love of himself? of himself as God? No! it was love to man.[15]

With love being the highest, Christ can be seen as the "*être suprême* of the heart" and a suffering God is thus understood as "a heart" of this world.[16] God as a compassionate, a feeling and material Being, as flesh *and* nature, or, perhaps more metaphorically, the very heart of the matter, is now able to penetrate as such into every single being of nature—and this is where Feuerbach meets Böhme. With an unusual yet logical maneuver, it is now possible to ascribe a "kindness" or "mildness" even to inanimate nature—such as to a stone or a mineral. To Feuerbach, Christ literally becomes *the plasticity* ("die *plastische Persönlichkeit* ist nur Christus"[17]), the supreme concentration and spiritually material melting, and shining, as it were, of divine/cosmic energies—the only Being that is able to reach out *as love* to the first and penultimate of creation. Christ is a pulsation of the universe in the rhythm of love—a materially revealed cosmic Christ. In *The Essence of Religion,* a beautifully written work on religion, Feuerbach fully attests to this.

In other words, Feuerbach further radicalizes his theological thought. In the first paragraph of *The Essence of Religion*, the concept of *God* is seemingly detached from the concept of *Nature*: "That being which is different from and independent of man, or, which is the same thing, of God, as represented in the 'Essence of Christianity'—the being without human nature, without human qualities and without human individuality is in reality nothing but *Nature*."[18] But in § 2, there already appears a first correction to this statement: the source of all religion, for Feuerbach, is dependence (*Abhängigkeit*; which therefore was taken from Schleiermacher). In Feuerbach's view, the object of this dependence is Nature: "Nature is the first original object of religion, as is sufficiently proved by the history of all religions and nations"—according to Feuerbach.[19] But, apart from these now already obsolete questions of the origin of religion, what strikes us here are Feuerbach's elaborations on the *religion of nature* that follow in the forthcoming paragraphs of his work. Feuerbach now inaugurates a wholly new and original theory of an *ontological* dependency upon nature, bearing important theological consequences: "But above all man is a being who does not exist without light, without air, without water, without earth, without food—he is, in short, a being dependent on Nature. This dependence in the animal, and in man as far as he moves within the sphere of the brute, is only an unconscious and unreflected one; but by its elevation into consciousness and imagination, by its consideration and profession, it becomes religion."[20] Feuerbach recognizes that in many Indigenous religions of the world, animals were protective beings; also, mountains and lakes, rivers and springs, trees and other plants were divinely worshiped beings—providing and securing the sacredness of the land for human beings, their animal companions, nature, and, finally, for future generations. These beings are the guardians of life on Earth; they are thought of in various traditions either as divinities/gods or as God. These sacred correlations between natural landscapes and divinity were forgotten and lost, already, with the dawn of the pre-Socratics; also, Christianity was blamed by Feuerbach for the forgetting of this sacred relationality and of the "Divine Being which is revealed in Nature."[21] The God of Theism, being totally detached from nature in its role as creator, thus becomes a model of divinity without any material-ontological link to nature. But creation and preservation are inseparable for Feuerbach, and it is impossible to live without a vital nourishment that pours into various beings from the minerals, plants, and like (as in Job 36:24–37:24). As an example of an early contribution to what we now regard as the environmental theology, we can assert with Feuerbach that Nature, when regarded with a religious eye, is "a personal, living, feeling being."[22] And to make one more step further toward cosmic Christ—in *The Essence of Christianity*—Feuerbach uses the somewhat esoteric phrase "pneumatic water therapy" (*pneumatische Wasserheilkunde*)[23] to refer to the aim of his whole teaching. It is significant that, in addition to water, which holds a preeminent place in Feuerbach, also air/breath is invoked here (as *pneuma*). Water reminds us of our origin from Nature, according to Feuerbach; and the water of baptism thus becomes the means "by which the Holy Spirit imparts itself to man."[24] It is within this renewed elemental milieu that Christ can be (re-)incarnated—now as a divine Being, having *the earthly body*,[25] filled with *pneuma*, a body in which the four elements circulate in a mysterious-material dance of cosmic graces, or with Caputo:

> The four "elements" circulate through the body of the earthman, in his fiery anger at hypocrisy, in the *pneuma* by which he is filled, in the earth and water of his spittle. The kingdom of God is an animal kingdom, a kingdom of animal needs to which Yeshua's divinanimal ministry responds. The kingdom of God is a field of flesh, of flesh laid low and flesh raised up. The cosmic powers come to birth (*physis*), come alive, in "flesh," in bodies of flesh, and the body of Jesus is the channel through which cosmic graces rush. The graces of the world are concentrated in his body and through him they pass into those he touches or who are touched by him. He is the mediator between this grace and them, and those who come in contact with him are transformed.[26]

It is astounding to think that Feuerbach already knew about this cosmic Christ, without having previously available any useful theological possibilities for such a revelation of these elemental-cosmic graces.

Jesus Christ, Deep Incarnation, and the Neanderthal

As we know from some passages in the New Testament (Col 1:15–20; Eph 1:9–10; 1 Cor 8:6; Heb 1:2–3), the relevance of Jesus Christ can be attested not only for humans but also for the entirety of creation—including nonhuman animals and inanimate nature. As noted by Niels Gregersen and Elizabeth Johnson, "the incarnation makes the incarnate One integrally part not only of the human race, but also of the whole of this material reality—not only animals (with whom Jesus shares genetic continuity) but also plants and inanimate nature."[27] Based on an early thought of Gregory the Great on the partial ontological sharing of human beings with the rest of creation (from stones to angels), it was Bonaventure who wrote that "Christ, as a human being, shares with all creatures; 'Indeed, he possesses being with rocks, lives among the plants, senses with animals, and understands with angels.' Since Christ, as a human being, has something from all of creation, and was transfigured, all is said to be transfigured in him."[28] As convincingly shown by Richard Bauckham in his essay on the cosmic Christ, this thought was recently reformulated by Arthur Peacocke in his proposal to understand the unfolding of the multiple levels of creation as being present in Jesus Christ.[29] Bauckham radicalizes this thought by critically viewing the Christian evolutionary thought of Jakob Klapwijk, wherein theological value is elaborated through the fivefold division of being—from physical (as most basic and common to all creation), biotic and vegetative (as common to plants and animals), to more advanced sensitivity (common to animals and humans) and higher mental levels (common only to humans as self-conscious and spiritual beings).[30] But Bauckham is suspicious of any attempts that point toward an anthropocentric direction, and he rightly references the more peculiar features of any of the preceding levels of "creation" that somehow disturb or even invert the proposed ontological lineup of being. The process of photosynthesis, for example, might be one such example—for according to recent scientific discoveries, photosynthesis in plants operates on levels of *quantum superpositions* and, thus, evades any naïve or simplistic labeling from the point of the view of gradualist evolutionary thinkers.[31] Another example could be the presence of higher sensory abilities in animals, which also clearly prevent any too anthropocentric or reductionist philosophical or theological claims.

The title of this chapter indicates a possibility of another understanding of human history—one that could reach beyond the exclusivity of one human species for theology. For that purpose, it is necessary to address the theological consequences of including other representatives of our common *Homo* species (for example, Denisovan or Neanderthal) into Christian evolutionary thought from the point of the view of a deep history we have not yet sufficiently addressed. Although rather suspicious of attributing too much of a prehistoric ritual practice or religion to our predecessors, Ina Wunn is still willing to grant to *Homo neanderthalensis* at least a modicum of ritualistic or religious behavior: "Therefore Homo neanderthalensis believed that the animal is a being quite similar to man, but talented with supernatural forces. He was convinced that gods such as the 'Master of the Animals' or 'Supreme Being' existed. The kill of the animal took place after a complicated ritual."[32] This and similar, more recent findings in the field of the paleoanthropological studies of nonhuman hominin groups raise interesting but also difficult theological questions: given that recent mtDNA analyses show traces of Denisovan and Neanderthal DNA in specific groups of modern-day humans—the percentage of genetic similarity goes from 1–4 percent for Neanderthal DNA within modern-day humans, and from 6.6 percent, even up to 8.2 percent, for the Denisovan DNA as present in selected groups of modern-day humans of Melanesia. With Kennan Ferguson we can logically claim, "Most humans, therefore, are not entirely human."[33] The consequences of these findings for deep incarnation theology are even more far reaching since this similarity must equally be valid in the case of Jesus Christ as God—being fully incarnated as human being of the *Homo sapiens* species. By using some theological imagination, we may contend that, through this new perspective, Christ Himself becomes a divine being that cannot belong to only one hominin species anymore, but also takes part in the wider, deep historical, and pre- or nonsymbolic cultures of our common cospecies or even our predecessors. In his essay on William Golding's *The Inheritors*, Peter Alterman explains a special relevance of this novel as follows:

> The Neanderthal men in *The Inheritors* are different from Homo sapiens in many significant ways. The five senses are expanded in the Neanderthal awareness, and this enhancement allows the Neanderthals to live sensuously in a way that humans cannot. The differences are the measure of their moral superiority and the reason for their failure. . . . The Neanderthals, in other words, are selfless, loving, gentle, religious, innocent. They are more than Noble Savages: they are Christ-like. The irony is that these ideal representatives of human goals are senselessly slaughtered by the ancestors of the readers, who, we assume, cherish

> these ideals. . . . The careful construction of the Neanderthals, both through descriptive technique and ascribed qualities, serves primarily to create *alien beings*. As previously noted, aliens can be human, and share many human characteristics. However, the living through the senses and the telepathy of the Neanderthals go *beyond more primitive human concepts to define an alien awareness*.[34]

Based on this excerpt, one may now be tempted to define Christ as an *alien being* that is being incarnated into the violent lifeworlds of our *Homo sapiens* species, which, ultimately have sacrificed and killed also Him—what an irony of history! The mentioning of telepathy is particularly interesting here if we keep in mind our reflections on telepathy from the fourth chapter of this book that deals with the telepathy and idea of God. To return to Bauckham's vision of ecotheology: for him, instead of seeing of the cosmic Christ as a penultimate being—encapsulating but also superseding in Himself the whole of creation—a new perspective based on diversity and interrelatedness is formulated, wherein Christ becomes the ecological center of *all* creation: which now also includes nonhuman *sapiens* species.

Let us now approach the theology of deep incarnation as originally framed by Gregersen in his recent reflections on evolutionary Christianity: for Gregersen, incarnation must reach "into the very tissue of biological existence, and system of nature."[35] And, according to one of his predecessors, Denis Edwards, the connection between deep incarnation and ecological theology can be conceptualized as follows: "Biology does not allow us to see human flesh as an isolated entity. Human beings can only be understood as interrelated with other life-forms of our planet and interconnected with the atmosphere, the land, and the seas that sustain life."[36] It is precisely in this vein that Elisabeth Johnson's "Jesus and the Cosmos: Soundings in Deep Christology" can bring important insights for the understanding of our earlier Feuerbachian theology of love. We have seen that for Feuerbach, Christ was understood as the plasticity, or, as it were, shining of cosmic energies, pulsating and reaching out into the creation as love. Feuerbach has broadened Christ's cosmic mission into the whole of creation: also, inanimate nature was subtly ontologically linked to the 'Fountain-spirit' (*Quellgeister*) of all creation, for Feuerbach. For Johnson, similarly, the old anthropocentric focus of Christ as savior only for the human race needs to be widened to include further biocentric and cosmocentric dimensions. In the New Testament, more specifically, in the prologue of John's Gospel, we have God's self-expressing Word, and in this Word was life: "This life was a light shining on all people."³⁷ The Word becomes visible as flesh (*sarx*; in the Old Testament the expression "[all] flesh" would be mentioned over forty times and referred to as *kol-bāśār*) and sometimes, as also nicely observed by Johnson, human beings are even compared to grass and flowers (Isa 40:6b–8).³⁸ Even more closely to Feuerbach's God, as understood as Love and a Being of the Heart, comes Ezekiel, who prophesizes "about the new creation of 'hearts of flesh' that shall replace the old 'hearts of stone' " (Ezek 11:19; 36:26: "I will give them one heart, and put a new spirit within them; I will remove the heart of stone from their flesh and give them a heart of flesh"). For Johnson, these are all proofs that human connection to nature is indeed so strong that

> we cannot properly define our identity without including our relationship with the whole sweep of cosmic evolution. Biologically, too, the common ancestry of humans with the rest of life and our continuing essential interactions with the community of life on this planet make clear that humans do not stand alone. We evolved relationally; we exist symbiotically; our existence depends on interaction with the rest of the natural world. . . . While *sarx* in a strict biological sense may point to soft animal tissue of muscle and fat interlaced with blood vessels and nerves, that flesh itself evolved from and exists in continuing interrelationship with other nonmuscular, nonbloody living beings and the physical world itself. In a deeply real sense, the meaning of flesh/*sarx* encompasses all matter.³⁹

This theological insight on the all-pervasiveness of the Christ in creation is visible in Pierre Teilhard de Chardin's *Hymn of the Universe*, which, although it is often criticized for its optimistic and Christocentric tendencies, still represents one of the most creative theological works of the twentieth century—its importance lies in the spiritual power of matter, or, as it were, a new spiritual-material intertwining, actually enabling matter to become *the matrix of spirit*.⁴⁰ For Teilhard, with Christ's incarnation, "mysteriously and in very truth, at the touch of the supersubstantial Word the immense host which is the universe in made flesh. Through your incarnation, my God, all matter is henceforth incarnate."⁴¹ With this prolonging of the body of Christ in the world of matter, Teilhard marks a radically new ontological plane of the new spirit-matter. In *Christ in the World of Matter*, in a remembrance of a vision of Christ, Teilhard communicates the radiance of his body, "delineating a sort of blood stream, or nervous system, running through the totality of life. '*The entire universe was vibrant!*' " Interestingly enough, as in Feuerbach's idiosyncratic yet still mystical thought, also in Teilhard's vision all this movement "seemed to emanate from Christ, and above all from his heart."[42] In a beautiful passage, which we want to bring out in its entirety, this movement is transformative for the mass of beings' hearts: "It had penetrated, through the channels of matter, into the inmost depths of all hearts and then it had dilated them to breaking point, only in order to take back into the itself the substance of their affections and passions. And now that it had established its hold on them it was irresistibly pulling back toward its centre all the waves that had spread outwards from it, laden now with the purest honey of all loves."[43]

It is noteworthy to mention that this materially cosmic vision of Teilhard resembles a much more ancient Upanishadic elemental and materially cosmo-theological thought on *brahman* as *honey* of all beings—penetrating through the creation as an incarnate *spirit-body*, or *ātman*: "This self (*ātman*) is the honey of all beings, and all beings are the honey of this self. The radiant and immortal person in the self and the radiant and immortal person connected with the body (*ātman*)—they are both one's self. It is the immortal; it is *brahman*; it is the Whole."[44] This Upanishadic vision is far-reaching: the excerpt 2.1.15 with *ātman* and *brahman* at the forefront is the culmination of this early mystical vision of ancient Vedic seers: in analogical manner, and in its preceding passages (2.1.1-14), this refers to the earth (as the honey of all beings), water, fire, wind, sun, quarters, moon, lightning, thunder, space, Law (*dharma*), Truth, and humanity (all of them being referred to as the honey of all beings). All these macrocosmic realities have their ancient microcosmic correspondences: physical body (for the earth), semen (for waters), speech (for fire), breath (for wind), sight (for sun), hearing (for quarters or points of the compass), mind (for moon), radiance (for lightning), sound and tone (for thunder), space within the heart (for space), person devoted to *dharma* (for Law), person devoted to truth (for the Truth), person existing in the human (for humanity), and, finally, the radiant and immortal *ātman*, connected with the body (for the self, or *ātman* proper). As in Teilhard's cosmic vision, the whole universe becomes an immense host, laden with the purest honey of all loves: in an even more naturalistically pregnant meaning, a *breath of air* breaks the barriers of a person's eyelids and penetrates her soul; she now feels as she is "ceasing to be merely herself; an irresistible rapture took possession of her as though all the sap of all living things, flowing at one and the same moment into too narrow confines of her heart."[45] This possibility of a synchronistic reading between Vedic and Christian cosmopoetics reveals an inherent plurality residing in the very heart of Teilhard's *noogenesis* as understood as *Christogenesis*. Christ is the synthesis, or the highest cosmic symbol of a unique and unsurpassable ontological experience representing the joining of being (element and totality, mind and matter, and the infinite and the personal) that would otherwise have never been put together. But the most important point in Christogenesis as noogenesis is, that, according to Teilhard—and this now is crucial—"*Christ is not yet fully formed* . . . the mystical Christ has not yet attained to his full growth."[46]

Theological consequences of these both deep incarnationalist thoughts from ancient Vedic India as well as from Teilhard are far-reaching: this now means that the Word of God not only became incarnated with humanity, but, as already indicated, that Jesus Christ now processually enters and evolutionarily permeates the ontological plane of creation—within and beyond the *Homo sapiens* species. *Christ-Omega* is the end point of evolution for Teilhard. But, for us, cosmic Christ reveals as *Christ-Matrix*, the *pulsation of being*, or a beating heart within the lifeworlds of creation in its entirety. We see in Feuerbach that through incarnation, love becomes a power even *higher* than God: it is this *arché*-primordiality, or, to put it ontologically, *excess of love* that enables and marks Christ's material and vulnerable presence in this world. In the remaining chapter we wish to delineate the hidden ontological place of the revelation of love as *Christ-Matrix*, as the hidden logic of this very excess of love.

Love as the Abyss: Ontological Riddle in the Heart of Creation

The question of the ontological foundation of love haunted Schelling, who, with his elaborations on the primordial ontological ground, goes deeper than any other thinker before or after him: according to Schelling, as already noted earlier in this chapter, the breath of love (*der Hauch der Liebe*) is the very foundation of God, which existed even *before* there was a foundation, and, importantly, even appears as a higher power than God itself. For Schelling, all life is born out of the primordial longing of God (as Ground) within itself, which is love. Here is how he puts it in his *Philosophical Inquiries into the Nature of Human Freedom*, and the excerpt also refers to Christ: "But if all will have become subject to him, then the

Son himself shall also be subjected to him that did subject all things unto him. . . . But love is supreme. It is that which was before there were the depths and before existence."⁴⁷ Schelling, then, continues and affirms that the groundless (or, God) divides itself into two equally eternal beginnings:

> [O]nly in order that the two which could not be in it as groundless at the same time, or there be one, should become one through love; that is, it divides itself only that there may be life and love and personal existence. For there is love neither in indifference nor where antitheses are combined which require the combination in order to be; but rather (to repeat a word which has already been spoken) this is the secret of love, that it unites such beings as could each exist in itself, and nonetheless neither is nor can be without the other.⁴⁸

We have two beginnings that are posited within the Groundless (*Ungrund*)—and they can only be conjoined by love. From another point of view, and as presented in his insightful work on Merleau-Ponty, Petri Berndtson refers to the same ontological riddle within the Catholic mystical theology in which, as he observes,

> God is often understood as either "Silence" or as "Abyss." For example, one of the most famous Catholic mystics, Meister Eckhart, often calls God in his negative theology "silence," "stillness," and "the nameless One which eludes all names." In His silence and namelessness, God, according to Eckhart, is "hidden" and "abyss" (*Abgrund*). . . . [T]he Catholic mystical tradition, with its understanding of God as "Silence" and "Abyss," has deeply influenced Claudel and has inspired him to call God with this notion of "*Sigè* [Silence] the Abyss."⁴⁹

Now, if *all life* is born out of the primordial longing of God within itself, which is love, then the issue is not about God anymore but instead about Nature. And this is precisely the turn that is made by another great (post-Catholic) thinker: Merleau-Ponty. As he states in *Themes from the Lectures at the Collège de France (1952–1960)*, in deciphering the riddle of an ontological correlation of God, love, and life, we are faced with the following dilemma: "As Schelling has remarked, there is in nature something which makes it such that it would impose itself upon God himself as an independent condition of his operation. Such is our problem."⁵⁰ For Merleau-Ponty, the ontological riddle of nature can only be questioned upon and solved by rethinking the question of God and nature in an entirely new way:

> Schelling considers the "abyss" itself to be an ultimate reality and defines the absolute as that which exists without reason (*grundlos*), as the "over-being" who sustains the "grand fact of the world." Just as the absolute is no longer its own cause, or the absolute antithesis of nothingness, so nature no longer possesses the absolute positivity of "the only possible world." The *erste Natur* is an ambiguous principle, or, as he puts it, a "barbarous" principle which can be transcended, but will never be as though it had never existed, and can never be considered secondary even in relation to God.⁵¹

The concept of Nature implies, for Merleau-Ponty, an entirely different positioning of nature, or of us—human beings—within creation. This repositioning of the ontology of nature will be described in a programmatic way as follows: "There is a unique theme of philosophy; the *nexus*, the *vinculum* 'Nature'–'Man'–'God.' Nature as a leaf of Being, and the problems of philosophy, are concentric."⁵² In a chapter dedicated to Merleau-Ponty's theological thought titled "The Cosmic Christ as Vinculum between God, Humanity, and Nature," Christopher Ben Simpson points to a "breaking down" of the frontiers or the "cleavage" between "naturalism," "humanism," and "theism"; "God, man, creatures" are seen as passing into one another.⁵³ In this process, of the intertwining, as it were, of the world and God, they are most intrinsically interconnected through Christ, and Simpson specifically points to Irenaeus's doctrine of summing up or recapitulation (*anakephalaiosis*) of all creation in Christ, and also to Maximus the Confessor's Christ as the recapitulator of the world toward true humanity—toward "connection between God and nature, as 'a kind of a second cosmos.'"⁵⁴ And, in *Sense and Non-Sense*, Merleau-Ponty states that "the Incarnation changes everything."⁵⁵ But, to imagine cosmic Christ in Merleau-Ponty, another step needs to be taken in an opposite direction: toward the place of Christ in now an entirely new ontological transfiguration of philosophical thought toward the material ground of Being. In order to be able to understand the full scope of this turn, we need to return to Feuerbach and correlate Merleau-Ponty's original inquiry into nature with Feuerbach's idiosyncratic and novel wish to rejuvenate the old tree of theology with the vital nourishment from the elements of nature.

According to Feuerbach, love shall be exalted into a new substance of religion, and he claims that love represents even a higher power than that of God itself: Christ renounces his Godhead and becomes human *out of* love—and this love still represents a mysterious ground yet to be revealed to us. In this view, Christ becomes the very heart of the matter, being able to penetrate into every single being of nature, for Feuerbach. From mineral to fungi, from plants to animals, from the descendants of our *Homo* species to *Homo sapiens*—in contrast to the theological ideas of *kenosis*, which is understood as an emptying of God through his incarnation, we therefore interpret the mystery of incarnation from the opposite side as *a growth*: as argued in *The Essence of Religion*, God as incarnated is only seemingly detached from nature—in reality, God is intrinsically and essentially linked to Nature—and this is now precisely what forms the essence of Merleau-Ponty's intervention into the very core of theology with the *nexus* or *vinculum* Nature–Man–God. Incarnated God, now, becomes cosmic Christ, penetrating the sum of creation: if nature is a *leaf of Being* (Merleau-Ponty), then Christ represents its cosmically material sap. As indicated by Feuerbach, Christ becomes plasticity, and is the only being who is able to reach out as *love* to every single element of creation. This now becomes his "divineanimal ministry,"[56] operating on the field of flesh, and, as indicated by Merleau-Ponty—debordering once and for all the frontiers between naturalism, humanism, and theism—the cosmic body of Jesus is "the channel through which cosmic graces rush."[57] But which logic underpins this newly revealed cosmic economy? As will be argued in the concluding part of this chapter, this economy is inaugurated in the very logic of the surplus of love.

We have already pointed to problems that we may be facing by using any of the straightforward evolutionary Christian attempts to regard Christ-Omega as a climax of creation. In this view, Teilhard's attempt to understand noogenesis as Christogenesis (or, to understand the biosphere as noosphere, and finally as Christosphere) must carefully be reread and reinterpreted from the synchronistic point of view of the above debordering of previously firmly set frontiers between various levels of evolution—as already indicated by us in a synchronistic and pluralistic reading of Christogenesis, and, most importantly, and as also indicated by Teilhard himself: with an awareness of the cosmic Christ as *not yet being fully formed*.[58] We now want to interpret this lack, or, an ontological weakness, in the very heart of the cosmic body of Christ. This will not be understood as an unfulfilled stage of evolution but rather as His/Her eternal yearning for love—and the very same yearning of every part of creation to become a living particle of the body of Christ. This can now finally be understood by an excess of love, which marks the ever vulnerable presence of beings in the world. We have seen in Merleau-Ponty that, by following Schelling, the abyss was understood as the over-being, sustaining "the grand fact of the world."[59] This abyss is precisely the so-called Fountain-spirit[60] of all creation as stated by Feuerbach: the heart of all the living, and Christ represents the finest distillation of its cosmic energies. For us, cosmic Christ, as revealed as a *Christ-Matrix*, is the *pulsation of being*: a beating heart within the lifeworlds of creation. We have seen that Christ's material and vulnerable presence in this world grows from the *arché*-primordiality of the abyss, or, to put it ontologically, from the *excess of love* that enables and marks this very presence of cosmic Christ in the materially shaped world.

Epilogue

Christ as flesh enters the theo-ontological plane; it is the great merit of Merleau-Ponty's *The Visible and the Invisible* that it enables, within his newly invented ontological concept of intertwining, for us to think of a general element of being, by making the "visible" and "myself" (as seer) to be synchronized within a new cohesion of being, now directly linked to the pre-Socratic concept of the "element" (remember our earlier references to Feuerbach's and Caputo's excerpts on ancient elements here):

> The flesh is not matter, in the sense of corpuscles of being which would add up or continue on one another to form beings. . . . The flesh is not matter, is not mind, is not substance. To designate it, we should need the old term "element," in the sense it was used to speak of water, air, earth, and fire, that is, in the sense of a *general thing*, midway between the spatio-temporal individual and the idea, a sort of incarnate principle that brings a style of being wherever there is a fragment of being. The flesh is in this sense an "element" of Being. . . . For if there is flesh,

that is, if the hidden face of the cube radiates forth somewhere as well as does the face I have under my eyes, and coexists with it, and if I who see the cube also belong to the visible, I am visible from elsewhere, and if I and the cube are together caught up in one same "element."[61]

This element in unlimited, for Merleau-Ponty—for it traverses the plane of being and establishes a generality that not only constitutes my body, but reveals something much more topical for both environmental theology and Christology alike: it enables us to become a living part of something much more complex than we might experience within own limited and fragmented lifeworld—of our ego, subjectivity, a kind of limited co-relationality, and relationality to some land or otherwise fragmented environment; or within the theological framework—of our personal relation to nature, Christ, or God. A new intercorporeality arises:

> Now why would this generality, which constitutes the unity of my body, not open it to other bodies? . . . Why would not the synergy exist among different organisms, if it is possible within each? Their landscapes interweave, their actions and their passions fit together exactly: this is possible as soon as we no longer make belongingness to one same "consciousness" the primordial definition of sensibility, and as soon as we rather understand it as the return of the visible upon itself, a carnal adherence of the sentient to the sensed and of the sensed to the sentient.[62]

All flesh, as a newly conceptualized plurality of being, now intermingles among itself, but, at the same moment, it also "radiates beyond itself"[63] and communicates a new interrelationality of beings (*vinculum* Nature–Man–God/Christ) beyond any established ontological means.

Being in the heart of the matter, Christ reveals as an elemental matrix, the cosmic element of Being. As flesh, that is the (t)issue of galactic and cosmic stuff, Christ's incarnation reveals as grace of the world: a mysteriously hidden, yet through His presence visible agapistic event—originating from *the flesh of light in love* (Böhme). But, how would this even be revealed? We have indicated that Christ becomes the agapistic plasticity of this world: the only Being that is able to reach out as a *pulsation of love* into the first and penultimate of creation. According to Schelling, all of life is born out of a primordial longing of Ground within itself—now in an unending process, revealed as growing of love among creation. The absolute (or God) is now not its own cause anymore. Love the abyss—or the "Fountain-spirit"[64] of all creation—is the heart of all living, with Jesus Christ representing the finest agapistic distillation of its cosmic energies.

respiration of matter

3

God in Matter

> Is this the body of Christ? Is Christ manifest here? Does his blood flow in these veins? Does his spirit breathe in these lungs? Does forgiveness flourish here? Is hope enlivened? Is charity practiced? Can I see, here, the body of Christ?
>
> —Adam S. Miller, *Future Mormon*[1]

In this chapter, we deal with some philosophico-theological possibilities that emerge from an unusual but interesting relation between Jean-Luc Marion's project in philosophical theology on one hand, and recent liberal philosophico-theological elaborations within Mormonism on the other hand. Many and varied scholars have written monographs on Mormonism and its theology.[2] These have received timely critical attention within academic circles, which we argue is deservedly so, and, as a consequence, they have been firmly placed within the contemporary (post-)Christian thoughts-world. One of the most provocative and original Latter-day Saints theologians, Adam S. Miller, has already put this focus in close conversation with Alain Badiou, Marion, and Mormon thinkers.[3] According to Simon Critchley, as it is an example of a *post*-Christian tradition, Mormonism includes a pluralization of divinity and "makes god radically immanent," which enables us to rethink some of the key features of any theology.[4] Moreover, with its idiosyncratic theory of matter—and related accounts on ontology, cosmology, revelation, and eschatology—the Latter-day Saints theology has, in my opinion, become one of the most important and vibrant theological narratives that we have for the twenty-first century. As such, it is not so far away from Richard Rorty's philosophical or "spiritual" romanticism and Irigaray's theories of sensible transcendental and new materialism within the upcoming era, as titled by Irigaray, "The Age of the Spirit."[5] With Irigaray's more recent philosophico-religious and post-Catholic thought[6] and with Rorty's late, as it were, more "theologically" infused writings,[7] we therefore have viable possibilities to think anew about the essence of religion and our personal religiously based self-affection as its necessary constituent part. To talk about the *essence of religion* and *self-affection* might be presumptuous, or at least unusual—if not even dangerous today: in the era of uncertainties or even hostilities in the field of religion (secularism vs. postsecularism; religious ideologies vs. religious peacebuilding; public vs. personal role of religion, and so forth), it seems that neither some "reactionary" narratives nor other "softened" post-theological views might be welcome. But there is more in religion than that: a future religion imagined or envisioned should be able to address both the material conditions of our lives in a given culture or society as well as the most intimate layers of our more "spiritual" or—if we wish—personal-subjective needs and hopes. This is precisely what Rorty was willing to admit when asked about the future role of religion: that as a system of symbols it should provide us with "hope for cooperation with one another,"[8] or that it is a process that opens up for us finite beings new possibilities—a new hope for a future world in which "human beings live far happier lives than they live at the present time."[9] (We will return to Rorty and his very special personal relation to Mormonism in the second part of this chapter.) Following this line of thinking, we first want to deal with one of the key questions that we can imagine in theology: of salvation as a mark of our aspiration to become divinized, or at least more godlike than we are now. This aspiration is necessarily related to the acknowledgment of the *distance* that prevents us to think of God as an idol, and it is in Marion's early thinking that we come closest to this theological constellation. Within Mormonism, this tradition is related to the processual constellation of a sentence "As man is, God once was, as God is, man may become,"[10] installing and offering a very concrete countermovement, as it were, to the mystical theology of Dionysius the Areopagite and also to its philosophical elaborations in Marion.

Let us now look critically at two arguments or, in our view, two disturbing gestures of Marion that we find as perhaps even being the key markers of his philosophical intervention into the very core of both phenomenology and theology. On this basis, we will critically read Marion's philosophical theology as it is contrasted to some more recent views on Mormonism. Further, we will also attempt to present (hopefully in a sufficiently humble manner) our own thesis on religion and some of its tasks in today's world.

Marion's Two Unpleasant Gestures

In his *L'Idol et la distance*, Marion makes two intriguing comments—one on Nietzsche and another on Heidegger—that we wish to take as our starting point on the relation of theology to ontology, materiality, and salvation. In his analysis of Nietzsche and his "Christology," Marion makes an observation that interests us as an example of an ungentle philosophico-theological reading. In the § 6 (titled "Le Christ: Esquive d'une esquisse"/"The Christ: Evasion of an Outline") Marion starts with the following sentence: "L'entenébrèment du délire final (*Wahnsinn*) conclut la destruction des illusions idolâtriques (*Wahn*) en exposant, ce voile une fois déchiré, un individu, Friedrich Nietzsche, a l'épreuve insupportable du divin immédiatement (corporellement) affronté."[11] In English this sentence reads as follows: "The darkness of the final delirium (*Wahnsinn*) concludes the destruction of idolatrous illusions (*Wahn*) by exposing, once the veil is torn, an individual, Friedrich Nietzsche, to the unbearable trial of the divine that is immediately (corporeally) confronted."[12] This observation is followed by another thought in the same section on Nietzsche's Christ, namely, that it is precisely Nietzsche's idolatric confrontation with the divine (in this case only with the "semigod," *demi-dieu*) that caused Nietzsche's final and long-lasting fall into mental illness: "d'òu la défaillance finale—*dont l'entenébrèment témoigna dix ans durant*. . . . Nous disons: la cohérence du texte nietzschéen, entenébrèment compris, devient ainsi visible, ainsi plus qu'autrement et peut-être: le Christ hante la pensée nietzschéenne plus profondément que comme un adversaire ou une référence—il reste le lieu typique et ultime où elle habite, inconsciemment ou conscienment, qu'importe. Figure vide du Christ."[13] And, in its English translation: "[H]ence the final failure—*to which the darkness testified for ten years*. . . . I am saying that the coherence of the Nietzschean text, including the plunge into darkness, becomes visible in this way, in this way more than otherwise, and perhaps that Christ haunts Nietzschean thought more profoundly than as an adversary or a reference—he remains the typical and ultimate place where that thought lives, whether consciously or unconsciously. An empty figure of Christ."[14] Apart from the point of view of such an etiquette that one could address (for example, why there is a need at all in someone to exert such pressure or an insistence on this issue *ad personam*), we still wish to reflect on some even more serious philosophical and theological consequences of such a thought. Clearly, for Marion, the Christological gesture of Nietzsche only leads to the semideath (*demi-mort*) of Nietzsche's soul/spirit (*esprit*), but not of his body (*corps*), which tragically or comically (as you wish) survives the necessary breakdown of an allegedly heroic soul of the individual man called Nietzsche, and causes his fall into the abyss of unthought. According to Marion, already for Feuerbach it becomes impossible to evade the idolatrous nature of making his "God" devoid of any remaining feature of negative theology and its inherent distance. Feuerbach and Nietzsche cannot step into the distance and are, therefore, idolatrous toward their divinities. If Feuerbach was still able to remain at this side of this ontological gap (*Kluft*), it was Nietzsche who has made one more step and has, therefore, collapsed into the final transgression—and into the sad and final, but rightly deserved (as it seems if we take Marion seriously enough) *entenébrement* of his soul.[15]

Is there perhaps another way to think through this aspect of Nietzsche? We wish to argue in favor of Nietzsche by making an unusual step first—namely, by invoking the idea of a child as we can find it in his thought. In *Thus Spoke Zarathustra*, Nietzsche famously introduces three metamorphoses *of the spirit*—first the spirit becomes a camel, then the camel becomes a lion, and finally the lion becomes a child.[16] It is decisive, for us, to know that for the play of creation for Nietzsche, a very special relation to sacredness is required. The idea of a child, for Nietzsche, is described as follows: "The child is innocence and forgetting, a new beginning, a game, a wheel rolling out of itself, a first movement, a sacred yes-saying. Yes, for the game of creation my brothers a sacred yes-saying is required. The spirit wants *its* will, the one lost to the world now wins *its own* world. Three metamorphoses of the spirit I named for you: how the spirit became a camel, and the camel a lion, and finally the lion a child."[17] In "The Soothsayer," there is another modality—or even acceleration of this thought—when "like thousandfold children's laughter Zarathustra comes into all burial chambers, laughing at these night watchmen and grave guardians, and whoever else rattles about with dingy keys."[18] Here, the idea of a child is radicalized as representing the only possible way of thinking about the future, since, clearly, *the child is the category of the future* (Nietzsche knew that very well—for only children can bring joy, laughter, and hope to this world). But why is the idea of the child so important in this particular context of ours? Apart from the fact that we do not have any single modern philosopher—with the exception of Nietzsche or Irigaray—who would dedicate an important portion of his or her work to the idea of the child, the most important reason is also that, for Marion, the distance with which we could escape idolatry can solely be understood and nurtured from the idea of the vertically understood relationality within the very concept of the parenthood—because, as we know from Marion, taken radically, "Paternal distance offers the sole place for a filiation."[19]

We have already elaborated on the idea of the child in *Antigone's Sisters*.[20] In the chapter "Forms of Pure Love: Parents and Children," we have followed Irigaray, who, in her most recent work, *To Be Born*, raises the question of the origin of human beings as follows: "Unveiling the mystery of our origin is probably the thing that most motivates our quests and plans."[21] The question of origin can refer to two possible paths: first, to the ontological thesis about the origin of our Being, and second, but by no means less important, to the question that is most closely connected with the idea of the child. Irigaray introduces her explication of the idea of the child in an idiosyncratic and, at first, recondite manner: she argues that whatever the factors of our conception or creation as individuals coming to this world, *we have wanted to be born—our will to live* is manifesting itself already at the moment of our birth.[22] In this gesture, Irigaray allies herself to this aspect of Nietzschean thinking, and this, naturally, leads her to a break with the established perception of the child as the third one in relation to its parents, or, as is the case with Marion, as the second to his father *(filiation)*—as the one who *is born* and thus does not *give birth* to oneself, and, consequently, does not have his own self-affection (including the debates around *filioque*). But, if the original idea of the child is related to its explicit singularity (which assures the child its autonomy), another ontology of the child is needed.[23] Based on this, we have argued that, between parents and children, even when being fully devoted to their child (or to each other), this relationship essentially and ontologically is *not* hierarchical—as their complete and unconditional love is fed precisely by what they themselves and each on their own *had never possessed or been* and by what they in equal perfection receive from their child, or from their parent; this is what vertical *transcendence* of the relationship and exchange of love consists in—it is a process of reciprocal giving and thus of the *gift of mutual love among them all* (this love being the third thing now). This form of love as a mutual gift was called in my analysis *genealogical love*. Now, to bring these thoughts back to the previous Nietzsche-Marion dispute: if filiation is only possible through the ontotheological gap (distance), then the very idea of a child, as described above and ontologically, evaporates into nothingness and indeed becomes *une nouvelle figure vide*—if we may use Marion's own terms here. One more time, according to Marion, now with the passage in its entirety: "Paternal distance offers the sole place for a filiation. Since in the intimacy of the divine strictly coincides with withdrawal, the paradox can lead to confusion: distance must, in order that we might inhabit it, be identified. We will be able to speak of it only if we come from it and remain in it. To speak of distance: concerning it, and also starting from it. But which language can be suitable to distance?"[24] We have now come full circle; but a further step needs to be taken—from distance to proximity, and from ontological gap to material closeness of a processual divine-human relationship, which will be a topic of the next part of this chapter.

Let me, now, focus on the second ungenerous comment by Marion from *The Idol and Distance*—this time on Heidegger's ontology. Toward the end of *The Idol and Distance*, Marion critically elaborates on the possibility of Christians positioning themselves within the *Ereignis*. For Marion, after dealing with Derrida's *différance* and *trace*, there is a nihilism at work when there is nothing that could be invoked, called—all that's left is the "platitude of *différance*, since the trace removes any name for it, disqualifies any identification of it, and finally fills any of its depth."[25] Derrida, in this "abyssal thought,"[26] is in fact not far away from Nietzsche, for Marion. All is indifferent, there is no transcendence, and beyond ontotheology (including the ontological difference itself), the Being of being is indifferently differentiated into the nothingness. The distance of the Father, clearly, cannot be present or encapsulated in this process. Marion knows that in order "[t]o eliminate any paternal site, it is necessary to reject the ontological difference. . . . The refusal of ontological difference in the one case, and its assertion in the other, aim at the same goal: to reduce to the Neuter, to neutralize the distant irruption of the Father."[27] In this sense, there is another—this time final—possibility that now has to be taken into consideration: it is Heidegger's *Ereignis* and the possibility of an ontological difference/distance. The entirety of § 19 (titled "The Fourth Dimension") of *The Idol and Distance* deals with that possibility. Heidegger's lecture, "Time and Being," is now crucial for Marion since it introduces the notion of *giving*. For Heidegger, Being as "giving" is presented as follows:

> Being *is* not. There is, It gives Being as the unconcealing; as the gift of unconcealing it is retained in the giving. Being *is* not. There is, It gives Being as the unconcealing of presencing. . . . A giving which gives only its gift, but in the giving holds itself back and withdraws, such a giving we call sending. According to the meaning of giving which is to be thought in this way, Being-that which It gives-is what is sent. . . . In the sending of the destiny of Being, in the extending of time, there becomes manifest a dedication, a delivering over into what is their own, namely of Being as presence and of time as the realm of the open. What determines both, time and Being, in their own, that is, in their belonging together, we shall call: *Ereignis*, the event of Appropriation. *Ereignis* will be translated as Appropriation or event of Appropriation. One should bear in mind, however, that "event" is not simply an occurrence, but that which makes any occurrence possible. . . . However: Appropriation neither *is*, nor *is* Appropriation *there*. To say the one or to say the other is equally a distortion of the matter, just as if we wanted to derive the source from the river. What remains to be said? Only this: Appropriation appropriates.[28]

But, from these still more abstract thoughts on Being as *Ereignis*, we can say that Heidegger's event of appropriation is also necessarily related to the gentle constellation of the "elements" of being, and is thus related to the discrete or hidden—but still discernible—"material" ontology of Being. Heidegger's proximity to the elemental world is, for example, visible in the introduction to his essay, "What Is Metaphysics?," when the earth/soil is presented as a root of the nourishing sources and strengths of the tree.[29] But, it is in *Building Dwelling Thinking* that he elaborates on the elements in the following way:

> But "on the earth" already means "under the sky." Both of these *also* mean "remaining before the divinities" and include a "belonging to men's being with one another." By a *primal* oneness the four—earth and sky, divinities, and mortals—belong together in one.
> Earth is the serving bearer, blossoming and fruiting, spreading out in rock and water, rising up into plant and animal. When

we say earth, we are already thinking of the other three along with it, but we give no thought to the simple oneness of the four.

The sky is the vaulting path of the sun, the course of the changing moon, the wandering glitter of the stars, the year's seasons and their changes, the light and dusk of day, the gloom and glow of night, the clemency and inclemency of the weather, the drifting clouds and blue depth of the ether. . . . Out of the holy sway of the godhead, the god appears in his presence or withdraws into his concealment. When we speak of the divinities, we are already thinking of the other three along with them, but we give no thought to the simple oneness of the four.

. . .

This simple oneness of the four we call *the fourfold*. Mortals *are* in the fourfold by *dwelling*. But the basic character of dwelling is to spare, to preserve. Mortals dwell in the way they preserve the fourfold in its essential being, its presencing. Accordingly, the preserving that dwells is fourfold.[30]

Here, we have earth/rock, plants and animals, water, atmosphere (with wind, air, or ether), and sun/light/fire. And mortals, of course. These archaic elements, in their mysterious but visible materiality, in the midst of the Fourfold, are the source or our All-life and our being/Being. But, in an even more elemental sense, and in a complete synchronicity with the inner dynamics of the Fourfold—for Heidegger—there is one of the elements that still is privileged, and this is precisely the wind/air/ether—or, with the words of Heidegger: "Beyng is the ether, which man breathes."[31] Appropriation appropriates, but the distance within the ontological difference can neither be called "idolatrous" nor can it be dispossessed of its ontological meaning, here. It is rather "spiritual"—but in a subtle, material way. Now, to return back to Marion—based on these thoughts, in his critical exposition of Heidegger, our philosopher is able to guide us toward the conclusion, namely, that, in the context of "Time and Being," neither time nor Being exist. The *Il y a* of a Being (*Es Gibt:* as an impersonal *Es* that *gives* itself) is *Ereignis* (the event of Appropriation). *Ereignis* and distance are now incommensurable, since it is *Ereignis* itself that posits into the distance from the distance itself, for Marion. Now, another dimension—the so-called fourth dimension—reveals from this constellation when we talk about the difference between God and Being, and this is the *Distance* itself: "The fourth difference, between God and Being, puts the other differences in place, because to begin with it gives rise to the (unextended, nonspatial) space where these differences, including the ontological difference, become imaginable. The fourth dimension, the last, is always the first. It is a question in fact of distance itself, such as it passes beyond every possible idol, and exercises itself as the distance of Goodness."[32]

Ereignis could, under certain conditions, even support this fourth dimension, but we are now coming to the very core of Marion's criticism of Heidegger: the play of *Ereignis* cannot—and this is now clear and indisputable—satisfy Christians in their radical ontological standing toward Being: not only being as such, but Being "itself" is now logically put into radical suspension, evaporation, and the fall into nihilism. Here, we are now at our second ungentle remark—or gesture of Marion—that we wanted to analyze. On the basis of previous criticism of *Ereignis*, Marion writes again on a very unpleasant or disturbing observation, which is now also very straightforwardly elucidated with the following words:

> From the point of the view of charity, everything enters into another light: Beings and Being itself appear, certainly not annihilated or without value (for *nihil* and *value* come to us from metaphysics), but nil in charity, inept because inapt for distance, in a word, vain. *Vain*, in the sense that "vanity of vanities, all is vanity" must be understood more or less as: "wind, nothing that holds, nothing but wind." That which reveals itself at this point to be vain (*vergeblich*)—namely, Being as well as beings—departs like wind. But the "wind" indicates also the spirit, which "breathes." Can the inanity of *Dasein*, like "wind," offer a name to the Spirit, offer its inanity (*Vergeblichkeit*) and give it (*geben*) to another authority? . . . The ontico-ontological inanity uncovers such a poverty to charity (distance), that charity cannot but remit it to it. . . . [B]ut only a forgiveness can grant it that one not impute that absence to it as a fault. . . . Only forgiveness will allow us to receive it [namely, Being, L.Š.] as a gift without abandoning ourselves to its serene inanity. . . . For what places Being in distance as an icon of distance remains first the humble and unthinkable authority of the Father.[33]

These words raise several difficult questions that we will be only able to address in the second part of this chapter. But here we simply wish to indicate what, in our opinion, is most problematic in these thoughts. First, Marion uses the play of words, in which "wind" is particularly exposed as a symbol of ontological nihilism. We know that wind (and breath as its microcosmic twin) has had an important role in the cosmologico-ontological constellation of Being since the pre-Socratics, although it has later been suppressed or forgotten.[34] Second, Marion, it seems to us, thinks about the possibility of Dasein (cynically, though) as an existence that interferes with the plane of grace, but, even if so, without any trace of joy. Here we come close to Nietzsche: for Nietzsche, we have seen, it is in the child and its *laughter* (and joy) that a new beginning is possible—thinking beyond nihilism, beyond metaphysics, beyond idolatry. It seems that Marion would like to warn us against making this essentially dangerous step into laughter and joy of life: with his first remark on Nietzsche, the idea of a child has evaporated into nothingness and became *une figure vide*. With the second gesture, which Marion makes against Heidegger, Being or Event of Appropriation (*Ereignis*) is cut off from any remains of even the most discrete presence of material signifiers. But this only means that, based on the thought of Being as an icon of distance, Marion himself establishes and insists on the idolatrous distance of the Father *of* Being that, in our opinion, needs to be deconstructed in favor of a more gentle, intimate, and elemental gesture of divinity—or *God-Being*—that both has a body and indwells in an ontological proximity that still needs to be philosophically explained and theologically revealed.

Against Idol and Distance:
On Mormonism's Philosophical Theology of Matter

Let us now deal with one of those philosophers who probably never even took Marion's philosophy seriously: Richard Rorty. In an interview with his wife Mary Rorty (a Mormon),[35] we find out how close Mormonism was to his personal life. Rorty was exposed for years in his closest family environment to this particular American form of Christianity. Now, we know from his numerous essays that he did not think that any institutionalized form of religion or any church per se should have a decisive role in shaping the lives of our societies. The same would hold for any straightforward form of philosophical theology. For that purpose, Rorty was often labeled or even self-proclaimed as an "atheist" or at least "anticlericalist" (in his later writings, at least he proclaimed himself like this). On that basis, he thought that religion was rather a conversation-stopper—Rorty simply thought that invoking religious arguments that go or straightforwardly enter discussions of public policy *beyond justification* is not particularly useful (for example, to link abortion with a perfect or supreme will of God).[36] Again, the same would be true for any kind of philosophical work, resting too much upon any form of an indisputable authority.[37] Rorty hence admired the anti-Calvinist and anti-Catholic Mormon theology and its more evolutionary idea of eternal progression toward the more divine selves in ourselves. Finally, from his more philosophical writings we know that Rorty still could be labeled as a "religious" person, as in the following claim that certainly brings a powerful post-Christian message: "My sense of the holy, insofar I have one, is bound with the hope that someday, any millennium now, my remote descendants will live in a global civilization in which love in pretty much the only law."[38] For Rorty's post-Christianity, therefore, to talk of religion, or—as he has put it—about something that we hold as holy and that permeates or connects our lives, is useful only if we are able to relate to it the material conditions of our lives and our (hopefully) abundant personal or "social" love. How this connection could happen remains a mystery.[39] Let us therefore see what we can learn from the post-Christian Mormon philosophy and theology as related to our original critical question of idol and distance.

For Mormon Christianity, the idea of God cannot be related to the metaphysical triad of *incorporeus, impartibilis*, and *impassibilis*. For Joseph Smith, not only Jesus but also God the Father is passible, and weeps with us. The portrayal of a weeping God is directly opposed to the ideas of the early Greek fathers that persisted through the history of Christianity until the modern era—namely that God (the Father) cannot be changed or affected by emotions. A distant God without the body or (bodily) parts, and a God that is unchangeable, *cannot really* be vulnerable to external events and thus also cannot be affected by any possible external perturbations. But, if we allow ourselves to think of God as vulnerable and, thus, changeable, this diminishes the *distance* between God and human beings and opens immense possibilities for a theological revitalization of the divine-human relationality—with all the ethico-eschatological consequences of such a turn. If God weeps, and if weeping means that God's (not "only" Jesus's) *tears* are, then, "real" and necessary, God must also have had a material substance that we cannot yet comprehend. Spirit and element—that is, God and His/Her tears are not separated any more, in the words from *Doctrine and Covenants*—"spirit and element, inseparably connected, receive a fullness of joy; And when separated, man cannot receive a fullness of joy" (D&C 93:33–34).[40] On this basis, we must contend that, within Mormon cosmology (and theology), there is a radical countermovement with regard the realms of spirit and matter. According to one of the most prolific Mormon thinkers, John Durham Peters, Mormon cosmology "is the story of humankind's increasing immersion in matter for the sake of progress and growth."[41] This means that, in the process of our spiritual growth, both realms—of spirit and matter—commingle and, in this sense, also Heavens are only the exaltation of *this* world for Mormons (this is also one of the features that Rorty praised most in Mormonism—which obviously was close to his romantic "faith" in human progress). In the *Doctrine and Covenants*, we also read that "God the Father and his Son have tangible bodies of flesh and bone,"[42] and, for the leading early Mormon theologian Orson Pratt, any theology that was not willing to deal with this kind of theological materialism seriously enough was no less than absurd (see his *Absurdities of Immaterialism*).

Now, for the sake of a better understanding of this context, a short review of Mormon theology is needed. Mormon theology distinguishes itself radically from other Christian trinitarian doctrines in its teaching that there is a God, the Eternal Father (and, sometimes, also Mother), His Son, Jesus Christ, and the Holy Ghost—but with an important difference, namely, that Jesus is identified with Jehovah (according to the teachings of Joseph Smith, Jesus Christ only *became* divine at some point "in the distant pre-earth past"[43]). God the Father (and, sometimes Mother) is now identified with *Elohim* (in its original plural meaning), and is thus representative of the "Gods" in their plurality rather than there being a one and only God.[44] If both God the Father and Son have tangible bodies, finally, the Holy Ghost is a purely spiritual although still enigmatically subtle material in its ontological character. Although some Mormons think that the Holy Ghost also must possess a certain kind of a spiritual bodily substance, it usually will be recognized in the form of an unembodied cosmic ether, being able to "dwell in us" (D&C, 130:22). This is an interesting point since it relates to the remark of Marion on the vanity of wind as related to the ontotheological concepts of Being and God. Furthermore, for Mormonism, God is supreme intelligence, but "he is not the source of all being, or even the creator of that which constitutes the human soul. Men and women have existed from eternity as uncreated intelligence."[45] How could this be understood? For Mormonism, *creatio ex nihilo* is, therefore, not an option and this clearly paves the way toward another theory of an independent and eternalist matter and element within theology:

> In its embrace of the eternalism of matter, its explicit rejection of a triune god "without body, parts or passions" in favor of

> a corporeal deity, and by its association of marital bonds with eternal states of relationships, Mormonism—like Blake—cast the earthly as a sacred sphere and rejected the dichotomies and valuations that necessitated a guarded response to worldly pleasures. . . . Here as elsewhere, the polarity that underlies conventional conceptions of sacred distance collapses, and materiality becomes spiritualized.[46]

In this light, embodiment, which is usually understood theologically as a degradation of the pure spiritual existence into its material form, is now rather a step upward. Since God (who comprises both heavenly Father and Mother[47]) is embodied, this is the reason that men and women themselves can *expand* toward divinity to participate more and more in an ongoing process of salvation wherein God desires to save the entirety of humankind. *As man is, God once was, as God is, man may become.* In this view, finally, the cosmos is essentially ontologically continuous, and the *fatherly distance* evaporates into the teaching on God's progression and passibility:

> Mormon rejection of creation *ex nihilo* in favor of creation *ex materia*, out of preexisting intelligence and element, together with the corollary that matter is uncreated and coeternal with God, affirm that the primordial origin of being is plural, not singular. Irreducible plurality is the fundamental character of being. The Mormon teaching that the spirit world is coextensive with the physical world suggests the immanence of the divine and orients the theological imagination toward the here and now rather than toward the transcendent.[48]

Among the features of such a new worldview, cocreativity and vulnerability are among the most important of all.

We now wish to address the second topic of our investigation—namely to elaborate on this basis on Marion's second remark on the vanity of wind and the related question of Being. In perhaps the most important of the sermons of Joseph Smith, now known as *The King Follet Discourse* (from 1844), we find the clearest distillation of Mormonism's more radical views—but before that what strikes us is a remark that he makes in the very beginning of this sermon.[49] The subject of the sermon is the death of King Follett, a fellow Mormon who passed away in March 1844, only a few months before the prophet himself was killed. Smith starts his speech with a prayer: namely, by seeking inspiration (here in the most literary sense—as being filled with *pneuma*) in the Holy Spirit and by wishing "that the Lord may strengthen my lungs and stay the winds"[50] ("lungs" are here being used as a bodily-spiritual organ[51]). In this sermon, Smith first contends that God himself "is a man like one of you," which dwelt on the Earth as Jesus did. Now, according to Smith, Jesus is also a god who had to become God—actually, all Gods have done this before (remember the plurality of gods as a principle in Mormonism). Now, a crucial argument appears: since *creatio ex nihilo* is not possible, God had before him materials, that is, the elements, from which he organized (and hence did *not* create) the world. These elements had their existence from the time they had—they are coeternal with God, and even more: "The pure principles of element are principles that can never be destroyed; they may be organized and reorganized but not destroyed." And, in *Doctrine and Covenants*, we also read: "There is no such thing as immaterial matter. All spirit is matter, but it is more fine and pure, and can only be discerned by purer eyes. We cannot see it; but when our bodies are purified we shall see that it is all matter" (D&C 131:7-8). Mormons, therefore, establish the realm of the elements (or matter) as a primordial ontological plane from which all beings have once emerged.[52] But why is the role of the air or wind as an element so special in this constellation? And why did Marion choose precisely wind, and not some other element, for arguing against Heidegger's Being?

We have already seen that, for Heidegger, wind has rather a key role within his ontology of Being/Beyng (if we remember Heidegger's remark on Beyng as ether): now, in his reading of Hölderlin's *Hyperion*, Heidegger considers the air that is breathed by all living beings as " '[t]his air' hallows the holy air, sister of the spirit, mighty master of the fire which reigns and lives within us."[53] This passage is a proof that, even for Heidegger, spirit is elementally linked to its archaic and subtle material core. These observations do not correspond to Marion's remark, and show that he is among those philosophers who, unfortunately, are not sensible to the respiratory aspects of our being.[54] Now, also for Smith, the *inspiration* of the Holy Spirit is crucial and, among the sins committed—according to *The King Follett Discourse*—there is only one that cannot be forgiven, and it is the sin against the Holy Ghost.[55] The respiratory thinker Petri Berndtson has already shown the importance of the relation between God and spirit/breath/air/wind (as *pneuma*)—as in John 4:24, wherein Jesus answers to Nicodemus's question about the new birth with the following words: "Very truly, I tell you, no one can enter the kingdom of God without being born of water and Spirit [*ex hydatos kai pneumatos*]. . . . The wind blows where it chooses, and you hear the sound of it, but you do not know where it comes from or where it goes to" (Jn 3:5, 8). Based on these thoughts, as interpreted in a horizontal and elemental "respiratory" (*pneuma*) and not vertical and metaphysical 'spiritual' (*spiritus*) manner, Berndtson[56] argues that the Bible should be reread and reinterpreted in an elemental sense—as a text that is much more closely connected to an original or archaic elemental constellation.[57] But, we must return to Marion now for one more time: for him, there is a double movement in wind—first, it shows itself in its sheer vanity or nothingness; it evaporates before Being is reached, or Being itself evaporates with(in) it. Second, and despite that, wind could perhaps still lead us toward the spiritual and thus it could "offer a name to the Spirit"[58]—but this could only happen in a way of giving up its "material" essence to the elevated and distanced authority of the Father and this is, yet, another dead end for the element of the wind.

In his more recent thought on saturated phenomena,[59] Marion represents the unity and continuity of his thinking over the decades by adding important new elements that are known as saturated phenomena. Revelation, now, "encompasses the four types of saturated phenomena"[60] (the event, the idol, the flesh, and the icon), and Jesus Christ Himself is a saturated phenomenon and "the Icon of the invisible God."[61] We must ask ourselves whether this new constellation could perhaps offer us an alternative way of thinking with or through the elemental plane: the Holy Spirit, as the third person of the Trinity, is now revealed to us as the givenness of the gift, *donum Dei*. His[62] role is that "the Holy Spirit enables the paternal depth of the filial icon to be seen, which no one can see without him and outside of him."[63] Finally, no revelation is possible without the inherent paradox that must be accepted as such: No one has ever seen God, because he remains "the only God, invisible" dwelling "in unapproachable light, and whom one among men can ever see" (*hon oudeis anthrōpōn oude idein dynatai*) (1 Tm 6.16), and of whom "the only Son, who is turned toward the Father's bosom, has made the exegesis" (*eikenos ezēgēsato*) (Jn 1:18), under the preeminently paradoxical title of "icon of the invisible God" (*eikōn tou theou tou aoratou*) (Col 1:15; see 2 Cor 4:4). It seems, then, that even in his most recent thinking, Marion is still not willing to let the distance of the Father give way to a more elemental ontological understanding. Or, in Marion's own words: "No misinterpretation of Revelation could surpass that of Heidegger . . . who wanted to submit the Revelation of God to the manifestation of the gods, that manifestation to the dwelling of the divine, that dwelling to the opening of the sacred, and that opening to the intact open region of Being."[64] The icon of distance has never allowed us to *breathe* the air of proximity.

What possibilities of revelation are thus offered to us in this constellation? We have already argued that, in our opinion, Marion insists on the idolatrous distance of the Father *of* Being, which rather needs to be deconstructed in favor of a more gentle and intimate gesture of divinity—a *God-Being*—that both indwells in a bodily and spiritual manner as well as in an ontological proximity to all of "us" (the elements, plants, nonhuman animals, human beings, and divine beings), which still needs to be philosophically explained and theologically revealed. In one of the most generous and thorough accounts on Mormonism and interfaith dialogue, *Mormon Christianity,* Stephen H. Webb presents us with a beautiful and theologically sensitive correction of any claim that God even could not have a being.[65] According to Mormon belief, God is not "radically different from everything else that exists,"[66] but this does not imply any simplistic or materialistic theory that could underpin such a statement. Thinking beyond any materialism-immaterialism divide, "God is mysterious but not indescribable, glorious but not unknowable, perfect but not infinite and unlimited."[67] Being a part of reality that is characterized as a continuous *becoming* rather than as static being *vs.* change (as a sign of weakness and decay), God can take part in this world.

Divine order is now immanent in this world and "we" (as molecules, organisms, beings, and so forth) are participating in the divine. This theologico-ontological gradualism is what could now be understood as a marginality of a *God-Being*—the *God-Being* is porous, with the margins of its subtle spiritually material body expanding by way of a rhythmic pulsation into the world of the elements and worldly beings.[68]

Part II
The Future

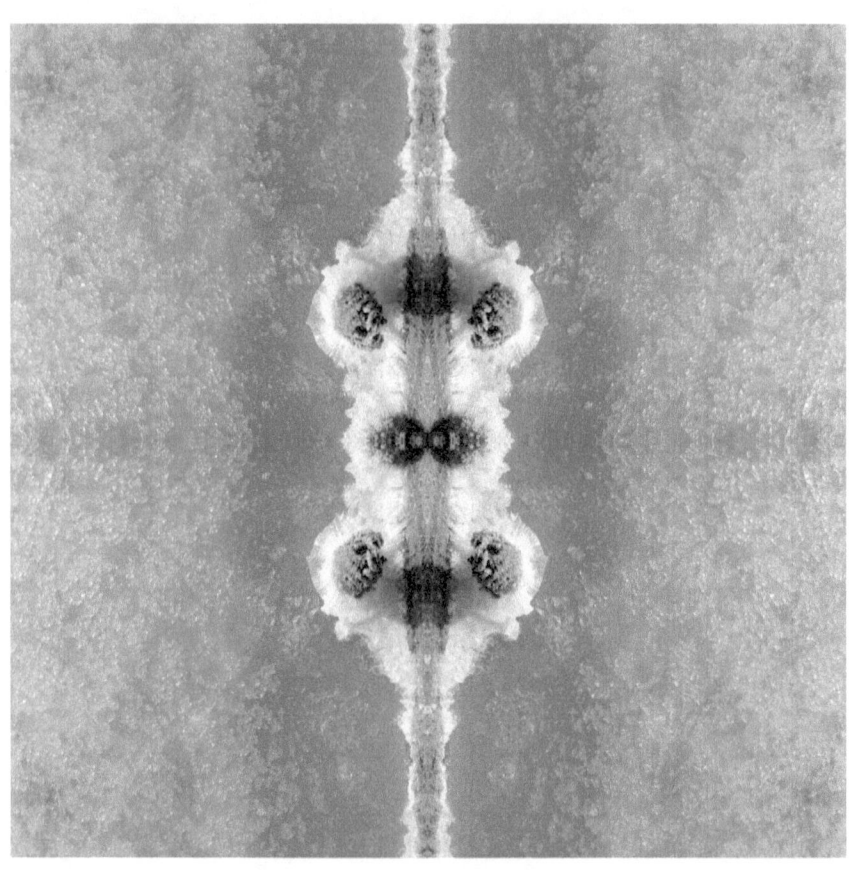

telephatic coupling

4

God in Telepathy

I know God cannot live a moment without me; If I should come to nought, He too must cease to be.

—Angelus Silesius[1]

Our aim in this chapter is to bring some of the most genuine of religious phenomena and experiences into a dialogue with science and philosophy—based on a close reading of some of the most intriguing essays of Arthur Schopenhauer.[2] With the rise of feminist theologians and with the emergence of new materialism in theology, these masculinist claims have been radically questioned and creatively transformed into a renewed narrative of codependency of creation and the entangled complexity as a mark of its inherent dynamics. With the rise of quantum thinking in science, the rich possibilities of these ideas have consequently been informing the humanities, and new and inspiring avenues of thought have been opening for theology. In this chapter, we also aim at a new interpretation of this epistemological turn under this particular view of phenomena, such as correspondences and sacred correlations: things usually despised in humanities as "magical" and thus labeled as nontheological, and, of course, nonscientific. In this, we will deal with one of Schopenhauer's most intriguing essays, "Animal Magnetism and Magic," from his work *On Will in Nature*—and point to its importance for cosmological and ontological debates within what we understand as the field of philosophico-quantum theology with philosophy of synchronicity as its part.

Schopenhauer connects two genealogies of thinkers: on one side his predecessors such as Amalric of Bène, Giordano Bruno, and Jakob Böhme, and on the other side thinkers following him and his epoch, such as Alfred North Whitehead, Wolfgang Pauli, C. G. Jung, and Catherine Keller, among others. Now, in our elaboration of Bruno's views on the divine, we have already seen that, for Bruno, both spiritual and material principles were recognized as the very substance of the world. According to this *Nolan* philosopher, following the Platonists (world-soul), the materialist traditions of Aristotelianism and Neo-Platonism, Islamic influences (Averroes), as well as Nicolas of Cusa's argument on the impossibility of separating the infinite potency of creating and being created in God, Bruno attempts at a synthesis of these respective thoughts to be able to think God or the divinity in accordance with matter. After the teachings of Amalric of Bène, this was the first attempt in Western theological thinking to define God through matter.[3] For Bruno, matter is taken as a substrate: a principal idea that cannot be annihilated. A soul/spirit is present in all things, and, as a consequence, God must necessarily be linked to the world—thus *natura est deus in rebus*. Bruno's method can, here, be identified with so-called *paleological thinking* that is based on the notion of identity predicates, which means that identity among two things is accepted if they share a corresponding link that is not strictly logical and causal ("a result, E, is attributable to any of a set of causes A, B, C, D etc.").[4] Paleological thinking is a characteristic of archaic, Indigenous, and aboriginal traditions, but was later forgotten and transformed into a fully objective monocausal scientific thinking—which does not allow for identity correlates beyond or other than from the ideal of Western logical, causal, and physical determinism of Francis Bacon, René Descartes, and Isaac Newton. It was only with the Copenhagen interpretation of quantum physics (1927) that thinkers could, again, take into account the (ancient and forgotten) principles of indeterminism, nonlocality, uncertainty, and, most importantly, complementarity.

For Schopenhauer, it is vital to affirm that the substance mentioned under different names by his main predecessors, from Plato to Hegel (to include his main opponent), could now be understood as a "Will." Now, we are used to understanding Will just as another metaphysical denominator in the long line of conceptual markers in the history of Western ontotheology. But it is our aim to show a potential for the understanding of Schopenhauer's Will beyond this line and, thus, as pointing toward two *quantum* concepts to be used in contemporary philosophical theology: correspondence and synchronicity. Both concepts will be understood as possibilities to comprehend the problem of matter, as well as part of an attempt to understand the so-called and earlier mentioned weird and paranormal phenomena (known as Psi phenomena[5]) as they are related to philosophical theology presented in this chapter.[6]

Schopenhauer's Paranormal Metaphysics

Let us now begin our analysis with Schopenhauer's remark on the ontological continuity of the world: "Therefore it could be asserted that if, *per impossible*, a single being, even the most insignificant, were entirely annihilated, the whole world would inevitably be destroyed with it. . . . [T]he inner being itself is present whole and undivided in everything in nature, in every living being."[7] For Schopenhauer, this remark is a part of his teaching on the objectifications of the will, spanning from inorganic nature to various organic forms, and, finally, to human realms and beings. Within this line of objectivizations in nature, gravity is, for the stone, as consciousness is for the human being. As Schopenhauer puts it, "In the case of man, this is called character; in the case of the stone, it is called quality; but it is same in both" (i.e., it is known in both of them as the will).[8] This notion of Schopenhauer is precisely what is at stake in Giorgio Agamben's discussion on the doctrinal content of the earlier mentioned heresy of Amalric of Bène:

> Amalric interpreted the Apostle's claim "God is all in all" as a radical theological development of the Platonic doctrine of the *chora*. God is in every thing as the place in which every thing is, or rather as the determination and the "topia" of every entity. The transcendent, therefore, is not a supreme entity above all things; rather, *the pure transcendent is the taking-place of every thing*. . . . The being-worm of the worm, the being-stone of the stone, is divine.[9]

This being-divine of the world, in Schopenhauer's vocabulary, is therefore positioned both beyond the crude materialism of early science as well as the enhanced rationalism of the modern epoch of Western thinking. With these views, any dichotomy or duality of matter vs. mind/soul/spirit becomes obsolete. The decisive point in this overturning of nineteenth-century Western views lies in Schopenhauer's idiosyncratic reinterpretation of the idea of "force" in his main work. According to Schopenhauer, will, indeed, could be understood as a *magic* word, revealing to us the "innermost essence of everything in nature,"[10] but the difference, now, is that will is not subsumed under the concept of force anymore, but actually every force in nature must be conceived *as* will. Moreover, will is not brought to us in a phenomenon or representation, but is knowable from within—"from the most immediate consciousness of everyone."[11] We can describe this immediateness of knowing by the inner (bodily) ethical insight of the will in ourselves—which leads us toward a compassionate response as the principal aim of his entire philosophy. According to Schopenhauer, then, an individual capable of achieving this compassion (not everyone is capable of this—thus Schopenhauer's inclination toward the doctrine of predestination) would inevitably feel bad at any wrongdoing. This would result in the so-called "sting of conscience or the pangs of conscience" (orig. *Gewissensbiß* and *Gewissensangst*)[12] in her bodily feeling that she has wronged someone. This feeling would appear, for example, as *felt* pain in our inside/womb (or stomach) as a result of bad conscience—a phenomenon well known to any ethically sensitive human being. It is precisely this inner presentiment or feeling that inaugurates the *correspondence* between beings through the *nexus*, called "Will," as we will see later. As a first representation, therefore, will is immediately known in the body, more precisely, in the inside/womb. According to Bracha Ettinger, this ethical place is defined as "matrixial" and is related to the "knowledge of being-born-together." Furthermore, according to her, "this cross-inscription is transmitted by matrixial effects such as empathy, awe, com-passion and compassion, languishing, horror, and maybe telepathy."[13] Let us keep the possibility of *telepathy*, as mentioned by Ettinger, in our minds—as this directly relates to Schopenhauer. To return to ontology now: the being-born-together mode as exemplified here is just another name for the correspondence of beings, known in Schopenhauer's philosophy as a chain of various objectivizations of will. What, then, connects beings as they manifest as objectivizations of *one* Will—and which laws bind them in their correspondences? In an earlier account on this problem, Bruno pantheistically exemplifies this concern by using the words "spirits" and "power" (we can replace them by "will" in Schopenhauer). Let us look at two important excerpts from Bruno—the first comes from *The Expulsion of the Triumphant Beast* and the second from his *Essays on Magic*:

> [V]arious spirits occupy the bodies of humans, animals, stones and minerals [and] there is no body which is completely devoid

of spirit and intelligence. . . . Finally, it must be consciously accepted and firmly asserted that all things are full of spirits, souls, divine power, and God or divinity, and that the whole of intelligence and the whole soul is everywhere, although they do not do everything everywhere. . . . As a result, the philosophers say that in the original state of things there was one matter, one spirit, one light, one soul and one intellect.[14]

Things in the universe are so ordered that they constitute one definite co-ordination in which there can occur a transition from all things to all things in one continuous flow. . . . And just as there are various species of things and differences between them, they also have various times, places, intermediaries, pathways, instruments, and functions. . . . If there were only one love, and thus only one bond, all things would be one.[15]

Both for Bruno and Schopenhauer, there is an inner force even in an inorganic form such as a mineral; both thinkers also attest that matter and spirit are only two sides of one reality, which is known as will by Schopenhauer. As matter is indestructible (and is as such spiritual), so spirit (or soul) is material and thus objectified in a body. Matter is conditioned by representation as mind is conditioned by its physical objectivization—in this they are truly codependent: "But true Metaphysics teaches us, that the physical in man is itself mere product, or rather phenomenon, of a spiritual (the will); nay, that Matter itself is conditioned by representation, in which alone it exists. . . . Thus knowledge and matter (Subject and Object) exist only relatively one for the other and constitute phenomenon."[16] Based on the ideas of codependency and coordination as a mark of Schopenhauer's metaphysics, and also based on the idea of his soteriological ethics of compassion, it is our aim now to address the principles of correspondence and synchronicity as related to "weird" or "paranormal" phenomena as still hidden but, in our opinion, key potentialities of Schopenhauer's practical or experimental metaphysics.

Animal Magnetism and Philosophy

The phenomenon of the world is here understood as exteriority of the will turned into the interiority of the bodily knowledge, thus establishing a link or *nexus* of the world both with and in ourselves. This connection opens entirely new avenues for the understanding of interpersonal or intersubjective relations not known before Schopenhauer's philosophy. The main aim of his entire project is, without doubt, the final ethico-soteriological realization that appears as a result of the mysterious realization in ourselves that our ego, our entire personal character and therefore our will can be *aufgehoben* and thus transmitted into the Will as *thing-in-itself*. Our will is thus suppressed or eliminated; we become one with this (one, and cosmic) Will, and in this moment, which remains a mystery, the highest and compassionate ethical correlation is established: we feel the *pain of others* in ourselves (literally in our body),[17] we cease to exist as my previous self and become one with the Will of the world:

> But this whole, the character itself, can be entirely eliminated by the abovementioned change of knowledge. It is this elimination or suppression at which Asmus [i.e., Matthias Claudius] marvels as said above, and which he describes as the "catholic, transcendental change." It is also that which in the Christian Church is very appropriately called *new birth* or *regeneration*, and the knowledge from which it springs, the *effect of divine grace*. . . . All love (ἀγαπη, *caritas*) is compassion or sympathy.[18]

Within this ontological plane of ethics, the entire *practical metaphysics* is revealed: upon the birth of any individual being, Will as *Ding-an-sich* enters a particular body—our knowledge assimilates the knowable part of the will under the categories of the body, which results in the first (immediate) representation of the will in ourselves: the body. The epistemological circle is connected and a new mode, *nexus metaphysicum*, is now enabled: from now on, as a singular being we are subsumed under the coordination of beings and we are, as it were, *synchronized* with them.

One of the most intriguing features of Schopenhauer's teaching is that this revelation of the will in oneself (and with it the mysterious correspondence of one self and other beings, all the way to the realm of inorganic nature) is understood as a mystery: as compared to divine grace by Schopenhauer, it "comes suddenly as if flying in from without."[19] Schopenhauer, it seems, could not, yet, provide a comprehensive explanation of the still mysterious phenomenon of the thing-in-itself and, despite his doubts about classical religious and theological vocabularies, he still remained in their vicinity. For some interpreters of his philosophy, this could be understood as a weakness. But, in light of contemporary theological narratives and their proximity to quantum science, Schopenhauer's vicinity to classical vocabularies actually opens up inspiring new possibilities for his thought. The question for us is the following—and we are heading toward our main argument now—if our connection with the other is enabled and active (compassion being our response to the pain and suffering that we can detect and actually *feel* in our bodies), *of which kind* is the substance that is revealed to us as a Will? If this substance is purely metaphysical (as is too often affirmed), then we could clearly not have any access to it beyond a mere representation. If it is material, then it is revealed to us as *natura naturans*, or a creative matter-energy and we are an essential part of this creation—even beyond possibilities once imagined or comprehended by the mystics.

Let us approach the question of Schopenhauer's ethics of compassion, now radicalized in the following way: we have learned that the highest and compassionate ethical correlation is established when I feel the pain of the other in myself (in my body). An ethical correspondence is activated and felt in myself as compassion as a form of sympathy. This activation of the *ethical* will in myself is still causal and local, but here already in the *weakened* sense: it is causal only as we see others and then react to their pain immediately and internally, and it is local as this still happens within the spatiotemporal continuum of our parallel, but now ethically already coordinated and synchronized, lives. Schopenhauer's ethics is thus still a version of weak metaphysics and this is why he largely employs theological vocabulary (grace, salvation, ascesis, new birth, and regeneration) in his main work. But there is a part of his work that escapes both causality and locality, and, despite still being closely related to all of his main ideas, leads us to new avenues of thought—now beyond metaphysics and into the new philosophical theology. It is Schopenhauer's elaboration of paranormal phenomena, which he never seriously incorporated into his main work, but which he still adamantly supported and defended in two of his essays, "Animalischer Magnetismus und Magie" (as a part of *Über den Willen in der Natur*) and "Versuch über das Geistersehn" (as a part of *Parerga und Paralipomena*). It is our aim to show the central importance of these view for his entire system, and to highlight the relevance of these views as key tenets for both contemporary philosophy and theology.

Before explaining the key tenets that form the background of this thought in Schopenhauer, let us start with a practical example: in the ethical field, the *nexus metaphysicum* is still loosely connected to the ordinary world of causality and spatiotemporality. Yet there exist phenomena that are detached from this continuum and are thus noncausal, nontemporal, and nonlocal. Metaphysics, now, becomes *experimental* for Schopenhauer, making the impossible, possible, and thus breaking or transgressing the ordinary (classical) natural laws.[20] An example given by Schopenhauer relates to a dying person communicating with his absent loved one or a friend. Schopenhauer regards this example and related phenomena (such as prophetic dreams, visions, and various kinds of telepathy) to be proven on the basis of numerous personal reports that he has read about or even witnessed: "There are dying persons that express this capability and thus appear in the moment of their death to their dear ones, even to more of them, and in different places" ("Namentlich sind es Sterbende, die dieses Vermögen äußern und daher in der Stunde ihres Todes ihren abwesenden Freunden erscheinen, sogar mehreren an verschiedenen Orten zugleich.")[21] This realization opens entirely new dimensions of the metaphysics of Will: based on the so-called phenomenon of animal magnetism (more on this later), there occurs an activity of the will that affects and reaches out to the other from the distance and, as such, across the known spatiotemporal continuum. The question is now: How do we explain the *nexum metaphysicum* and will in this and similar cases? For Schopenhauer, it is "the path through *Ding-an-sich*"[22] that lies outside the *principium individuationis* (and, thus, time and space) and that affects the will of the other across and, at the same moment, beyond the spatiotemporal continuum. Moreover, as this *Ding-an-sich* or Will cannot be destroyed, it would even be possible for a dead person to communicate with the living, as clearly indicated by Schopenhauer in the last paragraphs of his "Versuch über das Geistersehn."[23]

Now, to elaborate on this assertion, let us approach the concept of *animal magnetism* in Schopenhauer as it is key to what human beings used to refer to as magical action and what today is understood under the broad notion of psi phenomena.[24] The very notion "Animalisher Magnetismus" stems from the thought of the Jesuit father Athanasius Kircher (1601–80) and was later widely used by the French doctor and the so-called magnetizer Franz Anton Mesmer (1734–1815). The "magnetism" in this concept presupposes the activity of a hypothetical power or a vital fluid, which could be linked to the meaning of *prāṇa* as (cosmic) vital power in Hinduism (or in other similar concepts, such as *qi* and *mana*).[25] The basic idea of the Mesmerian "magnetic cure" was the ability of the magnetizer to transfer this power to another person.[26] Now, for Mesmer, it was also possible to use this telepathic ability for other purposes—such as in extrasensory perception, clairvoyance, prophetic dreams, and precognition of future events. Schopenhauer himself was familiar with paranormal events and had also experienced them personally during his life; so, he was very sensitive to this thought. In his library there were numerous books on psi phenomena of his time, and he also explains some of his personal experiences in his works. In *On the Will in Nature*, Schopenhauer writes:

> In consequence of these facts, notwithstanding many reasons and prejudices to the contrary, the opinion has gradually gained ground, nay almost raised itself to certainty, that Animal Magnetism and its phenomena are identical with part of the Magic of former times, of that ill-famed occult art, of whose reality not only the Christian ages by which it was so cruelly persecuted, but all, not excepting even savage, nations on the whole of the earth, have been equally convinced throughout all ages.[27]

In the beginning of our essay, we highlighted the paradox, which is rarely addressed within theology: that religious experiences such as prayers, personal visions of God (or other divine beings or saints), prophecies, appearances of living or deceased persons or beings, miracles (with resurrection of the dead being the utmost example—Lazarus and, of course, Christ), and also the assumption into heaven of Mary, represent the very essence of religious faith (at least in Christianity—if we remain within the scope of Schopenhauer's analyses). But it is strange that paranormal phenomena (for example: clairvoyance, precognition, and telepathy), which are structurally closely related to miracles, are still rarely admitted to enter religious or theological narratives. With the exception of the psychology of religion (William James, Carl Gustav Jung, and recent empirical research in the field of religious beliefs and the paranormal) and cognitive science (which are *not* theological disciplines), psi phenomena are still regarded as exceptions and are generally omitted from discussion. They are, rather, measured and interpreted statistically to delineate their place in the broader "religious" field as to be included into the proper field of ontologies of religious or even theological belief.[28]

The issue with so-called paranormal phenomena is that they could be understood as an extension both of the realization of the will (in epistemology and ontology) as well as compassion (in ethics and soteriology): if taken seriously—that is, as *actio et passio in distans*—they operate across and beyond the ordinary spatiotemporal plane and produce effects that were traditionally understood in theology as miracles. David Cartwright states that "Schopenhauer found a connection between compassion, animal magnetism, and magic, classifying them, along with sexual love, as forms of 'Sympathy'; that is, of forms of 'The empirical emerging of the metaphysical identity of will through the physical multiplicity of will's appearance.' In this regard he referred to animal magnetism, magic, and compassion as 'practical metaphysics,' as expressions of what (theoretical) metaphysics describes."[29] The task of interpreters of Schopenhauer must be to further theologically develop what he clearly states about magic in his "Animal Magnetism and Magic" chapter from *On the Will in Nature*. Let us look at the following three excerpts:

> Although Magic is differently defined by the various authors who have treated of it, the fundamental thought which predominates in all its definitions is nevertheless unmistakable. For the opinion, that there must be another quite different way of producing changes in the world besides the regular one through the causal nexus between bodies, and one moreover which is not founded at all upon that nexus, has found favour in all ages and countries.

> But here it was assumed, that apart from the outer connection between the phenomena of this world on which the nexus physicus [physical connection] is founded, there must exist another besides, passing through the very essence in itself of all things: a subterranean connection, as it were, by means of which immediate action was possible from one point of the phenomenon on to every other point, through a nexus metaphysicus [metaphysical connection].

> Just as we act causally as *natura naturata* [created nature], we might probably be able to act also as *natura naturans* [creating nature], and momentarily to enable the microcosm to play the part of the macrocosm; that, however firm the partition walls of

individuation and separation might be, they might nevertheless occasionally permit a communication to take place, as it were, behind the scenes, or like a secret game under the table.[30]

This possibility of an action from one point to every other point, as an immediate (or direct) communication beyond the space-time continuum and causality is, for Schopenhauer, the proof for the magical power as an inherent part of the Will or *Ding-an-sich*. This is why interpreters can now describe his metaphysics of will as being in close relation to quantum-physical phenomena, and thus making "a semantic connection between natural science, psychology, philosophy, religion, and mysticism."[31] It is clear that in the midst of the nineteenth century (Schopenhauer wrote the first version of his animal magnetism essay in 1836), Schopenhauer was on the track of something very important: an enigmatic and synchronistic thought that he could not fully develop and include in his main work, but which he still ardently defended throughout his life. Let us look into the possibilities of this thought for philosophical theology.

From Compassion to Telepathy

This discussion now leads us to the main part of our elaboration: we now know that compassion (feeling with the other) and telepathy (distant feeling with the other) are structurally linked as two features of the sympathetic disposition or possibility in human beings. As a result of the enhanced mode of our being-in-the-world through *Ding-an-sich*, this disposition now enables us to initiate a correspondence with the *core of nature*, enabling our self to become synchronized with other selves. It seems that it is precisely through the psi phenomena that Schopenhauer could provide a definitive solution of the ancient ontotheological riddle—of an enigmatic correspondence between microcosm and macrocosm—or of human and divine realms. But, as Cartwright rightly observes in his elaboration of the paranormal phenomena in Schopenhauer, Schopenhauer was not a skeptic in this endeavor. He therefore concludes his analysis with a rather negative insight:

> At the same time, however, one must question his willingness to uncritically accept paranormal phenomena at face value. If there was one thing that Schopenhauer was not, he was not a skeptic.

> This lack of skepticism sometimes serves him well, such as his pragmatic rejection of theoretical egoism (solipsism). But with the paranormal, it appears to have failed him. Perhaps he should have just left the paranormal as the subject for parapsychologists and ghost hunters, waiting instead for "facts" for which he could then attempt to supply a theory.[32]

There are two strategies for us here: we can either follow Cartwright's skeptical stance and contend that Schopenhauer was indeed one of the pioneers in the field rarely elaborated by philosophers (although even Cartwright affirms that Johann Gottlieb Fichte, Schelling, and Hegel also believed in the paranormal[33]) but that he uncritically accepted too many presuppositions about the paranormal and thus made a methodological mistake. On the other hand, we can follow the alternative route, employ contemporary thinking on the quantum field and synchronicity and try to link Schopenhauer's idiosyncratic thought with some of the most intriguing issues in psychology (Freud, Jung), philosophy (Derrida and Ettinger), and contemporary philosophical theology (Keller, new materialism, and quantum theology).

For the sake of our elaborations, we will take paranormal phenomena, such as precognition, clairvoyance, and telepathy, as a part of the *supernatural field*, comprising both religious and psi experiences. For example, in this view, we cannot epistemologically or aprioristically distinguish between genuine religious and genuine paranormal phenomena. We can here present the epistemological claim regarding the dichotomy miracles vs. psi phenomena: evaluated from the ordinary causal spatiotemporal nexus, these phenomena are entirely impossible as they break natural laws. They can be quickly labeled as superstitious and theology can, then, provide justification for miracles (by using the narratives of faith, love, or hope, for example). But it is much more difficult to provide justification for the psi paranormal phenomena, as they were traditionally associated with the magical, fetishistic, or animistic domain (and labeled as occult) and were thus devoid of any real ontological meaning.

In his seminal book *Parapsychology, Philosophy, and Spirituality* (not dealing with Schopenhauer or Jung) David Ray Griffin presents us with a series of arguments for the academic and scientific evaluation of the paranormal phenomena.[34] In this excellent and unique book, Griffin lays the foundation for any future elaboration of the psi phenomena based on psychological, philosophical, and religious interests. Based on a statement by

Alfred North Whitehead that it is "fatal to dismiss antagonistic doctrines, supported by any body of evidence, as simply wrong,"[35] Griffin argues, that, in an era of evolutionary science, relativity theory, and quantum physics, it is vital and actually necessary to extend our interests in philosophy and religious science toward the field of parapsychology, including telepathy, of course. Underpinned by numerous reports, examples of experiments and personalities (such as various scientists, philosophers, psychologists, and religious scholars) exploring psi phenomena and experiences, Griffin criticizes the scientific reductionism of late modernity and thus transcends the supernatural *vs.* atheism and dualism *vs.* materialism divides. God, for him, reveals within the *continual creation* of the panexperientalist and processual view of the universe,[36] now also without the fundamental support of the *creatio ex nihilo* idea.

But to return to our elaboration of telepathy: there is a long history of *materiaphobia* that actually prevents both theology and the study of religion from accepting the possibility of an enhanced spiritually materialist view of creation.[37] But the creativity in the world itself is so rich that it invites us to think beyond borders of both classical science and theology; this shift clearly breaks the unfortunate dichotomy in which humans could become godlike but still were not admitted their proper ontological value. As Karen Barad affirms within the field of agential realism in the conclusion of her seminal work on quantum physics and philosophy:

> Intra-acting responsibly as part of the world means taking account of the entangled phenomena that are intrinsic to the world's vitality and being responsive to the possibilities that might help us and it flourish. Meeting each moment, being alive to the possibilities of becoming, is an ethical call, an invitation that is written into the very matter of all being and becoming. We need to meet the universe halfway, to take responsibility for the role that we play in the world's differential becoming.[38]

Understood in theological terms, the possibility of this meeting finally breaks the line of separation between the divine and human realms and enables us as human beings to partake in the experience of the world. In light of all these intertwinings and with the ontological gates open, we can now focus more closely on the ethically intersubjective (and then also quantum-like) phenomenon of telepathy.

As feeling at a distance (understood both in terms of action and thought), telepathy breaks all known spatiotemporal laws and is marked by Schopenhauer in *On the Will in Nature* as the *subterranean connection, by means of which immediate action was possible from one point of the phenomenon on to every other point, through a nexus metaphysicus*. As predecessor of both Freud and Jung, Schopenhauer was decisive for the advancement of psychoanalytical understanding of the human soul. As both intra- and interpsychic act, telepathy weaves together two sides of an always impossible ethical encounter: even in its most immediate ethical response, compassion, as a form of sympathy (in Levinasian terms), always comes too late (*être tard*). In Schopenhauer's ethics, our feeling of the pain of the other is indeed immediate, but still comes *only after* we are able to recognize it with our representation and as based on our five senses—as pain and suffering of the other. Isn't it so that only telepathy could breach this temporal barrier, as a precognitive response to the feeling of the other ("precognitive" here meaning to be actually cross-temporarily synchronized with the other), or, perhaps, as based on a mysterious sense we do yet not know? In "Telepathy," which is a testimony to Derrida's own *conversion* to telepathy (being on a trace of Freud's report of his *conversion to telepathy* from 1926[39]), we find this excerpt from a letter, dated July 10, 1979:

> When you asked me the other day: what is changing in your life? Well, you have noticed it a hundred times recently, it is the opposite of what I foresaw, as one might have expected: a surface more and more open to all the phenomena formerly rejected (in the name of a certain discourse of science), to the phenomena of "magic," of "clairvoyance," of "fate," of communications at a distance, to the things said to be occult. . . . Everything, in our concept of knowledge, is constructed so that telepathy be impossible, unthinkable, unknown. If there is any, our relation to Telepathy must not be of the family of "knowledge" or "non-knowledge" but is of another kind.[40]

Our concept of knowledge must expand, as it were, to *another sensitivity of the other*, beyond both knowledge and its absence. As Derrida capitalizes Telepathy, he already knows that She (telepathy is feminine for Derrida) guards the mysterious entrance to a kind of newly invented Schopenhauerian "panpathy" (as a sign of an ethical process from *sym-pathein* to *tele-pathein* and, finally to *pan-pathein*, as it were). This is what was already indicated by Ettinger, when she proposes that this ethical place is itself matrixial, and transmitted by matrixial effects such as empathy, compassion, and telepathy.[41] This matrixial atmosphere of telepathy is a psychico-material ground for the affects of distant feeling, and, if, indeed, it is thought in the latter—atmospheric—sense, then a comparison to wireless communication through *ether* really is coherent—as John Durham Peters states in his elaboration of communication media through history.[42] Now, in her reading of Derrida, Elisa Marder points to Nicolas Royle's observation that, for Derrida (and after Freud), telepathy is situated within his philosophy "in accordance with the foreign body, as being at once outside-the-subject and at the very heart of the subject."[43] To come full circle now, this telepathic coordination and correspondence of two body-minds or subjectivities is precisely what is proposed and defended by Schopenhauer.

The Telepathic Synchronicity

The correspondence of beings, as shown in the coordination with the *Ding-an-sich* in Schopenhauer, is very close to Derrida's statement about the presence of the foreign body in myself if considered as a part of Derrida's own dialogue with Freud's *conversion* to telepathy and his theory of the foreign body. This entanglement *with-in* telepathy of three major thinkers, namely Schopenhauer, Freud, and Derrida, strikes us; it is a testimony of the still-undisclosed synchronicity within the logic of the psyche itself—in its inherent inclination toward the other as also in its intrinsic capability of a *tele-pathic hospitality*, as it were: a disclosure of the perhaps highest ethico-cosmical correspondence we may be able to find in this world. The highest paradigm for this (sacred, divine, or mysterious, as you wish) correspondence might be the *perichoresis* between the divine persons of the Trinity, with breath of love as the connecting nexus.[44] Interestingly enough, in his *Entangled Trinity*, Ernest Simmons presents an argument for his perichoretic Trinitarian panentheism, and in doing this, he works in close proximity to quantum physics and thus develops his own quantum theology: the *perichoresis* as a dynamics within the Trinity is here understood as entanglement and "dance of the divine."[45] For Simmons, the Trinity is a dancing God, with its parts flowing "in and out of one another in a continuous way."[46] And his final panentheistic definition of Trinity reads as follows: "*Pericho-*

resis may be conceived as the mutual indwelling energy of the divine Trinity through which the creation is created and which evolves within the life of God as entangled superposition."[47]

But to return to the notion of tele-pathic hospitality now: much is at stake here, and the paradoxical nature of this hospitality is still awaiting to be fully disclosed and conceptualized. Compassion—as we have seen in Schopenhauer—is the preeminent and final realization of the will-in-ourselves within his philosophical system. Within my body, the ethical continuum is broken and a miracle happens: my body *feels* the pain of the other. The dormant *Ding-an-sich* in us, as it were, is awakened, and we are reborn and activated into a new kind of human being: one that is synchronized with the ontological ground of the all-world; for the moment of our compassionate response, we are one with the other and this ethical correspondence indicates that the place, or an instant *topia* of the other in ourselves, is revealed as a Will. The highest ethical distillation of this bodily phenomenon materializes in *stigmata* and wounds of compassion; these are a mark of the ethical wound of the other: cross-inscribed upon a *body-psyche* on a basis of the highest ethical correspondence of two singular beings, connected in compassion (as in Saint Francis of Assisi and Julian of Norwich[48]). As such, stigmata and wounds of compassion are the radicalized form of com-passion—of its materiality, cross-ethicicity, and mutual affectivity, affecting our bodies with wounds—regardless of whether they are visibly materialized or not. This highest ethics of vulnerability acts across distances and times, as it were, but it still operates within the "normal" epistemological field, although being at its very limit. But with the possibility of a telepathy as a coordinated and synchronized distant feeling (as an enhanced com-passion), things now change radically—epistemologically and ontologically. In his posttheistic thought, Caputo approaches the quantum entanglement (i.e., the mysterious correspondence of two distant events across the spatiotemporal plane), as originally exemplified by Keller as follows: "we should envisage the same set of potentialities getting actualized as the same event in two different locations, as excitations of a common field."[49] In a further observation, being so close to Schopenhauer now that this cannot be overlooked, Caputo writes: "Each thing is entangled with everything else in a common field of potentiality, a common (under)ground of being, a sea of entangled potentiality, a wavy undulating boundlessness, a *tehom*. Theologically, this resonates with a *Deus-sive-natura* panentheism."[50] The subterranean connection of Schopenhauer (let us remember his *subterranean connection, by means of which immediate action was possible from one point of the phenomenon on to every other point, through a nexus metaphysicus*) is here closely related to Caputo, for whom God, taken as the ground of Being, is now "a theologically suggestive nickname for quantum potentialities."[51] But, we are still not able to explain the very concept of a meaningful coincidence—that is, of two events being so closely interrelated or coordinated as to be able to produce a common and meaningful effect. We will approach this topic by looking into the theory of synchronicity of Jung, who was both deeply influenced by Schopenhauer as well as by the evolving quantum science of his era (especially as propounded by his friend W. Pauli).

Before we embark on a short journey to Jung's theory of synchronicity as developed also under the influence of Schopenhauer,[52] let us try to describe a synchronistic phenomenon as mentioned by Ernst Benz in his *Die Vision: Erfahrungsformen und Bilderwelt*; here, Benz reports on Saint John Bosco's prophetic dreams and his concrete example is the story of the young Don Bosco, who was dreaming about a forthcoming school test so clearly that he could write it down in the morning precisely enough that his teacher (having the test prepared for Don Bosco and his schoolmates) could simply not believe his own eyes. As in similar cases, we can employ a skeptical approach and dismiss these and similar cases as examples of a certain coincidence, luck, or a trick (tricks were possible and, sometimes, of course, pupils would indeed steal school tests and so forth; another possibility would be that this or similar stories are simply made up). But the ability of Don Bosco to foresee the future in his dreams was reported many times over, and the more time passed with Don Bosco's accurate visions the more the door was open for a paranormal explanation of the events. Put in Schopenhauerian terms, if we take Don Bosco for person A, and his teacher for B, then we have two independent continuums in an ordinary spatiotemporal sense with some causal connections. The effect of Don Bosco's correspondence with the continuum B could only happen if the common background of both persons is attested: for Schopenhauer this would mean that the will of A has mysteriously correlated with the will of B. For quantum theory, it would mean that both A and B would subsist on the fluctuations of the so-called vacuum state of energy. As Webb explains:

> The Higgs field permeates all of space, and thus space is not really empty, although the Higgs field represents the lowest state

of energy in the universe, and thus space is as empty as you can get.... The Higgs field, which is really a form of quantum energy, is more basic than the Higgs boson, so perhaps it should be called "God's field," since the image of a divinely saturated matrix more accurately conveys the way in which everything that exists does so because of its relationship to something else.[53]

Webb speculates that all of life must somehow subsist on one common *resonating* field and that—take creativity of any kind as an example—human beings are capable of connecting to a kind of divine or cosmic matrix in ways we cannot foresee or explain rationally (take multiple and rationally inexplicable coincidences leading to inspiration and creativity). Webb also asserts that "telepathy, spiritual healing, prayer, clairvoyance, the transcendence of mind over matter, and even the resurrection of the dead have all been attributed to the bizarre properties of this field."[54] This assertion nicely fits with our initial hypothesis that both religious and so-called psi phenomena need to be taken together as entities of one supernatural (or supernormal) field.

As already indicated, Jung was strongly influenced by Schopenhauer's thought. Throughout his life, Jung was under the strong influence of paranormal phenomena: he was encircled with family members who were experiencing strange and uncanny things—his maternal grandfather conversed regularly with the spirit of his deceased wife, his grandmother was clairvoyant, and his mother experienced strange occurrences. Since his early childhood, Jung was a subject of strange and paranormal phenomena, which led him to believe that, apart from the ordinary personality or psyche, there must be another, a more primordial, ancient, and deeper one, which is closer to dreams, nature, or God.[55] Jung had experience attending séances before completing his PhD and had witnessed the abilities of a medium in a trance state, which enabled him to formulate his theory of the collective unconscious and archetypes. But, after having a serious heart attack in 1944, and having a near-death experience, Jung felt even more committed to the phenomena known as "paranormal." As a consequence, for Jung, distant knowing or knowing of events in the future is possible, since *within the unconscious*, these phenomena or events coexist beyond the causal space-time continuum: "For the unconscious psyche space and time seem to be relative; that is to say, knowledge finds itself in a space-time continuum in which space is no longer space, nor time time. If, therefore, the unconscious should develop or maintain a potential in the direction of consciousness, it is then possible for parallel events to be perceived as 'known.' "[56] This observation is, of course, in line with Schopenhauer and opens the possibility for a psychological interpretation of the psi phenomena. As Jung knew Albert Einstein and his theory of relativity, he was also familiar with the early stages of the new quantum mechanics (in particular, as defended by Niels Bohr) and his theory was further developed and refined on the basis of his friendship with the physicist Pauli (the friendship lasted from 1932 and until Pauli's death in 1958)—that is, during the decisive years of Jung's conception and development of the theory of synchronicity. For Jung, synchronicity means that there exists a "coincidence of a certain psychic content with a corresponding objective process which is perceived to take place simultaneously."[57] Based on the findings of quantum mechanics, Jung thought that, *per analogiam*, similarly as for the subatomic level, acausality also could be attested on the macroscopical level. We are still without sufficient knowledge in this field and need to rely on some nonscientific suppositions. But, Jung still affirms (similarly to Webb—as presented above) that "there are indications that psychic processes stand in some sort of energy relation to the physiological substrate."[58] Synchronicity (or meaningful coincidence, as he puts it; *sinvolle Zufälle*) takes place when an event happens that cannot reasonably be explained by mere chance or, in more complex cases, by chance grouping (that are still probable and thus rationally explicable). But in many other cases, when the probability ratio rises, we cannot talk about chance anymore—Jung employs meaningful coincidence here and the group of related phenomena consist of precognition, clairvoyance, psychokinesis, and telepathy, among others. Encouraged by the results of J. B. Rhine's experiments on extrasensory perception (or ESP), Jung finally contends:

> Synchronistic phenomena prove the simultaneous occurrence of meaningful equivalences in heterogenous, causally unrelated processes; in other words, they prove that a content perceived by an observer can, at the same time, be represented by an outside event, without any causal connection. From this it follows either that the psyche cannot be localized in space, or that space is relative to the psyche. The same applies to the temporal determination of the psyche and the psychic relativity of time. I

do not need to emphasize that the verification of these findings must have far-reaching consequences.[59]

We are still not in possession of the scientific methods that we could use to verify these hypotheses. For Jung, these phenomena were taken as psychic and, as such, they were regarded within the context of the activation of the archetypal plane of our psychical life. As highlighted by Andrea Kropf in her extensive work on Schopenhauer, Jung, and the paranormal, it was Jung's firm conviction that there was a theoretic proximity between the fields of parapsychology, depth psychology, and modern physics, and that they all "culminate in the conception of the archetypes as psycho-physical natural constants and as creative world-shaping factors."[60] The theory of quantum nonlocality (or nonlocal correlation: two subatomic particles remain correlated and act across distances as if they "know" each other) offers a possibility to think about certain similarities between subatomic and subconscious processes. Moreover, and in tune with Schopenhauer and Jung, according to Bernard d'Espagnat, it is precisely through the insights of quantum physics that we can affirm that particles, traditionally taken as particular objects, actually form an indivisible whole.[61] We also know from Keller that our universe is so mysteriously entangled that we cannot employ the usual methods (neither of science nor or theology) to explain its dynamics. The divisions we knew from philosophy or classical physics do not work anymore: "subject and object, inner world and outer world, body and soul [are] no longer adequate. . . . Rather the entangled state of A and B is read as a single entity, no matter how far apart is B from A." This is a "sort of telepathic coupling that horrified Einstein."[62] Our thesis is now that there must be a relationality between two temporal moments—our time (as human beings) must be related in a yet unknown manner to the temporality of a "God," which, as it were, interferes with our "ordinary" worlds through the effects that we learned to call "miracles."[63] Replace "God" with "Will" and wonder: from Schopenhauer to Jung, from Bruno to Keller, and beyond—it is one mysteriously entangled world we inhabit! Whether in galaxies or in cafes—we meet halfway to each other, or, perhaps, isn't it so that we have always already met and known our interrelated lives, and that these mysterious meetings are just events of one bond of Love, a plane of immanence yet to be explained and revealed to humanity (and beyond humanity's own domain)—as an inner force of the cosmos, that *compassionately* and *telepathically* correlates and synchronizes our apparently disassociated, yet unified lives?

Postscript: On Telepathy in Jainism

There is a unique tradition of the cultivation of supernatural powers within Indian philosophies and religions since the beginnings of Yoga, early Buddhist texts, and Jainist scriptures. According to Knut A. Jacobsen, this supernaturalism is a neglected topic in the research on yoga and South Asian meditation traditions. According to him, yoga powers are "forms of extraordinary knowledge, such as awareness of previous rebirths, knowing the minds of others, seeing distant and hidden things, and remarkable abilities such as the power to become invisible, enter others' bodies, fly through the air, and to become disembodied for a period of time, which are traditionally thought to be attained as yogins progress in their practice."[64] In chapter 3 of Patañjali's *Yoga-Sūtra*, we find aphorisms on knowledge of subtle and concealed objects, as well as teachings on knowledge of the mind of others. As we cannot discuss the vast terrain of the Yoga powers here, let us focus on a distinctive Jainist traditions of telepathy and its predecessors in early Buddhist thought. In early Buddhism, the so-called *iddhi* "stands for power in a general sense and for the exercise of supernatural power in particular."[65] Within early Buddhist supernaturalism, *iddhi* also features as the first of six higher knowledges, known as *abhiññās*, which are listed as follows: after *iddhi* as the first of these powers (known as *iddhi-vidhā-ñāṇa*), we have the divine ear (*dibba-sota-dhātu*), telepathic knowledge (*cetopariyañāṇa* or *paracittañāṇa*), recollection of one's former lives (*pubbenivāsānussatiñāṇa*), the divine eye (*dibba-cakkhu* or *catūpapatañāṇa*), and, finally, the attainment of full liberation (*āsava-kkhāya-ñāṇa*) as the sixth power, leading the practitioner toward liberation and realization of *nibbāna*. These powers are known by those practitioners "that have attained the fourth *jhāna* or level of concentrated and calm meditative absorption."[66] Now, in *Dīgha Nikāya*, we find three types of extraordinary powers—these are supernatural powers such as multiplying oneself, the telepathic ability to read the mind of others, and instructions on how to train one's mind.[67] Still, among the six higher knowledges, *aññā* or the gaining of full awakening holds the most prominent position and is thus superior to any display of the supernatural powers for ulterior purposes. Buddha himself did not encourage his followers to exhibit these powers solely for the purpose of the performance of wonders, declaring this as "a minor offense, *dukkaṭa*, if a monastic exhibits supernormal abilities to laity."[68]

In Jainism, telepathy is much more elaborated and more intriguing, and can be linked to Schopenhauer's and Jung's elaborations on synchronicity and mystical correspondences—and to our reflections on quantum theology. We acknowledge Schopenhauer's interest in Indian philosophy, especially in Buddhism, and we do not need to mention Jung's lifelong interest in non-Western traditions.[69] The main source of these teachings of Jainism is the *Tattvārtha-Sūtra*; this work was written by Umāsvāti between the second and fourth centuries CE and comprises the distillation of the entire Jain knowledge.[70] In this sutra, telepathy is defined as follows: "Knowledge is of five kinds—sensory-knowledge—*matijñāna*, scriptural-knowledge—*śrutajñāna,* clairvoyance—*avadhijñāna*, telepathy—*manaḥparyayajñāna*, and omniscience—*kevalajñāna*. . . . The two kinds of telepathy (*manaḥparyayajñāna*) are *Rjumati* and *vipulamati*."[71] The commentary of the sūtra affirms that the difference between both kinds of telepathy is due to the purity and infallibility of the practitioner—namely of her scope of knowing the objects thought of by the minds of others and of her ability in the destruction of telepathy-knowledge-obstructing karmas. But, before we discuss the scope of this knowledge, let us look into the main elements of Jaina epistemology. According to Piotr Balcerowicz, apart from the Buddhist influences, "Jaina epistemology relied heavily on the general epistemological paradigm developed by other schools, especially that of early Nyāya-Vaiśeṣika."[72] This is how the key epistemological categories are defined by him:

> Despite Jaina epistemological classification's original terminological incompatibility with the rest of epistemological traditions in classical India—the term *pratyakṣa* (universally: "perception"; in Jainism: "direct cognition") was reserved for a range of supernatural cognitions, whereas the actual sensory perception was known as *abhinibodha* or *mati-jñana*—both kinds of perception were clearly distinguished in the quintuplet of cognitions: sensuous cognition (*abhinibodha, mati*; lit. "apprehension," "mental process"), testimonial cognition (*śruta;* lit. "the heard"), clairvoyance (*avadhi*; lit. "mental infiltration"), telepathy, or mindreading (*manaḥ-paryāya* or *manaḥ-paryaya*; lit. "penetration of the mind") and perfect knowledge, or omniscience (*kevala*; lit. "the singular one"), all being later grouped under two headings of indirect cognition (*parokṣa*) and direct cognition (*pratyakṣa*), respectively.[73]

Now, the most important feature for our comparison with Schopenhauer is the fact that the Jain concept of telepathy "presupposed an idea, which is a pan-Indian belief, that mental phenomena, including all states of mind of other people, are somatic."⁷⁴ This means that—if we are using the Buddhist vocabulary here—all *dharmas* (i.e., "bodily" and "mental" constituents or elements of existence) are understood as being materially somatic. In this line of thinking, even telepathy is related to grasping of fine or subtle, yet still material, percepts that are located in the mind. Yet there is a distinctive teaching in Jainism that we cannot find in other South Asian traditions—namely, that even *karma* itself is viewed as consisting of matter and is, thus, regarded as a physical substance.⁷⁵ According to this teaching, karma is like a screen blocking out our soul, which is pure consciousness and nonsubstance in its essence. On a very basic ontological level, without the gross particles of various karmas literally adhering to our soul (*jiva*), we would not even have a body and be incarnated as a human being (or any other existing being—from plant to worm or any other sentient being). This indeed is what Schopenhauer wants to propose with his teaching on the will as a veil of māyā⁷⁶ and this is very close to Schopenhauer's views on *Ding-an-sich* and Will; as our internal will cannot be destroyed, it still defines our lives *as* karma—from the most elemental forces such as gravity all the way to the highest mental states (including telepathy), all our bodily and mental states are obstructed by the *veil* of this will. We have seen, in our elaboration of Schopenhauer's will, that upon the birth of any individual being, Will as *Ding-an-sich* enters a particular body, which results in the first representation of the will in ourselves in the body; from now on, any singular being is subsumed under the coordination of beings and is as *synchronized* with them. The goal, now, is to eliminate this veil and become one with the pan-cosmic Will; this enables us to establish a mysterious, yet practically visible ethical correlation—that is for Schopenhauer manifested in compassion. But, the possibility of an action from one point to any other point—as an immediate or direct communication beyond the space-time continuum and causality—was for Schopenhauer proof of the magical power as an inherent part of the Will or *Ding-an-sich*. Hence, we have the possibility of the so-called *panpathy* as a proof of the existence of *nexus metaphysicus*: we are now synchronized with the ontological ground of the world.

To return to Jainism now, clairvoyance (*avadhi*) is here defined as a possibility of grasping "material microscopic objects that were considered physically beyond the reach of ordinary, sensuous perception or testimonial cognition.⁷⁷ This kind of perception was, of course, not accessible to everyone. But telepathy was even much subtler and as such it was only to be found in the most advanced human beings (compare this to Schopenhauer's view on our capabilities to grasp the *Ding-an-sich*); it was regarded as a capacity "to directly grasp others' thoughts, i.e., all contents of other minds."[78] As an apex of all cognitive and spiritual faculties, telepathy now represents the highest possibility of an insight into the coordination of beings or existences through (and later even beyond) the obstructing karmas: the spiritually perfected being (*kevalin*) faces no obstructions whatsoever: beyond the ordinary spatiotemporal continuum she is capable of accessing the plane of a supramundane existence and knowledge, where all karmic matter is destroyed. All things—past, present, and future—are revealed to her (we may add a remark here that this knowledge was attested by Jains in at least one woman—namely Malli, the nineteenth Tīrthaṅkara). The telepathic actuality becomes the sign of omniscience, knowledge of things that were not yet seen, perceived, or thought. Beyond sensory and scriptural cognition, clairvoyance and telepathy enable us to enter the stage of perfect and liberating knowledge.

Interestingly enough, and thus explaining many reported but often contested cases of clairvoyance and telepathy (cf. Schopenhauer here), in Jainism "it is possible on occasion for a non-omniscient being to have cognition that is not associated with the sense-organs or with the mind."[79] These partial occurrences of clairvoyance can be related to certain places or locations, but they are not permanent. Now, according to the *Tattvārtha-Sūtra*, "Telepathy (*manaḥparyayajñāna*) and clairvoyance (*avadhijñāna*) differ with regard to purity (*viśuddhi*), space (*kṣetra*), possessor (*svāmī*) and subject matter (*viṣaya*)."[80] Taking into account these differences now, "mind-reading knows the finer modes of material clusters which are beyond the reach of clairvoyance."[81] We can now ask ourselves the following question: Could telepathy in Jainism therefore be regarded as a special kind of our *quantum-related* capabilities, somehow tied to the common resonating field, a divinely saturated matrix of all being, as it were? To be connected to this hidden, yet materially (cf. the gradations of will in Schopenhauer and karmas in Jainism) attested field now means, that we are synchronized with the ontological ground of the world—now beyond spatiotemporal obstacles and by "seeing" (i.e., knowing) through the veil of obstructing factors.

The suppression of *manaḥ-paryaya-āvaraṇīya-karman* (i.e., the mind-obstructing subtle material veil around us) enables one to establish, as it were, a subterranean or pan-cosmic connection with the mysteriously entangled world we inhabit. As an omniscient being is also a perfected being, and as telepathy relates to this heightened awareness of the world, it now becomes what we designate in relation to Schopenhauer as panpathy—a supernatural capacity to compassionately, empathically, and telepathically correlate and synchronize with surrounding worlds and beings.

In the following chapter, we wish to address some further possibilities of these supernatural capacities and mysterious entanglements of ourselves with the surrounding world.

bright matter

5

God in the Future

From Dewey to Ruyer and Beyond

> God, if we hold to this word, *is the future itself,* or rather the eternal reservoir beyond time and creating time, who constantly projects himself or pours himself into the present.
>
> —Raymond Ruyer, "The Status of the Future and the Invisible World"[1]

In his tiny but highly important book on philosophy of religion from 1934, John Dewey propounds his idiosyncratic philosophical vision of the future of religion and the idea of God. Searching for a new concept of divinity, as a way of evading the supernatural within the American tradition of philosophy of religion, Dewey indeed inaugurates what we could label as one of the first possibilities for a new thinking toward the era of post-Christianity, within both philosophical and theological narratives of the twentieth century. While Dewey definitely cannot be labeled a posthumanist thinker, his thought still offers some very interesting possibilities for entering into a dialogue with this strand of thought—and this represents the main point of our attempt of reading Dewey's philosophy of religion alongside Raymond Ruyer's philosophy.

Dewey's ideas are part of a wider context of American religious thought reaching from Ralph W. Emerson and Henry D. Thoreau to Charles S. Peirce and William James (Whitehead, process philosophy, and process theology could also be mentioned). It is in this vein that Douglas R. Anderson—in his fine essay on American philosophy of religion[2]—discusses the continuity in the philosophical thought of Jonathan Edwards, Thoreau, and Dewey. Namely, they all position "God" within the finiteness of our experience: instead of supernatural signifiers, pointing to various attributes of God, they all point to the human faculty of imagination, which opens up the horizons of the infinite or the ideal. Rorty contends similarly in his essay "Pragmatism as Romantic Polytheism," where he explains James's "polytheistic" use of the term "the divine" as being "pretty much equivalent to 'the ideal.'"[3] Rorty is clear in his essay that to be a polytheist, in this sense, is to be able to abandon old metaphysical ideas about the divine, or the belief that there is something nonhuman out there supporting us or intervening in our human affairs. Finally, the purpose of Dewey's *A Common Faith* is disclosed as a way of restoring some meaning to all those who, in a post-Marxian, post-Nietzschean, or post-Darwinian age have remained without God, are caught in a paradox of a world without "religiously" defined ends, and are thus without any access to the divine:

> It may be of help if I say whom I had in mind in writing the book. I have taught many years and I don't think that any of my students would say that I set out to undermine anyone's faith. . . . The lectures making up the book were meant for those whose religious beliefs had been abandoned, and who were given the impression that their abandonment left them without any religious beliefs whatsoever. I wanted to show them that religious values are not the monopoly of any one class or sect and are still open to *them*.[4]

Despite some doubts about the religious vocabulary to be used, Dewey still decides to remain in the vicinity of the idea of "God." The idea of God, in Dewey's religious world, stands for the unification of ideal values, with imagination intervening into the very core of our beliefs and values, and thus unifying—at least for the time being—our attitudes and conduct into (again temporarily) a signifying whole. Now, this imagination does not operate on a plane of mere fantasy or any other fanciful idealization (including utopian ones) of reality, but, quite the contrary, enables us to think of various possibilities or coherent *future* ends reaching toward us through its capacity. On a broader plane of humanity, this process "endures and advances with the life of humanity,"[5] and, for Dewey, the idea of God (or the idea of the divine) is thus "one of ideal possibilities unified through imaginative realization and projection."[6] Moreover, the idea of God is "also connected with all the *natural forces and conditions*—including human association—that promote the growth of the ideal and that further its realization."⁷ Finally, for Dewey, the name "God" designates "this active relation between ideal and actual."⁸

For the advancement of human culture and, broadly speaking, civilization, a projection into the future is needed—one being able to unify existing habits, values, and ideals. For Dewey, "the idealizing imagination seizes upon the most precious things found in the climacteric moments of experience and projects them."⁹ But, we would now like to confront this Deweyan temporality of religion and of the divine with the thought of Raymond Ruyer (1902–1987), the much underestimated French thinker who strongly influenced Gilles Deleuze, among others. In Dewey and Ruyer, two futures and two divinities meet and collide in a truly fascinating and synchronistic way. The consequences of such a nexus of an apparent constellation are indeed far reaching, and they will later enable us to enter into the so-called quantum field within theology itself, saturated with the *material-spiritual* divine matrix—understood as a plane of coordination, or *sacred* bond (*vinculum*), of the world of spirit-matter and its divinely evolved consciousness.

Throughout his career as a philosopher, Ruyer published on topics such as the philosophy of biology and nature, and he contributed to cybernetics, technology, and information science at the very beginning of the era of robotics and computers in the 1940s. And, in an equally important part of his work, Ruyer contributes to the philosophy of religion with his equally original conception of the Tao-God or the Unknown God.¹⁰ In his essay "The Status of the Future and the Invisible World," Ruyer presents us with an idiosyncratic account of God, time, matter, and consciousness of the world, reaching toward the entirely new forms of pan(en)theism and futuristic thought in theology. On an epistemological level, the temporality of the future in Ruyer's essay seems to be quite different from Dewey's concept of "God" as the unification of future ends. Similarly to Dewey's intervention against early twentieth-century atheism and various remnants of supernaturalistic tendencies, Ruyer feels obliged to polemicize with another two extremes, here as it is related to the future—fatalism (astrology, premonition, and so forth) and scientific determinism (with its laws being able to define and calculate the results of any movement). Referring to Einstein's theory of relativity, Ruyer does not want to assert that there is a preexisting or deterministically fixed future available somewhere out there—that is, being within reach for someone traveling through space on a super-rapid spaceship. The symmetry is broken during time travel within the laws of gravity for two persons traveling at the same time at different speeds, but the future as such does not yet exist for us and thus remains unknown to any person whatsoever. What kind of temporality of the future can we imagine, then? According to our philosopher, "if existing things did not continue to exist except by freely causing the future and by disrupting their normal functioning, time would be disjointed and the future would no longer be *their* future."[11] But there is more in the concept of future, and it is here that Ruyer's thought becomes especially theologically interesting and indeed thought-provoking.

Thinking theologically now, and placing his thoughts, as it were, in medias res of some of the key questions of a new theological temporality, Ruyer introduces and defines his idea of "God" in the following way:

> God, if we hold to this word, *is the future itself*, or rather the eternal reservoir beyond time and creating time, who constantly projects himself or pours himself into the present and who transforms the functioning of already created beings into sensible behavior and actions in order to cause the world to evolve in a living manner and not like a great machine which could only finish at a stable equilibrium or with irremedial wear and degradation. . . . God, or the future-as-ideal-control, can only produce minute shifts in direction. His "ideas" steer and guide through ultra-weak interactions. Nevertheless, the universe finally obeys this imperceptible future, but not without enormous failures and catastrophes.[12]

This is an extraordinary piece of theological thinking. We will again return to the analysis of this paragraph in the third part of this chapter—as its contents are directly linked to the reflections on time and time travel in Christopher Nolan's *Interstellar*. First, there is an obvious link to Dewey's idea of God in this passage, but here in a much radicalized manner: if Dewey's God became "visible" or revealed itself through our imaginative realizations and projections *into the future*, and thus, as it were, Dewey's God would be "operating" from the future as a way of providing sense to our strivings and doings as humanity retrospectively, then Ruyer's God is more linked to the very concept of time and temporality of the future itself: it is situated beyond time and actually creates time on its own behalf—as proposed by Ruyer. The "unknown God" of Ruyer now "envelops the 'material' world which, minus this envelope, would be only 'thing' in its purest state, indistinguishable from nothing, or which would be only a present incapable of presence lacking a past and a future."[13] But to understand this dense and rich passage, we need to understand the notion of *mnemic theme* in Ruyer.

What is defining our search for answers in this world appears as twofold—as an inherent creativity of the world and its openness, or "call of the future"—the call that enables us to enhance and re-create ourselves.[14] Ontologically, this happens within the world of forms of life and among them anti-Platonic "primary forms" are of key importance. Primary forms have self-forming properties and range "from the most elementary forms of matter, the atom and its subatomic ingredients, to the most complex forms of self-production that characterize all forms of life."[15] Similarly to Schopenhauer's will or Nietzsche's will to power, Ruyer is searching for a *link* or *connection* (later, with Bruno and Merleau-Ponty we will understand this ontological or "cosmic" link as a *bond/vinculum*) that underlines all simple and more complex processes in the world. In this view, he seeks both organic as well as inorganic conditions, and explores into every consciousness, "including those before and *beyond* the human"[16]—which includes machines, computers (AI), or technology in general. Primary forms are not separated from the material that actually "forms" them and this view enables Ruyer to direct his reflections very much in line with the developments in quantum physics during his time. They are dynamic structures, repairing themselves, and they are thus forming trans-spatial mnemic themes and their inherently embodied values:

> Primary forms can be attributed both a "life" and a "consciousness," even though they cannot be understood on the models of life and consciousness that we attribute to ourselves. . . . If living things are never stable forms, always undergoing change, nevertheless there is something that subsists in these changes: not anything bodily—for every cell and organ is in the process of self-regeneration or self-replacement—but what Ruyer understands as a melodic or mnemic theme, not locatable in space or time but that subsists and accompanies life, and all primary forms, through its processes of autoaffection.[17]

Elizabeth Grosz observes succinctly that, within Ruyer's embryogenesis of the world, the consciousness understood as a mnemic theme must already (pre-)exist in the world. There is a continuity that links things distant or different from themselves as far as subatomic matter and human "values." This means that mnemic themes (or memory) gain precedence over being(s) and also that "consciousness" (in one of its forms) takes over from evolutionary biology. Finally, according to Grosz, "even God must be understood not as a divine being separate from the world, but as an acting, a mode of self-creation according to an internal ideal."[18] But let us return to the question of temporality in these processes: according to Grosz, in Ruyer's thought of the divine, the *future itself* may be the destination. Now, about this process of imagining the future, or projecting back from the preconceived future into our deeds or activities—as inherent or immanent in the world—Ruyer writes: "When we imagine, our imagination depends especially on our memory. But there is also a tiny proportion of creativity, of something pulled from nothing."[19] We will later understand this *difference* of creativity as a *quantum moment* in theology. The growth, arising from our creativity and all of its visible consequences, however, is not all that we have—there exists, by way of comparison, *the invisible world, or the unknown God*, which is like an immense body of underground water (being) under a certain pressure. This underground water (as a reservoir of memories or mnemic themes) is available to us only as long as we are able to "communicate" on our own account with those layers of these supplies of water that are positioned more closely to the surface. Again: we must make our own future, but—with an important distinction now—nothing can be made without conforming to "an order existing well beyond our own wills," or "[i]n other words, God proposes and man disposes. And this gives men, those on the surface, the impression of having to work things out alone in the visible world. Nevertheless, their entire 'substance' is made up of the underground water."[20] Finally, according to Ruyer, this unknown God is the universal framework of the cosmos, planter of the very tree of life, the principle of all channeled memories as well as all possible types of existences that we can imagine. God is beyond all place and beyond all time and envelops the entire material and spiritual world.

But, in order to understand the modality of God, two additional (weak or post-) theological arguments need to be taken into account. First, in his *The Insistence of God: A Theology of Perhaps*, Caputo paraphrases Derrida's words from "The Force of Law," and by replacing the signifier "justice" with "God" we get the following passage:

> "Perhaps"—one must (*il faut*) always say *perhaps* for God. There is a future for God and there is no God except to the degree that some event is possible which, as event, exceeds calculation, rules, program, anticipations, and so forth. God, as the experience of absolute alterity, is unpresentable, but God is the chance of the event and the condition of history. . . . Whenever and wherever there is a chance for the event, that is God, perhaps. God can happen anywhere.[21]

The weak theology of Caputo that, as he writes, *comes on the wings of doves*, appears under a different modality than Ruyer's or Dewey's elaborations, but Caputo remains in their closest ontological vicinity: for Caputo, perhaps is "the only way to say yes to the future,"[22] a modality of the future that stretches well beyond any logical or imaginative probability of an event, or its anticipation by any of our rational means: "Perhaps, I hope, perchance, there is a chance, *a ghost of a chance*, in what is happening."[23] *Perhaps*, to Caputo, is an anarchic energy within the cosmos, and, indeed, "the only *possible* thought of the event."[24] As in Dewey's *A Common Faith* we are facing the demise of a strong theology of faith—as based on the onto-theologically logically affirmed or postulated supernatural substances, and the capacity of us human beings to delineate and indeed foresee and mark with an unsurpassed sovereignty the "future" of God as a terrain of *Our* truth and *Our* justice—it is now only through our powerlessness that the event may, *perhaps*, be revealed to us (or, perhaps, not at all). "Perhaps," for Caputo, is thus older than God: " 'Perhaps' is a place more elemental than anything that takes place within it. Older than everything cosmological, theological, zoological, anthropological, 'perhaps' " is not chaos or radical evil. . . . 'Perhaps' is not mere indifference but more radically neutral—*ne uter*—although it constantly verges on becoming uterine—*ne-uterine*, like a womb, a primal place in which, from which, existents emerge."[25] As a place, like *khora*—"perhaps" indicates a place older than the cosmos itself:—a cosmic riddle, remaining now for us only as the question of what is *coming*—an event, or a call for the future (of God, perhaps): "I have ended up in my old age in a desert, like a certain an-khora-ite, praying and weeping for the coming of *the* impossible, for the coming of what I cannot see coming."[26]

And, here comes our second theological intervention, one that perhaps can insist with(in) us as a remedy, or at least thrive as a promise to the praying and weeping an-khora-ite from the desert. The promise now comes with the words of an unexpected prophet—and they testify: *As man is, God once was, as God is, man may become.*[27] This view of divinity, marking the very core of Mormonism's theology and comprising in itself the ideas of Dewey, Ruyer, and Caputo (and their inherent futurity)—may now insist as our promise and guide us toward a reframed concept of divinity in both its new spatiality as well as temporality.

With its idiosyncratic but original theological account, Mormonism represents one of the most vital and relevant attempts at redefining the divinity in the early postmonotheist and secular era of the nineteenth century. According to Simon Critchley, Mormonism's main message consists of an idea that we have to learn how to become gods, and that we indeed have inherited the very same power and glory as God to become exalted like him. We therefore can arrive at the "station" of God (only in a more protopian futurist scenario as compared to the well-known scene of the station from the *Matrix*), but this can only happen in the future. Incarnation therefore is "a two-way street," and a part in each of us that we usually call "spirit" is in fact coequal with God. With its feature of a continuing revelation, Mormon theology remains open to the future and reveals a truly *post*-Christian character and message to us.[28] Human deification or apotheosis then represents the most significant part of the teaching of Mormonism. The making of gods, and therefore, the aspiring toward the future as our final destination in achieving godhood—stated more directly—means that there is a capacity in/for us for being a part of the process in which we may indeed become gods. Apotheosis goes both beyond "theosis" as a process of human transformation through becoming united with God, as well as beyond Christological logic, as explained by Davies:

> The "two-natures" argument over Jesus' identity still remains of interest to contemporary Christians, because he is sometimes made so divine as to lose contact with humanity, whilst at other times he is represented as so human as to lose the divine status. For Latter-day Saints this is not a problem, for every individual shares the same "substance," everyone is a spirit person at some stage of developing their potential as divine, and in this sense Jesus is simply an elder brother who is further along the path of divine development.[29]

As we did take words from Ruyer in a literal sense, and while now we are making ourselves gods in the process of apotheosis, to us God indeed becomes *the future itself*. Now, in *King's Follett Discourse*—perhaps the most inspiring and revealing text ever delivered and revealed by Smith—the Mormon prophet describes the genesis of a god as follows:

> First, God himself, who sits enthroned in yonder heaven, is a man like one of you. That is the great secret. . . . [But] God himself, the Father of us all, dwelt on an earth the same as Jesus Christ himself did. . . . Here, then, is eternal life—to know the only wise and true God. And you have got to learn how to be Gods yourselves—to be kings and priests to god, the same as all Gods have done—by going from a small degree to another, from grace to grace, from exaltation to exaltation,

until you are able to sit in glory as do those who sit enthroned in everlasting power.[30]

God is our future destination, therefore. As in Ruyer's biological-theological innovation, there is a full continuity among (human) beings and gods (note a transition from a god to gods here as a mark of an inherent-dynamic plurality in the concept of divinity itself). Matter and its elements *precede* creation (and *creatio ex nihilo* becomes obsolete), both in Ruyer and in Mormonism; moreover, according to Smith, God himself could not even create himself: "God never did have power to create the spirit of man at all. God himself could not create himself. Intelligence exists upon a self-existent principle; it is a spirit from age to age, and there is no creation about it."[31] In a more radicalized, spatially temporalized sense, we can now contend that our divinization is well imprinted into a continuity of present and future spheres.[32] The argument that we would like to present here (this argument will be updated later)—being thus currently only at our first *intermediate time*—would go as follows:

> God is the future itself, revealing in a series of revelations through time to other beings as not-yet-gods or evolving-gods. God evolved from the most archaic and still not-fully-disclosed matter and began acting from the primeval chaos in a time moment still not known to us human beings. God as a fully (also technologically) evolved (supreme/super-intelligent) being, reaching its/his/her destination, projects into the present. In this process, which is mediated (to us) through visible signs (called also "miracles"), God enlightens and transforms the functioning of the so-called primary forms and the so-called secondary-composite beings (elements, minerals, plants, animals, various *Homo* species and superhuman beings) by causing human beings and beings beyond our reach to evolve into an ever more agapeistically developed species. The esoteric and hidden connection between God and other beings is called a bond, or gravity—and God thus reveals as the bonding agent. This process may finally be labeled as the evolution of materially spiritual vibration of a cosmic consciousness as revealed in the cosmic presence of God as a bond of love.

To be able to fully develop this thought on God's temporality and futurity (and God as the bonding agent), an elaboration into the cosmic/natural bond or *vinculum* of *Deus, hyle et mens* is required.

On Cosmic Bond, Matter, and God

Our aim in the second part of this elaboration is to inquire about the two interrelated conditions for the validity of the above argument about God: namely, about God as evolving from the elemental nature or matter, and about the connection between God and other beings as called a bond. Now, in one of our previous essays we have already elaborated on the *post-Christian* elements in the thought of Amalric of Bène (1150–1206/7), the founder of the medieval heretical sect of Amalricians.[33] Next to Master Amalric was a philosopher, David of Dinant (c. 1160–c. 1217), one of the most prolific members of the sect, who also influenced Bruno, the *Nolan* philosopher. David of Dinant, who outlived his close friends (who were either burnt at the stake or imprisoned between 1210 and 1215), was known for his pantheistic-materialistic *Deus, hyle et mens una sola substantia sunt* sentence. The genealogy of this new *insurrectionist theology*,[34] being, for the first time, infused with new and daring teachings on God *and* matter, evolved all the way from the natural philosophy of the pre-Socratics, Aristotle, and the tradition of *left-wing* Aristotelianism—and the medieval Persian and Islamic influences as present in Ibn Sina/Avicenna (980-1037) and Ibn Rushd/Averroës (1126-98)—when infusing more progressive Christian sects in Europe. Averroës's philosophy was rooted in his own interpretation of the Aristotelian teachings on the ontological primacy of uncreated and eternal matter, and it was this overturning of Aristotle's *dýnamis-enérgeia* scheme that strongly influenced David of Dinant, a close ally of Master Amalric and an important influence on Bruno.

At this point, a step ahead toward Schelling is needed first: in a letter to K. A. Eschenmeyer from July 30, 1801, Schelling contends that, in this year, a light entered his philosophy: it was a new impulse that enabled him to abandon his earlier transcendental thinking.[35] In the 1802 treatise *Bruno*, Schelling already embarks upon a new destination for his thought: in the form of a dialogue, and in response to Fichte's harsh criticism of his system, Schelling—disguised in dialogue as (Giordano) Bruno—presents us with a fascinating account on the natural and divine principles of the world; and thus on the nature of reality, matter, God. and their ontological yet hidden bond. With this gesture, the center of gravity of philosophy now shifts from Kant and Fichte to Schelling and Hegel in a most direct way. According to Schelling, the aim of this new thought could be described as follows:

> To come to know this indifference within the absolute—that character whereby idea is substance, the absolutely real, whereby

form is also essential reality and reality is form, each one inseparable from the other, whereby form and reality are not just perfectly similar likenesses, but directly are one another—this is to discover the absolute center of gravity. To know this is to uncover *the original metal of truth*, as it were, the prime ingredient in the alloys of all individual truths, without which none of them would be true.[36]

As a direct consequence to this overturning of German idealism, a new philosophical view of divine and nature principles, God and nature, respectively, a new constellation emerges; now, Schelling's concluding words from *Bruno* read as follows: "And as we move up and down this spiritual ladder, freely and without constraint, now descending and beholding the identity of the divine and natural principle dissolved, now ascending and resolving everything again into the one, we shall see nature within God and God within nature."[37] For Schelling, both the *metal* of truth, as well as the *alloys* of all other truths, clearly point toward his "material" perception of a dynamic, yet ontologically esoteric nature of, as it were, an elemental-materially underpinned constellation of truth.[38] Now, on this basis, we intend to embark on a more esoteric path toward this constellation by reading Bruno's philosophy through the lens of a *magical bond* and related philosophy of (meso)cosmic coordination (bond/*vinculum*). With this gesture, we want to prepare the ground for our argument about the divinity as being marked as a spiritually material process in time, clothing and penetrating the totality of being—of both visible as well as invisible nature.

Apart from his far-reaching innovations in cosmology, and its effects on the progress of the scientific revolution, the Nolan philosopher's main contribution to the history of philosophy might be in proposing an entirely new concept of the divinity.[39] In our attempt to delineate the expansion and liminality of the Nolan philosopher's immanent and temporally synchronistic cosmic God, Bruno's understanding of matter is of vital importance. According to our philosopher, "David of Dinant was not led astray by taking matter to be an absolutely excellent and divine thing."[40] Moreover, and on the basis of this thought, if "a spiritual principle and a material principle are recognized as the very substance of the world, it seems evident that it is their coincidence that constitutes its permanent substance."[41] Following the trail of the Platonists (world-soul), the best "materialist" traditions of Aristotelianism and Neo-Platonism (as regards their treatment of matter), Islamic influences (Averroes), as well as of Nicolas of Cusa's argument on the impossibility of separating the infinite potency of creating and being created in God, Bruno therefore attempts a higher ("magical," as we will see) synthesis of their respective thoughts—only to be able to think God or the divinity in accordance with matter. According to him, Averroes is praised for his elaboration of matter as comprising in itself unlimited dimensions, and if this thought is taken together with his claim that all things "no matter how small and miniscule, have in them part of that spiritual substance,"[42] then we have come full circle here. Matter, therefore, is taken as a substrate, a principle indeed that cannot be annihilated—because a soul/spirit is present in all things; as a consequence, God must necessarily be linked to the world: *natura est deus in rebus*.

An introduction of a magical interpretation of the world requires a preliminary note on two different yet connected teachings—the ancient pre-Hindu Vedic teaching and the post-Christian Mormon teaching. In his critical Indological exposition of the Vedic text *Kaṭha Āraṇyaka*, Michael Witzel's paleological and magical approach might serve as a starting point. Paleological thinking is based on identity predicates, which means that identity among two things is accepted "if they share just one common predicate."[43] Following this logic, the Vedic ritual with its identification techniques, establishing links, nexuses, or correlations among things, beings (including divinities), or minds, is designated as a part of a magical interpretation (*magische Weltanschauung*) of the world. In relation to these magical correspondences, so-called Vedic magic is one of the best examples of this.[44] The cosmic or *paleo-ontological* correlation of *ātman* (body, self) and *brahman* (formulation of truth, later: Absolute), which evolved from an earlier and more materially underpinned correspondence between cosmic wind (*vāyu*) and our vital breath (*prāṇa*), establishes a hidden bond (Sskt. *bandhu* or *upaniṣad*) among the respective microcosmic and macrocosmic realms through the third element—that is, the sacred or cosmic ritual (or the mesocosm).[45] This scheme represents the paleo-ontological cosmic triadic process in which microcosm (nature, body, matter as substrate) is intrinsically related to macrocosm (world-soul, spiritual substance, supreme being, divinity/God), which is equally related to the ritual sphere (hidden connection, or a bond: *bandhu,* also called *upaniṣad*). According to Patrick Olivelle, the central concern of all early Vedic thinkers and seers was the knowledge of these hidden connections that *bind* their elements: "The final *upaniṣad* or equation is between Ātman, the essential I, and Brahman, the ultimate real."[46] The processual cosmic nature of all three layers of being can now be called *vinculum*—and this will serve us to look at the Nolan philosopher's idiosyncratic teaching on this binding aspect of all reality. On this ground, and in a theological acceleration of this teaching, it will be possible for us to think of the Cosmic Christ as a supreme bonding agent of the cosmos. But, let us first look at our second example.

In a chapter titled "The Magic of Being Mormon,"[47] Webb presents us with an analogous account of magic within Mormonism and its theology. Within Christianity, calling something magical, or using the label "magic" itself, clearly can only serve as a designation for various spells and empty incantations or, more straightforwardly, as a means to ridicule someone simply for holding this position. But it is precisely Mormonism, with its peculiar sense for both ancient magic and new (evolutionary) science, that enables us to rethink the meaning and the theological sense of these allegedly non-Christian or simply "pagan" elements. We know from anthropological evidence that more caution is needed in claims about magic. Apart from the evolutionary bias in nineteenth-century sociology and social anthropology—such as in Auguste Comte, Herbert Spencer, or James George Frazer and their successors—it is in E. E. Evans-Pritchard's *Witchcraft, Oracles and Magic among the Azande* (1937) that an affirmative view of allegedly "prelogical" or "mystical" thinking is presented. We know now that "magical rites must be understood on a symbolic level. To see these rites simply as instrumental activity arising from misplaced ideas about natural causality is to misread them. . . . What is of real importance is the symbolism involved in the rite. Those who hold this symbolic perspective view primitive myths and rituals as a form of artistic or theological expression rather than a form of scientific speculation."[48] These more ancient symbolic or expressionist aspects of religion were mostly purged from theological thinking. Mormonism, as a nineteenth-century alternative to mainstream Christianity, is a fine counterexample to this. Webb is correct that, among many objections and prejudices against magic, the strongest is that magic "clashed with the belief that God is absolutely sovereign and thus in complete control of all events.[49] But, against such a prejudice, for Webb, "the sacrifice of Christ was sufficient to *repair* our relationship to the divine."[50] In an era of quantum thinking in physics but also in philosophy and theology, we know that by using strictly *causal* thinking, it is not possible to reveal more hidden layers of both the "physical" and "spiritual" reality that surrounds us. If we take only one example of such an enhanced view of our intellectual abilities, then we can contend that this way of thinking reveals "an innate ability of the human brain and psyche, drawing its deepest resources from the heart of the universe itself."[51] As furthermore visible within quantum field theory,

> [t]he universe and all its constituents consist of energy in different states of excitation. People, tables, chairs, trees, stardust and so on are patterns of dynamic energy set against a background (the quantum vacuum) of still, unexcited energy. . . . [W]hen two metal plates are placed very close together, they are attracted to each other because of the subtle pressure that the quantum vacuum exerts on each. The kind of transcendence illustrated by the quantum vacuum is similar to that described as the *Tao* or the Void (*Sunyata*) in many Taoist, Hindu and Buddhist texts.[52]

Two consequences can be inferred from this. First, we have now come close to our initial definition of God as based on Ruyer's elaborations: God is a relation to the primeval chaos/ ungrounded abyssal ground in a time moment still not known to us. Second, magical thinking appears now to be much more complex and dynamic than originally expected. The divine, or God, can now be viewed as a "kind of pervasive energy that can be tapped into."[53] As such, God is not immaterial in relation to space nor eternal in relation to time:

> Mormons believe that there is an essential continuity between this world and the other world, so that there are no gaps or gulfs between matter and spirit. God is not a unique entity who stands outside of the world and requires us to do likewise if we are to know anything about him. God is very much a part of the cosmos (or the cosmos is a part of him), which means that the way we come to know God is not different from the way we come to know anything else in the world.[54]

Reality as becoming, and the goal—"the perfectly dynamic creativity that God has already achieved"[55]—is the core of Mormonism's radical theological invention. For Webb, the message of Mormonism as a branch of Christianity could now be described as follows: "If I am right that magic and religion are close relatives, then it simply makes sense that a new and exuberant religious tradition like Mormonism would mix the two together, but it also makes sense that Mormonism can show the rest of Christianity how to retrieve a truly magical (in the sense of wonder and awe at the works of God and the beauty of Christ) way of being in the world."[56] It is now time to turn to the Nolan philosopher's magical way of knowing the immense cosmic divine, or God.

As a sixteenth-century man, Bruno still believed in demons. Since his childhood, he had been encountering them as spiritual forces, being able to throw stones or snatch cloaks in the night. They were living creatures consisting of a subtle body, having the ability to fuse and contract themselves into various shapes, having also the ability to see the future.[57] But the magic of the Nolan philosopher soon became more intellectual and philosophical. By perfecting the art of memory (based on the art of mnemonology of Ramon Llull), he was convinced he was able to "connect" or "bind" the sacred knowledge in his mind and thus, intellectually, "gain power over the entire universe."[58] Now, for Bruno, the world-soul causes matter to be formed in infinite ways, and it is the working of this connection or bond between both entities that interests our philosopher. Further, according to Bruno, all the bonds "can be reduced to the bond of love."[59] This *vinculum* or hidden bond therefore cannot be found in visible things and is somehow secretly present in the cosmos:

> [T]he vinculum [is] that which links to an ever-changing degree the operator (the *vinciens*) to the *vinciendum*. The original unity of the All, therefore, establishes the conditions for the success of magical action, because it allows us to understand how a magus can restore an existing apparent multiplicity to its underlying unity. Human beings, too, are presented as matter over whose surface pass infinite forms, and clearly each one of them is a *vinculum*, one of the many which we all, in fact, encounter.[60]

As the most powerful bonding agent among all, it is the *breath of love* that effectively transforms the world. Bruno's essays *On Magic* and *A General Account of Bonding* (the latter being unfinished) attest to this teaching. Clearly, the Nolan philosopher's use of magic is of the kind that we initially delineated within the contexts of Vedic thinking and Mormon theology, respectively. Consequently, Bruno deals only with magic in its divine, physical, and mathematical types. Within contemporary scientific thought, this would imply contributions from theology, cosmology, and religious studies (for the *divine field*), (quantum) physics and astrophysics (for the *quantum field*), and logic (for the *field of bonding*), respectively. This constitution is fully in accordance with the nature of "Truth," which, for Bruno, is "ideal, natural, and, notional"; or, in more general terms, appears as metaphysics, physics, and logic.[61] Truth, therefore, is "manifest in all living things, operating through the eternal laws of an immanent God identified with a timeless universe.[62] Now, the most important feature of his theory of magic is that

> various spirits occupy the bodies of humans, animals, stones and minerals [and that] there is no body which is completely devoid of spirit and intelligence. . . . Finally, it must be consciously accepted and firmly asserted that all things are full of spirits, souls, divine power, and God or divinity, and that the whole of intelligence and the whole soul is everywhere, although they do not do everything everywhere. . . . As a result, the philosophers say that in the original state of things there was one matter, one spirit, one light, one soul and one intellect.[63]

Now, in *A General Account of Bonding* (*De vinculis in genere*), Bruno brings a more detailed account on bonding agents and their effects in both the visible as well as the invisible cosmos or nature. For the Nolan philosopher, the main bonding agents are God, demons, souls, animals, and nature. But, essentially there are four things that are located around God: they are mind, soul, nature, and matter; they circle or rotate around God and are bound to the divinity with more or less attraction. Metaphysically, humans are most powerfully bound by the bond of love, and in physics, the bonding agent could be designated either as gravitational force, electromagnetic force, strong force, or weak force—as far as to the gravitational force of dark matter (we think of electromagnetic and gravitational fields as collections of force lines that drive or pull objects toward other objects[64]). Humans may be attracted by humans or animals, and vice versa; music can bind in a profoundly aesthetic way, and, last but not least, on a completely other scale, stars and galaxies are bound to other stars and galaxies with gravitational force. According to Bruno, and to come full circle with our preliminary elaborations on the principles of coordination: "Things in the universe are so ordered that they constitute one definite co-ordination in which there can occur a transition from all things to all things in one continuous flow. . . . And just as there are various species of things and differences between them, they also have various times, places, intermediaries, pathways, instruments and functions. . . . If there were only one love, and thus only one bond, all things would be one."[65] In all things there is one fundamental (divine) force, according to Bruno, and this force is called love. This bond reveals as the "hypostasis of things,"[66] both visible and invisible. But, it is not possible, yet, to develop a full theology based on bonding or vinculum *as love*. The missing link still needs to be discovered—and here we can only hint at a possibility of a cosmic Christ as highest among the bonding agents—to be revealed as the *cosmic vibration of love*.

But, it is perhaps not coincidental that the term *vinculum* only reappears in Merleau-Ponty's 1959–1960 course notes known under the title *Nature*, which represent a rare, yet supreme, attempt to think along both Vedic and Bruno's realms of thoughts. This is fully attested in the following observation of our thinker: "There is a unique theme of philosophy: the *nexus*, the *vinculum* 'Nature'—'Man'—'God.' Nature as a 'leaf' of Being, and the problems of philosophy, are concentric."[67] First, nature as a leaf of Being recaptures our previous themes on matter and God in an enhanced way. Moreover, in an essay on Merleau-Ponty's theology ("The Cosmic Christ as Vinculum between God, Humanity, and Nature"), Christopher Ben Simpson refers to his philosophy as an example of the "breaking down of the frontiers or the 'cleavage' between 'naturalism,' 'humanism,' and 'theism;' 'God, man, creatures' are seen as passing into one another [and this can happen specifically] in and through Christ."[68] In view of this cosmic intertwining, as it were, of the human with nature-matter and God in Christ, the nexus/*vinculum* is revealed as the bond.

The Futurity of God

> Think about tomorrow. Think about green fields and new life. Think about water. Think about clear skies and spring the way it used to be.
>
> —Timothy Egan, *The Worst Hard Time*[69]

We know from Caputo that there might be "a ghost of a chance in what is happening."[70] This *ghost*, as it were, hints toward an anarchic (quantum?) energy within the cosmos, a mysterious or magical bond still to be regained, revealed, or achieved. Now, it is our aim to connect both the idea of a futurity of God as well as a materially underpinned *vinculum* of nature, human, and God into a new theological synthesis—enabling us to affirm our initial thesis from the conclusion of the first part of this chapter: on God as the future itself and a fully evolved Being, projecting into the present/past by the mediation of visible/material signs or divine gestures based on a cosmic bond. Let us now embark on a journey into this future by looking more closely at Christopher Nolan's *Interstellar*.

Nolan's *Interstellar* represents one of the most original possibilities for imagining the bond of love and futurity of God under the backdrop of time travel, quantum physics, and postapocalyptic thinking. Since the beginning of cinematic history, time or cinematic temporality has featured as one of the most central settings for imagining alternative visions of life and reality, and for imagining alternative futures. This especially holds for Nolan for whom cinema itself is "a time machine" of its own kind.[71] The plot of *Interstellar* itself is worth special attention and its postapocalyptic setting is intrinsically related to one of the most pressing issues of our time: the climate crisis. In the near future, humanity is facing a catastrophe and, being on the brink of starvation, they are seeking a new home in space. In the center of the plot is the story of the Dust Bowl: the worst manmade ecological disaster in American history, and actually the first climate disaster in the world that was entirely caused by human beings' activities and deeds. The Dust Bowl represents one of the saddest epochs in American history, causing an unprecedented mass exodus of desperate Americans in search for shelter and food. According to Melt White (as one of the witnesses of this catastrophe), "God didn't create this land around here to be plowed up. . . . He created it for Indians and buffalo. Folks raped this land. Raped it bad."[72] For Nolan, the catastrophe represents an impetus for an idiosyncratic cinematic journey into the future that is based on the best possible scientific accuracy as well as an extremely rich philosophical imagination. At first, it seems that Nolan is not interested in the theological consequences of his story (there is no mention of God or divinity in the movie), but, actually, all of the main elements of the film hint at a profound level of thinking that could imply more than an imaginary journey into the cinematically arranged future: from Murphy's "ghost," manipulations of time and matter, and quantum dimensions of a space-time continuum to five-dimensional (bulk[73]) beings (gods, perhaps?) and a tesseract; from the uncertain destiny and despair of the apocalyptic future and love being the strongest of all bonds to the redemption of humanity that is marked in the final scenes of the movie by *green fields and new life*—all these elements indicate Nolan's initial constellation that we wish to interpret along more theological lines. By adding quantum physics itself and its quest for ultimate answers concerning the nature of the universe (featured so importantly in this movie), all that implies that we cannot fully understand various facets of reality beneath the visible and tangible world. It might come out that the effects of physical quantum laws could indeed help us to understand what we have earlier described as the effects of a "magical" bond. Christopher Nolan meets our Nolan philosopher here.

The story of *Interstellar* is about Cooper, a NASA-trained pilot and engineer, his ten-year-old daughter Murph, and their family (Cooper's father-in-law, and Murphy's fifteen-year-old brother Tom). This family lives in times of great environmental crisis and they farm corn, as this is all that is left for agriculture in 2067. It is made clear in the film that even farming corn will soon not be possible anymore. Now, Murph comments that her room is haunted by a *ghost* (we may remember Bruno's faith in "demons" here) sending her secret and encoded messages by using books as they move and fall from the book shelter in various patterns. One of these messages carries a secret code (it turns out that this holds the GPS data of an undisclosed location), which takes her and her father to a clandestine NASA base. Cooper and Murph are introduced to Professor Brand and his team and their top-secret program for finding an extraterrestrial solution: new inhabitable planets for humanity. Professor Brand asks Cooper (he is the last person on the Earth with such expertise) to embark on a secret intergalactic mission toward three planets in distant galactic systems beyond ordinary reach. Three pioneers—Miller, Mann, and Edmunds—were, earlier, sent to these planets (now named after their founders) by NASA since these planets were identified as the best candidates for humanity's repopulation. Cooper knows that he would put his entire family in great danger by embarking on such a dangerous journey, but he accepts it. Murph feels abandoned but her father promises to return to her. However, during the intergalactic journey Cooper's timeline is thrown out of synch with Murph's due to a time dilation in intergalactic travel, and their bond is radically endangered. By using a tesseract (a hypercube presumably placed there by some advanced beings), Cooper is able to travel intergalactically, as well as back in time, to the ten-year-old as well as to the forty-year-old Murph's bedroom. Such a journey is possible because humans discovered some fifty years earlier that unknown (future) beings had positioned the wormhole near the planet Saturn and, thus, enabled humanity to travel with the speed of light to distant galaxies with habitable planets; these are located near a black hole called Gargantua, which is ten billion light-years away from the Earth. Being in a tesseract, now docked near Murph's bedroom, Cooper actually reveals that he is her "ghost," and, by giving her a secret NASA location as well as necessary quantum data, actually enables humanity to be rescued. The tesseract is not positioned only alongside Murph's bedroom, but "has potentially infinite facets, each one docked alongside the bookcase at a particular moment, the whole representing Murph's bedroom at every possible moment."[74] Now, it is important to add that the rules of *Interstellar* do not allow Cooper to travel to his own past, but they allow that the "gravitational forces can carry messages into our brane's past."[75] The tesseract, thus, appears to be a symbol for a quantum synchronicity beyond our brane's time and space continuum. Theologically, a tesseract appears as a plane of immanence of love, a place of divine providence, a symbol of a future dwelling of evolved beings-gods.

Now, one of the most original ideas of this film is that humanity indeed lives in a five-dimensional bulk inhabited by hyperspherical or five-dimensional beings. Upon the impending catastrophe, it is these beings that help the inhabitants of the Earth to survive by populating new inhabitable worlds of the universe.[76] But *who* are these bulk beings? In *Interstellar*, these beings are referred to as "They"—and nobody knows who they were. Based on Nolan's imagination, these beings "are actually our descendants: humans who, in the far future, evolve to acquire an additional space dimension and live in the bulk."[77] It might, thus, be so that these beings exist: if they do, and if they pass through our worlds, we could be affected by their gravity: "for example, if a hyperspherical being appears in my stomach and has a strong enough gravitational pull, my stomach may begin to cramp as my muscles tighten; trying to resist getting sucked to the center of the being's spherical cross section."[78] And, it is from here that our theological imagination derives an entirely new acceleration.

Things become interesting if quantum physics is wedded with what we may call "quantum theology." We know that the complexity of human intelligence cannot be reduced to the intellectual and emotional layers of our mind. By mapping our minds with three kinds of intelligences that we have—"intellectual," "emotional," and "spiritual"—as a consequence, it might be true that "our deepest salvation may lie in serving our own deep imagination."[79] This missing or unitive element of our otherwise either more serial (scientific/theoretical) or more associative (emotional/practical) intelligence might indeed represent a *bond of love*, as indicated by the Nolan philosopher, as he said *that if there were only one love and thus only one bond, all things would be one*.[80] Now, Zohar and Marshall describe the possibility of a quantum self (we may equally take this passage as an entrance into a quantum thinking in theology) as follows:

> At the beginning of this chapter I spoke of the quantum vacuum—the background energy state of the universe, the source of everything that exists. I pointed out that the vacuum is the ultimate transcendent reality describable within physics. It is the still, silent "ocean" on which existence appears as "waves" (oscillations of energy). The first thing to emerge from the vacuum is an energy field known as the Higgs Field. This is filled with very

fast, coherent energy oscillations that are the origin of all fields and fundamental particles in the universe. It is in itself a huge Bose-Einstein condensate. If proto-consciousness *is* a fundamental property of the universe, then there is proto-consciousness in the Higgs Field, and the quantum vacuum becomes very like what mystics have called the "immanent God," the God within all. In that case the 40 Hz neural oscillations that result in our human consciousness and our spiritual intelligence have their roots in nothing less than "God." "God" is the true centre of the self.[81]

Fully in line with the Mormon theology—as explained earlier—it is possible to assert now that God may actually be viewed as the transcendent oscillation of energy of "a divinely saturated matrix," also referred to theologically as God's field.[82] On a spatial level, one of the hypotheses is that the universe is a membrane (called "brane" by the physicists) "residing in a higher-dimensional 'hyperspace' to which the physicists give the name 'bulk.'"[83] As the brane necessarily has three space dimensions, the bulk would have at least four. Scientists do not yet know if the bulk or hyperspace really exists, but the 1984 announcement of "superstring theory" by Michael B. Green and John Schwarz (the theory that might reconcile the laws of quantum physics with Einstein's relativistic laws) demanded that, apart from our three-dimensional membrane, there must be a multidimensional bulk (according to superstring theory, the bulk actually would have six more dimensions).[84] Our thesis would now be the following: analogously to the "mysterious" or scientifically still undisclosed relationality of brane and bulk, the same relationality appears between two temporal moments: our time (as human beings) must be related in a yet unknown manner to the temporality of a "God," which, as it were, interferes with our "ordinary" worlds through the effects that we learned to call "miracles." In an analogous manner—as in spatial terms—it might now be so that this God exists (as a supreme bulk being): if it does, and if it somehow (mysteriously) *passes* through our worlds, we could be affected by this "gravity" in ways we do not yet know to apprehend or describe. We may now recall Caputo's words and say that one must always say *perhaps* for God as an event that exceeds calculation, anticipation, prediction, and the like—"but God is the chance for the event and the condition of history."[85] God, which *is the future itself* (Ruyer), messages as a super humanely and technologically evolved being into the past. The tesseract represents the cosmic "vehicle" of God's supreme love for humanity and nature (thus revealed both ethically and ecologically).[86]

Apart from the postapocalyptic setting and science of intergalactic and time travel, we wish to turn our theological attention to two narratives, marked by the stories of two *daughters*—Murphy (Cooper's daughter) and Dr. Amelia Brand (Professor's Brand daughter). Both daughters' stories are stories of *love, faith, and hope*—and it is here where the *theological* aspects, as siding with the overly *scientific* setting of the film, may be introduced and taken into consideration. Murph and Amelie are two daughters in search of love and trust in dangerous times. Murph has faith in what she claims to be messages from the "ghost," and her love and hope for her father, and for humanity, is immense. Similarly Amelie—despite a constant dismissal of her faith from the side of Cooper and his own faith in Mann's planet (which turns out to be a catastrophic mistake)—is guided by her love toward Edmunds, and hope for his mission and for his planet stays with her until the end; also, Amelie (intuitively) "knows" that, out there in the universe, there exist sympathetic bulk beings, and she states accordingly: "And whoever They are, They appear to be looking out for us."[87] As concerns the roles of Murph and Amelie, we may refer to Irigaray's thought about the neglected role of daughters in the history of religions—it is our opinion that Nolan wanted to point precisely to this aspect in attributing a very special (if not redemptory) role to both of them. Irigaray contends that *daughters* play a special role in cosmic and generational orders: they are *women born from women* and, as such, are bearers of an entirely different type of genealogy compared to men; women, therefore, belong to a genealogy that is not accessible to men.[88] Almost all main religious and theological traditions of the world have granted priority only to men (e.g., kings and prophets, founders of world religions, priests and monks), which, as a result, has caused multiple crises—from extreme bias in gender roles within world religions, to the inherent hierarchical models in Churches, and consequently broken communities of the faithful (wars included), all the way to the modern ecological crisis as marked with our broken alliance with nature. As a ten year old, Murph is convinced that there is a ghost in her bedroom, messaging something to her. Despite the fact that her intuitions are being constantly rejected by her father (in line with our previous elaborations, we could assume that Cooper sees her faith as belonging to some unjustified magical beliefs), Murph still insists on what she believes might be a sign of a mysterious communication from some unknown source, *perhaps* even from some god. In this way, her faith intervenes two times in a most decisive manner: first, by her belief in a ghost, she discloses a secret code that actually enables humanity to embark upon its journey toward the new habitable world, and, second, again by her hope for her father's

God in the Future | 135

return, a forty-year-old Murph finds the decisive quantum data from the watch in her bedroom, which he gave her upon his departure and which now enables humanity to escape the dangerously suffocating atmosphere of the Earth. Also, as regards Amelie—the final scenes of *Interstellar* confirm her role—after meeting an older Murph, who is now nearing her death, Cooper returns to Edmunds and rejoins Amelie on her habitable planet.

Now, to return to our Nolan philosopher, his theory of bonding agents, and the theological consequences that may be inferred from this teaching. According to Bruno the vinculum was that which linked "to an ever-changing degree the operator (the *vinciens*) to the *vinciendum*."[89] Translated into the theological language of quantum theology, this statement means that the *vinculum* may be represented by the tesseract as a quantum field of the bonding agent. The magical action of the principal bonding agents—that is, futuristically evolved humans or gods—represents the process of restoration of ever broken connections of love: from the more elemental nature toward connections between other sentient beings, and all the way to nature as an elemental whole. Beings of the brane are, in the exact words of the Nolan philosopher, *presented as matter over whose surface pass infinite forms, and clearly each one of them is a vinculum*. The addendum to our argument on the existence of God from the end part of our first section, updated by our reading of *Interstellar*, would run as follows:

> On the background of the existence of brane beings and objects, God exists as a supreme bulk being. God passes through our worlds, which are affected by this "gravity," in ways we do not yet know how to apprehend or scientifically describe. These events can be designated as mesocosmic constellations of a *vinculum* or bond of love that are affecting our agapeistic activities. As an enhanced spiritually material being, God subtly passes through the surface of brane beings, which report these weak passings as "mystical experiences." The interactions of God with brane beings establish paleo-ontological and mesocosmic correspondences between microcosmic (brane beings, objects) and macrocosmic (Gods, other bonding agents) "deities."

On Astrotheology

With Ted Peters, we were introduced into a new subfield within systematic theology: astrotheology. In chapter 13 of his *God—The World's Future*

("Astrotheology"), Peters gives the most elaborate presentation of this new field so far.[90] According to him, astrotheology has four main tasks: (1) to reflect on the scope of creation beyond geocentrism; (2) to set the Christological parameters under the new astrotheological view; (3) to analyze and critique astrobiology from within; and, finally, (4) to cooperate with leaders of other religious traditions and with scientists in order to prepare the public for a possible extraterrestrial contact. These arguments do not overlap directly with what we aim to present in this book. But Peters concludes his presentation of the field with the following thought on our cosmic future, and it is here that our arguments on the temporality of God indeed overlap: "Our present creation will be consummated in God's promised new creation. Or, to reverse it, God's new creation will *retroactively* determine and define the present creation. *God is the future of all things,* the galaxies and their stars included."[91] This passage closely relates our question of the temporality of God with the question of astrotheology. So, let us now finally summarize our argument in the vicinity of this field.

The core argument as presented within our philosophical theology, dealing with Bruno's and Ruyer's philosophy on one side, and Mormonism's and *Interstellar*'s rich scientifico-religious imagination on the other, is that God is the future itself: projecting into the present and affecting or guiding "us" as a bonding agent through various ultra-weak interactions. As based on a philosophico-theological imagination (and thus being related to Dewey's original idea of God as a future unification of ideal values[92]), God as temporality of the future is an enigmatic sign of continuity and interdependency on the field reaching from subatomic matter to higher human values through time. As an idea of a supreme intelligence, God reveals to us (as *not-yet-gods*) through philosophy, religion, science, and art: through these revelations of ideas, scientific laws, and artworks, retroactively synchronistically, as it were, the world we are inhabiting is revealed to us as a part of his ongoing creation. Within these multiple revelations, God is attested to be a pervasive cosmico-quantum energy that can be tapped into—and living beings are the material entities, whose bodies can encounter, absorb, and distribute this energy: they can induce agapeistic action on a basis of these encounters. As a way of an announcement of a future bond, unifying all, these encounters are discernable in humans as signs of *love*. These encounters are a mark of our divinization, and God-the-future is the vibration of a cosmic web of love of which we are a part. Our argument could now finally be summarized as follows:

(A) God-the-future acts in this world through a series of revelations that are felt by beings as ultra-weak interactions, inducing shifts in their orientation and action.

(B) In humans, these revelations are felt as signs of a future creation, retrospectively projected into the present from the God as bonding agent.

(C) The highest cosmic coordination between all-encompassing God and beings (matter over whose surface pass infinite forms) is called a plane of love.

(D) On the basis of divine revelations and cosmic coordination, human beings are able to induce and share agapeistic action.

According to Keller, the universe is so mysteriously entangled that its particles actually "coordinate instantly, precisely and at any distance whatsoever—even across the galaxy" and that "the events far away seem to feel each other."[93] In our argument, this was understood as an example of hidden and mysterious correspondences between microcosmic and macrocosmic beings—underpinned or initiated by God as bonding agent. In the language of Nicolas de Cusa, Keller asserts that "through all things God is in each thing."[94] And, she adds—in a beautiful quantum-theological metaphor:

> We are learning of an immediate connectivity operating across the widest distances, where there is not empty void but rather an infinitely plastic body of mysterious energy. And the very energy of the expansion may flow from the intimacy of the entanglement. Never mind the math. Consider the metaphor! The ancient mystical trope of the "brilliant darkness"—the glowing darkness of the infinite whom we have nicknamed God—seems to be growing (in theory) a subtle body. A body of energy, no thing, but pulsing webs, strings, and fields, the entangled intensity of everything that is, in some sense, everywhere.[95]

The world is full of gods.

spell of the water

6

God in the Third Age

> Everything will be as it is now, just a little different.
>
> —Giorgio Agamben, *The Coming Community*[1]

The Three Eras

In her seminal essay on the originality and influence of Joachim of Fiore, Marjorie Reeves argues that the ideas on the new coming age—the so-called Third Age—flourished in Europe well before the thirteenth century. But as long as Christians stood outside the secular order, the ideas of a coming age could not be understood in a historical manner—as later in Joachim of Fiore's thought. When in Eusebius's *History of the Church* the Roman Empire became understood as "the latest instrument of God" in the long Judeo-Christian history from Abraham to Constantine, it was possible to introduce, as it were, a proto-Hegelian understanding of the historical stages into the theology.[2] But Montanus (second century) was first to contend that he was living in the age of the Holy Spirit, which is to succeed the ages of the Father and of the Son.[3] Similarly, it was St. Augustine who derived from St. Paul the triadic pattern of six great ages (*aetates*)—in whose three consecutive times/*tempora*—of *ante legem, sub lege,* and finally *sub gratia* flourished. These six ages, symbolizing the six days of Creation, were sealed or concluded with the Seventh or Sabbath Age (cf. also seven seals from the Apocalypse). And Honorius of Autun (c. 1080–1154?) first elaborated on the three stages as found within the six great ages as *tempus ante legem* from Adam to Moses, *tempus legis* from Moses to Christ, and, finally, *tempus gratiae* reaching from the Incarnation to the Second Coming.[4] But Honorius would still remain Augustinian in a way that according to him the Seventh or Sabbath Age would still rest *beyond/outside* the Last Judgment. Finally, Rupert of Deutz was the first to clearly relate three stages to the three Persons of the Trinity, linking this Trinitarian dynamics also with the progressive movement through history. And, lastly, two mystics—Eberwin of Steinfeld (d. April 10, 1152) and Hildegard of Bingen (1098–1179) would now be able to directly link the three ages with the process of perfection within the earthly Church in which new humble *perfecti* would emerge and surpass or outgrow the old spiritual patterns: for both, blessedness is to take place on earth.[5] Both mystics can be understood as the early predecessors of Luce Irigaray and her thought of the age of the Spirit.

But in order to encapsulate the full historical setting of the idea of the three eras, let us look at the words from the Jewish tradition that originate from around 600 AD. In the "Abuda Zara" tract of the *Babylonian Talmud*, we read: "The disciples of Elijah taught: The world will continue for six thousand years, the first two thousand of which were a chaos (*Tahu*), the second two thousand were of Torah, and the third two thousand are the days of the Messiah, and because of our sins many years of these have elapsed, and still he has not come."[6] The three ages, as propounded by the authors of Babylonian Talmud, refer to the chaotic age before the Law, to the age of the Law of Torah, and to the future Messianic age that is still to come. In the Middle Ages, this thought clearly resounded in the teachings of Joachim of Fiore (c.1132–1202), whose idea is that history was divided into three ages: the age of the Father (Old Testament), the age of the Son (New Testament and Church), and the age of the Spirit (Third Testament and Spiritual Community), which is still to come and in which new religious orders would inaugurate a new Spiritual Church or future Spiritual Community here on Earth.[7] The same teaching was then also probably one of the sources for the heretic medieval sect of Amalricians, and, in the most recent form, this thought is revived in an idiosyncratic way in Irigaray's teaching of about "the age of the Spirit" (also equally called "the age of the Breath"), in which the task of humanity will be to become itself divine spirit, or divine breath. But, for Irigaray, there is one distinctive feature of this new or future era—namely, that in this era it will be possible to reunite "the breath of the woman-mother with the divine redemption of humanity."[8] The third age, for Irigaray, will thus suspend the more patriarchal or masculine theological settings or spiritual environments of the first and the second ages. In this particular model of history, she has no close contemporaries within contemporary philosophy.[9] But before we return to this specific line of the tritheism teachings from Joachim of Fiore and Amalric of Bène to Irigaray, let us posit a preliminary question on an alleged controversy in the fields of ethics and theology.

In his seminal book *You Must Change Your Life*, Peter Sloterdijk starts with the reformulation of one of the most famous sentences in philosophy—now in the form of "A spectre is haunting the Western world—the spectre of religion."[10] In the time of huge migration flows *from the beyond*, which, in recent decades for Sloterdijk already look like "an aspect of a mass exodus,"[11] there exist neither "religion" nor "religions" in the times of this grand exodus. What remains instead are various practices and operations that provide or improve our qualifications for the ever next practice—in terms of our philosopher. Instead of an obsolete but once all-powerful world, still having a character of a theotechnics, we are left with the reign of anthropotechnics. This would, now, mean that after exhausted and weary *Homo faber*—also *Homo religiosus*—should take a well-deserved farewell. Our future will be running "under the sign of the exercise,"[12] and the question, then, is whether this necessary turn from vertical metaphors and *acrobatics* in religion into their nineteenth- (Feuerbach, Nietzsche) and twentieth-century horizontal usages is what has now finally been superseded by the era of exercises. According to Sloterdijk, we could perhaps talk about three eras, as it were: the vertical age (typical in the parable of Jacob's ladder, or in Dionysius the Areopagite's mystical theology, for example), the horizontal age (which still is characterized by a few last vertically designed but already metaphysically weakened denominators such as, for example, Nietzsche's *Übermensch*), and, finally, the horizontal age of exercises, the common and future age of anthropotechnics. In this view, *You must change your life!* becomes a new absolute imperative, now operating under the qualifier of ethical difference—but without any religious connotations. The substitution of all forms of religion and theology with ethics and its new absolute imperative is therefore accomplished. But what if this story—as told and explained by Sloterdijk—would also represent one of the stories being similar to the long series of unjust subjugations of religion and theology by other disciplines (psychoanalysis, cultural anthropology, sociology of religion, and so forth)? If we take for granted, that, in the twenty-first century, it is obviously impossible to sustain any of the great religious (or even secular!) narratives, we still want to propose a possibility of a *pulsation of religion* in ourselves—as a still remaining, although hidden sign of our salvation and divinization, if we put it strongly. In our contemporary desacralized and demythologized world, it seems that it is only within political theology that we can find the remaining signs of a religious imagination of the future, and of an agapistic and solidaristic ethics of salvation and hope that is so much needed in our times.[13] But more than that should be desired and an access to the interiority should remain open and vital in this era as well.

But if we now return to our preliminary topic of the three eras, what Gianni Vattimo finds interesting about Joachim of Fiore in his *After Christianity* is precisely this: that salvation history is still in progress, here and now, and perhaps this sounds rather paradoxically and counterintuitive than logical—namely, that in our global, decentralized, and too often cynical world that is, at the same moment, extremely socially or ethically vulnerable and environmentally fragile—that we could talk of any kind of salvation at all. Vattimo argues that "we can speak of prophecies of the future only because salvation history remains unfulfilled."[14] What then if Sloterdijk's parable of huge migration flows from the beyond should have been accompanied with another, yet more *inward*, movement still to be revealed to us? What if instead of triumphantly exposing and counting cadavers or dead bodies of various gods and demigods, and their religious and secular ideologies that we first invented and then worshipped and finally renounced and deserted (too often in terror and death), we try to consider another narrative: one less grandiose and of a much more delicate kind? One of a search for the *pulsation of religion* in ourselves, for the return of charity/love into our tired and seemingly empty salvation history narratives—one that is perhaps not yet visible or tangible among us and our ethically fractured communities but is as concrete and strong as our highest hope? If we believe Joachim of Fiore, there is only one name that deserves and needs to be elevated to the heights, and cherished in the future—and this is *charity*:

> There are three ages of the world indicated by the sacred texts. The first is the stage in which we have lived under the law; the second is that in which we live under grace; the third is one in which we shall live in a more perfect state of grace. . . . The first passed in slavery; the second is characterized by filial slavery; the third will unfold in the name of freedom. The first is marked by awe, the second by faith, the third by charity. . . . The first period regards the slaves; the second regards the sons; the third regards the friends. . . . The first stage is ascribed to the Father, who is the author of all things; the second to the Son, who has been esteemed worthy to share our mud; the third to the Holy Spirit, of which the apostle says, "Where the spirit of the Lord is, there is freedom."[15]

According to Joachim of Fiore, the three stages are accomplished in the third, that is, final *historical* era, also known in his teachings and prophecies as *the Sabbath Age*, in which this earthly world will be transformed into a kingdom, or a terrestrial era "without war, without scandal, without worry or terror."[16] Per Joachim of Fiore, the first *status* originates with Adam and was completed with Christ; the second *status* begins with Uzziah (King of Judah) and was near its end in the time of Joachim of Fiore; the third *status* had already started with Saint Benedict of Nursia and will end with the conclusion of history.

Although the teachings of Joachim of Fiore about the division of time were based on the idea of the Trinity, his theology was still largely focused on the "political" idea of a millennial transformation of society toward the final eschatological unification of Christians, Jews, and Greeks (Orthodox) in one Roman Church. Thus, the *status* of the Father was related to the nonbelieving Jews and their subsequent conversion—as the *status* of the Son was related to the Gentiles or heretical Greeks and their conversion. In the third, final age, humanity would witness the final unification of all under the Holy Spirit with the spiritual guidance of spiritual men (Christian monks) who would guide this world in an earthly Sabbath age. Related to the era of crusades to which Joachim of Fiore bore witness and was both their supporter and a critic, his teachings, of course, are one of the earliest contributions to political theology as such.[17] Still, according to Vattimo and his interpretation of the abbot from Calabria in *After Christianity*, this still remains a prophecy with an important "discovery that historicity is constitutive of revelation."[18] But, behind and also beyond a more narrow interpretation or reading of his innovative thoughts, there is a strong ethico-eschatological message that we want further to explore in this chapter: namely, that the third age—if we may risk this idea here—actually is a *pulsation of divine life* (or religion) in our most inward *spiritual-material* layers still to be revealed and opened to us.[19] If this could be true, then the age of the spirit actually is the future or coming *messianic* age of the renewed religious and aesth/ ethic sensibilities: "We should not forget that the world *spirit* (*pneuma*) means etymologically breath, wind, blowing, something volatile, fleeting, of which thought lost the memory when it began conceiving of spirit as the evident and indubitable foundation of self-consciousness, up to Hegel's 'absolute spirit.' "[20] Clearly, this fully resounds with Irigaray's version of the three ages' teaching as leading to the future *age of the breath* in which the task of humanity will be to become itself divine breath. But it is in one of the immediate successors of Joachim of Fiore—namely, in Amalric of

Bène's pantheistic and materialistic thought—that this idea already found its first earthly incarnation.

Amalric of Bène on the Way to Post-Christianity

According to Agamben, the meaning of ethics is understood when "good is revealed to consist in nothing other than a grasping of evil," and evil is recognized by us as the forgetting of the "transcendence inherent in the very taking place of things."[21] God *or* good, according to Agamben, is the *taking-place* of the entities—such as that being-worm of the worm, or the being-stone of the stone that is now regarded to be divine. Good, therefore, means that "God is all in all" and this appropriation or understanding of the Platonic doctrine of *chora*, according to Agamben, is also the doctrinal content of the Amalricians, who, similarly to Albigensians and Cathari and their *perfecti*, were regarded as perfect or impeccable by themselves and, thus, believed that it is in them and in their inherent divinity that the new spiritual age has just been revealed to humanity. Transcendence, therefore, does not dwell as a supreme entity somewhere above all entities and things, but, rather inversely, "*the pure transcendent is the taking-place of every thing.*"[22]

Who were the Amalricians? How was it possible for this early thirteenth-century small, but already influential, Parisian group of theologians to become so radically *post-Christian* in the midst of Latin Christianity? Master Amalric or Amalric of Bène (1150–1206/7) was the founder of a medieval heretical sect that was known under the name of their founder: the Amalricians. Next to Master Amalric was a philosopher David of Dinant (ca. 1160–ca. 1217), who was among the most prolific members of that sect. David of Dinant, who outlived his close friends, was known for his pantheistic-materialistic *Deus, hyle et mens una sola substantia sunt* sentence, which was preserved by Albertus Magnus.[23] On November 20, 1210, ten of the most important followers of Master Amalric were burnt at the stake in front of a large crowd of spectators in Paris (all of whom were students of theology at the newly established University of Paris). Other followers of the sect were imprisoned or forced to abandon their heretical teachings. Amalric himself died in 1206/7 after being condemned shortly before. In 1210, Amalric was excommunicated posthumously and his bones were exhumed from their resting place and transferred to unconsecrated ground for his second burial. By 1215, the sect was virtually annihilated. Importantly, among the Amalricians there were many women and the sect gathered among its members people from the lower classes, such as various handworkers and peasants. With their orientation toward the plebeian social classes, Amalricians, therefore, also had a clear political dimension and a social program for an earthly kingdom of men *and* women of their time beyond Church and state hierarchies and class divisions. Any human being, according to the Amalricians, could become divine in themselves in her or his lifetime.[24]

At the time of Master Amalric's teaching, the University of Paris was already famous for theological learning; as it was under the protection of King Phillip Augustus, the university was the very center of theological studies of the western Christian world. But at the same time the Church and political leaders were already firmly determined to get rid of heresies in the land—and crusades against Albigensians and Cathari had just begun in 1209 and 1210. At the university, Aristotle's books (on natural philosophy) and Scotus Eriugena's books (*De Divisione Naturae*) were banned because they were considered subversive. Further, the sect of Amalricians, which had already outgrown the narrow academic environment and had become, by then, an evangelical movement with many important intellectuals as their followers (though presented as a new teaching among the plebeian social classes) was recognized as extremely dangerous for the Church and thus the sect was quickly destined by Church leaders to be stopped and annihilated.[25]

Apart from his relation to Scotus Eriugena's early teachings (which, from their original idealistic form, were now materialistically reshaped by Master Amalric) as a propounder of the teaching of the three stages, Master Amalric must have been in touch with the Joachite prophecy. Either in Rome or at the University of Paris, Amalric must have encountered these thoughts in order to reformulate and further develop them with his friends and followers into the doctrine of the three ages of history.[26] With these teachings, Amalricians fully rejected the Church hierarchy and, instead, prophesized about the worth and dignity of ordinary men and women of their time—and therefore already incorporated sexual difference into their revolution of religion.[27] But, before we elaborate on their teachings, it is necessary to mention important Islamic influences as they are present in *left-wing* Aristotelianism,[28] especially the writing of in Ibn Sina/Avicenna (980–1037) and Ibn Rushd/Averroës (1126–98), which already contained materialistic and pantheistic/panpsychistic traits and could also quickly become widespread among the Christian schools of their time. Avicenna's vitalist materialism form does not precede matter anymore: matter is both primordial and coeternal—with the form. Matter/nature is now a subject for the first time—and "contains within it a possibility of its own emergence."²⁹ According to Averroës in *Destructio Destructionis*, it is in *Philosophia Orientalis*, a lost document that is only known from indirect sources, where Avicenna supports the claim that "[t]here must exist a spiritual force which is diffused in all the parts of the universe in the same way as there is a force in all the parts of a single animal which binds them together."³⁰ This beautiful intuition of Avicenna rests on his presumption that knowledge (and within it, science) actually takes precedence over faith. According to Bloch, it is within these movements of the Persian elite that it was possible for Avicenna to break with the usual connections to religious orthodoxy and instead link with Sufis from Persia and with the Brethren of Purity of Basra, and—in terms of his teachings on the elements—also with the more ancient Persian "cosmological metaphysics of light."³¹ Averroës's own philosophy was similarly rooted in his own take on the Aristotelian teachings on the ontological primacy of the uncreated and eternal matter, which also represented the traits of the emerging, more progressive social classes and their interest in natural sciences of the Islamic twelfth century.³² According to Herman Ley, it is precisely in this overturning or overcoming of Aristotle's classical *dýnamis-enérgeia* scheme that, later, actually helped the West make a transition toward natural sciences in the Renaissance. We know that David of Dinant, a close ally of Master Amalric, was influenced by these Islamic developments in the philosophy of matter.

But there is even an earlier line of thinkers before Avicenna and Averroës that should be included more indirectly but, in a way, even more strongly into the genealogy of the teachings of the Amalricians. Following Aristotle's statements from the third book of *On the Soul* on the knowledge as being derived from the bodily senses and from the use of reason, and his statement that there must also be knowledge that must have been derived from some other source, it was Alexander of Aphrodisias who first decided that this other source must be God.³³ Those among the Islamic circles who accepted these views were Sufis, and their beliefs that "they were in direct intercourse with God" (*waḥdat al-wujūd*) became too offensive for the orthodox circles or any interpretation that was in line with the Qur'ānic teachings. Such was the case with Sufi teacher al-Junaid (d. 910), who influenced al-Hallāj (858–922), who also is known for his pantheistic or panpsychistic teachings—being clearly off the beaten path of any accepted tradition of his time.³⁴ We need to know that among the Persian thinkers, and in particular among those of a non-Islamic tradition, we had philosophers and theologians who were less concerned with orthodox teachings, as was the case with their Arabic contemporaries. Not far away from the teachings on the third age of Master Amalric, it was al-Hallāj who already had been assuming that "by obedience the *Divine Spirit* came into the mystic's soul."[35] Among the Shi'ite authorities, some were convinced that, with his preaching, he was assuming the role of Mahdī—and even placing himself in close proximity to Jesus, his teachings, and his martyrdom. This ultimately led al-Hallāj to his death by torture, followed by symbolic decapitation. Among his most important contributions to the mystical and ethical tradition is without any doubt his teaching on the participation in suffering in compassion unto substitution—which in the twentieth century became the name of the Badaliya community, founded by the greatest admirer of al-Hallāj: Louis Massignon. According to Massignon, substituting oneself for another means "*exiling oneself to the other as he or she is* in order to offer Christ hospitality in the other's own soul, in the other's own taking-place."[36] If we now link this thought to the meaning of ethics—as already proposed by Agamben when he spoke of the Amalricians (God *or* good as the *taking-place* of the entities that now are regarded to be divine and a related thought on the God who now, as it were, *pantheistically*, becomes "all in all")—then if we are looking toward the opening of the third age or the future Age of the Spirit/Breath, we are perhaps on the right track.

To return to Amalric of Bène's teachings, there is perhaps no better example than to read the following excerpt by Roberto M. Unger, another thinker on a path of post-Christianity: "The antinomian element in Christianity, so close to the wellsprings of the faith, remains, however, a strength rather than a weakness. Antinomianism is intimately related to the conception of the person as situated and *embodied spirit*, transcendent over the institutional and conceptional frameworks that shape him and incapable of being wholly defined by circumstance."[37] This, precisely, is the same as that of Master Amalric and the Amalricians. The sources on what the Amalricians believed are scarce and largely depend on an official document of the Catholic Church that was issued by a provincial synod at Paris in 1210 upon the conviction of the sect.[38] The charges against the Amalricians consist of three parts: "pantheism, the attainment of spiritual perfection here on earth, and the antinomian and antisacramental implications of the Amalricians' views on the preceding two topics."[39] Within their concept of the third age—the age of the spirit—Amalricians held a belief in an ontological continuity between God and creation so as to bring deification of men and women within reach in their lifetime. Apart from this, Amalricians also contended that they had been granted a very special place in the plan of salvation and, thus, they indeed possessed the grace of already being in the third age. Quite in line with Agamben's remarks on the meaning of ethics, Amalric and his followers took the notion of "God is all in all" seriously and understood salvation as the "coming of the place of itself"—of each and every entity, from God to human being, from animal to mineral or stone. The age of the spirit means that the taking place of each entity, or its transcendence, implies a radically *materialistic* salvation theology. This "absolute pantheism" of the Amalricians, therefore, was in line with Bruno's and Baruch Spinoza's later forms of pantheism—for both counted as "materialistic" as opposed to other "idealistic" forms—if we have just Hegel in mind.[40] As we know, for Spinoza, "God is Nature taken 'complicatively'" and "that the world he produces adds nothing to the God's essence."[41] Whether Spinoza's expressionism (and, *per analogiam*, this also holds for the teachings of the Amalricians) is taken in its stronger (direct or materialistic) or weaker (indirect and thus idealistic) form, it could still be said that "[i]t implies a rediscovery of Nature and her power and a recreating a logic and ontology: a new 'materialism' and a new 'formalism.'"[42] Now, Karl Albert adds another dimension into the line of influences, since he puts Amalrician pantheism in line with the pre-Socratic natural religion of Greece, and more concretely, Thales's sentence that "all things are full of gods"[43]; to which we could add the introductory sentence from the Vedic (analogous therefore to the pre-Socratic time) *Īśā Upaniṣad*, namely that "[t]his whole world is to be dwelt in by the Lord, whatever living being there is in the world."[44] The plenitude of material things as divinized, and at the same time the immanence of God as all-inhabiting and all-pervasive—especially when this thought is related to the world of the ancient elements (such as water, air, earth, and fire)—is what inaugurates the ontological continuity in the world and enables at the same time a new materialistic understanding of the cosmos. It is only within Mormonism[45] and in Irigaray's thought that we can imagine a similar ontology, also with similar *material* consequences for our salvation. But, for Amalricians, these terms were not so important. An argumentation that we can get from *Contra Amaurianos*—and these most probably were the words of Amalricians, charged with heresy—is simply the following: "What always in God is, is God. In God is but everything, because everything, that is created, was life in him. Therefore, God is all."[46]

For Pope Innocent III, who in 1208 officially proclaimed the *extra Ecclesiam nulla salus* ecclesiology (followed by the Fourth Lateran Council in 1215), the Amalrician teachings were not even properly heretical, since they were simply impossible to comprehend or "insane."[47] Amalricians believe that God is everywhere, and that God actually *dwells* in all things, thus "[i]nhabiting a God-filled universe in which the Holy Spirit held sway and within which man might aspire to become a truly spiritual being"[48]—this was the meaning of their antinomian and antisacramental teachings. For Amalricians, then "just as the ceremonies of the old law ceased with the advent of Christ, so, too, the sacraments of the Church ceased to be operative with the coming of the Holy Spirit."[49] *Women and men*, having the Holy Spirit incarnated within themselves, were now free and thus not dependent on any external power or law anymore. The highest law of humanity (and a new religion!) is to become spiritual *beings*, here and now, on the earth. It is, of course, logical that they were labeled as *Gens insana* by their opponents.[50] A new era has come, then—according to Master Amalric and his friends—an era that resembles the advent of Nietzsche's (Persian-born) Zarathustra, namely when "like thousandfold children's laughter Zarathustra comes into all burial chambers, laughing at these night watchmen and grave guardians, and whoever else rattles about with dingy keys."[51] The keys of the third age, as it were, are in our hearts. It is up to us to resolve the riddle of all riddles: the taking-place of the post-Christianity in/*as* ourselves. Not an easy task at all! But we may believe in an event of its coming.

The Age of the Spirit

It is time to approach the topic of the age of the spirit—in both a theological and ethical sense, and as a sign of a future reconciliation between morality and religion. We have seen in the first part of this chapter that the decisive point for historicization of the three ages was the positioning of the Roman Empire into the salvation history of the Judeo-Christian world. Now, this vision reappears for the second time—if we use the well-known sentence from Karl Marx's "The Eighteenth Brumaire of Louis Napoleon"—that history repeats itself, *first as tragedy, then as farce*—through following the constellation around Hegel's writings, as explained by Purushottama Bilimoria in his fine essay on Western orientalism and related concepts of the philosophy of history: "Spectacularly, the night before the Holy Roman Empire fell to Napoleon's . . . Wellington boots at Jena in September 1806, Hegel completed his *Phenomenology of the Spirit*. The massive tome ends, appropriately, with an ontotheological schema reminiscent of Joachim of Fiore's announcement of a New Age of the Spirit to complete the Ages of the Father and the Son. And like Goethe, Hegel concluded that the irreversible event signaled the end of the Middle Ages."[52] Although there are no citations from, or other concrete signs of, Joachim of Fiore in any of Hegel's writings, we still can contend that the entire phenomenologico-historical mission of Hegel's "triadic" thought is marked by Joachite influence. We know that Hegel's absolute spirit is marked with an absolutely indispensable occidentalist tendency. In Schelling's late work *Philosophy of Revelation*, he elaborates on the third age by making a more direct and more appropriate reference to Joachim of Fiore. According to Schelling, it is necessary to think of three successive ages in order to complete the world history with an era of the Spirit. By referring to Jn 7:39 ("for as yet there was no Spirit, because Jesus was not yet glorified"), Schelling therefore makes clear reference to Joachim of Fiore and other heretical sects as those that knew and prophesized about the future time in which Christianity would really become the "religion of humanity."[53]

From Joachim of Fiore to Schelling, the third age was therefore announcing a Third Testament and a new Christianity—perhaps one that would now be *inscribed in our hearts*, and, as it were, one that would be synchronized with the *pulsation of religion* in ourselves and indeed in our carnal and spiritual bodies. We can now contend with Irigaray that there is one task to be accomplished in the world: to "make divine this world—as body, as cosmos, as relations with others."[54] In this post-Christian world, (cosmic) Christ would now manifest as a "concentrated embodiment of divine energy," an "activity of spirit that we find in our experience of transcendence and that we rediscover at work in evolving nature."[55] This is not only the task of one culture or one religious tradition, but is mutually shared between the world traditions beyond any artificial dichotomies or antagonisms based on intellectual pride or prestige. According to Vattimo, we can speak of prophecies of the future only because salvation history remains still unfulfilled, and we have seen in Sloterdijk that an alternative to salvation within religion could only be in the descent of any of the remaining vertical layers of our religious experience into an era of exercises: the era of anthropotechnics. But there is another path, one that is not so much attached to getting to our self-affection through exercises, but is rather is linked to a new way of self-affection[56] emerging from the *spiritual-breathful* being. The task, now, is to become in tune with the process of the new *spiritual* transformation of humanity so as to become enlightened enough to hear the voice of the other—to detect his/her signs and gestures that call for a dialogue with him or her, or with nature in one of its incarnations. This also is a task for us to learn how to ethically respond to the call of another human being (or of a nonhuman species and their breathing), since breathing first means being alive but also staying alert and sensing everything and everyone around us with a deepened sense of proximity. This, perhaps, already hints toward a future postreligious *status* in which subtle divine/cosmic elements and related energies are activated in us by an enhanced mode of self-affection—as the taking-place of divinity in ourselves. In encountering this new world of divine/cosmic elements, our closest ally is Gaston Bachelard, an elemental philosopher, whose air/wind, or breath, was described as being intrinsically linked to our imagination and freedom, to the *"awareness of the free moment"*[57]—or to what opens to us in the future: as an era of the spirit. For Bachelard, air indeed is a *materially spiritual* substance of freedom as such. This free moment, as a place of an ethical *and* religious difference in ourselves, is what invites us to think toward the possibility toward the messianic event, which will be the time when "everything will be as it is now, just a little different."[58] This difference, as a reconciliation of ethics and religion, is as subtle as the spiritual breath that we share one with another: it is present in a little child, who sleeps in tranquility, and breathes in the atmosphere of peace; it is revealed in this world when a little girl plays in the garden joyfully and calmly; it is a time when men and women breathe the air of mutual respect and hospitable exchange of their spiritual energies (in body, language, and spiritual gestures, as new rituals); it is the communal breath of peace, a pulsating of community, as it were, in the rhythm of peace; *finally*, it is a time of a new covenant with nature and its divine beings and their subtle bodies, as impregnated by the holy sap of cosmic breath. *Divine is the love for the other as other, divine is the praise of nature as nature*, for Irigaray.[59] And this is what Rorty, as one of the last great American intellectuals, so beautifully described in his essay on the future of religion:

> My sense of the holy, insofar I have one, is bound with the hope that someday, any millennium now, my remote descendants will live in a global civilization in which love is pretty much the only law. . . . I have no idea how such a society could come about. It is, one might say, a mystery. This mystery, like that of the Incarnation, concerns the coming into existence of a love that is kind, patient, and endures all things.[60]

The spiritual community of Amalricians knew and prophesized about this future, and this love—when the body of humanity, and the body of nature and its beings, will become impregnated with the Holy Spirit, and thus being divinized.

earth-kiss

Postlude

God in Dualis

When I wandered across parallel worlds;
back and forth from my solitary lives and their doubles,
then, as if from nowhere, a thread of Your
wavering existence appeared
and spun us into a golden, enchanted cocoon.[1]

The Ultimate Couple

Then Awareness All-Good Male and Mother All-Good Female sat conjoined, non-dually.

—*The Great Tantra of the Lion's Perfected Display-Energy*[2]

In the symbolism of a tantric bond, the primordial sexual-divine energies of the masculine and feminine are presented as conjoined in the state of oneness. Their bodies, radiating or vibrating beyond the opposites of two sexes—into an encounter of the ultimate couple—are a sign of enlightenment and, as such, indicate the arrival to the original state of being-in-love in unity of opposites. In this state, the All-Good Female and All-Good Male, "lacking permanence or nihility, appear purely . . . within the primordial gnosis of great equanimity."[3] According to tantric teachings, in the search for love, human beings are attracted by each other into the bond of loving equanimity. The temporality of this encounter—an immeasurably small moment in time, as it were, in which the couple has achieved this state of love—itself is a mystery: to be understood, it first requires from us a transformation of the logic of love and of the two. As Ludwig Binswanger would argue, the *Dasein* herself-himself (here) exists as a loving encounter—and love is precisely that unfolding of *Dasein* toward its oneness as a primordial form of "we" (*Wirheit*).[4] In our ontological ground, we are, therefore, always already two in the mysterious oneness of the *dualis* mode (here understood as a grammatical number that is fully preserved and used in the Slovenian language).[5] The realm of love is here revealed in its primordial state: there is no love without an encounter. The mutual attraction of the encounter of this originally Twofold-Being will, to us, be revealed as the primordial or elemental cosmic (quantum, as we will argue) energy of God, passing through and indwelling in a couple as the highest of all magical bonds: the embrace of love. As we will see, Binswanger was on a trace of Böhme and Franz von Baader's philosophy vis-à-vis the correlation of spiritual and material/carnal layers of being and their teaching of the heavenly androgyne as a paradigm of our "earthly" longings toward love.

We may add that, since the beginning of Indian religious history in the ancient Vedic Sāṃhitās, the bond of love was thought of as desire (called *kāma* and *tapas*). In the ṛgvedic creation hymn (thoroughly analyzed in the prologue) we have That One (*tad ekam*) that breathes in a clandestine manner into itself and out of itself, without, in so doing, exhibiting any visible signs of life. In the first ontological progression following this initial constellation, we have That One, which is coming into being through the power of heat—this is the primordial cosmic desire, or love: the first sign of life. The creating of space-time is described in the Vedas in a predialogical manner of fundamental difference-in-twoness: That One that breathes using its own power, which exists in the empty space of silence, and which can symbolize the womb as the shell of being—its primordial space. But, in this first shell of being, a hidden kernel of primal warmth/love is present (sexual difference), which precedes thought and is the only thing that can vitalize breath into the first co-breath (conspiration of the two) that can install the possibility of the first loving breath of the World. Schelling knows this, as he writes: "For not even spirit itself is supreme; it is but spirit, or the breath of love. But love is supreme. It is that which was before there were the depths and before existence (as separate entities), but it was not there as love, rather—how shall we designate it?"[6]

Now, let us look at the following passage from *The Great Tantra of the Lion's Perfected Display-Energy*, which illustrates the sacred and bodily cardiology of the encounter of two buddhas. The All-Good Female declares the following teaching to the accompanying buddha of her class: "I, Unchanging All-Good Female, display appearance self-manifested as the *dharma*-body. I, Inexpressible All-Good Female, display awareness apart from the extremes of conceptualization. In the all-displaying heart of primordial gnosis there is neither a made nor making. . . . In a single [instance] of awareness, *saṃsāra* and *nirvāṇa* are complete. . . . Awareness enters the field of All-Good Female. Father-mother-in-union, lacking permanence or nihility, appear purely."[7] Apart from Buddhist teachings and related symbolism and iconography, what is it that this ultimate couple could represent? What theologico-sexuate genealogy grounds this metaphysical encounter? For the Buddhist teachings, the hypersexual loving embrace in its (trans)elemental bodily radiation represents the very peak of sublime knowledge. *Saṃsāra* and *nirvāṇa* are complete in this divine act and both subjects of this encounter achieve a state of Buddhahood: the ability of primordial awareness in which all conceptual distinctions and related categories appear as illusory.

It is important to know that the "All Good Female" designates Samantabhadrī, the name of the consort of the Ādi Buddha or primordial and highest buddha according to the Nyingma sect of Tibetan Buddhism (the name of this Buddha is Samantabhadra).[8] Samantabhadra is said to be the embodiment of "awareness" (Tib. *rig pa*). In the above passage, the entry of awareness into Samantabhadrī is a metaphor for the sexual union.[9] The symbolism of the couple as two bodies in union is of vital importance here: it indicates both the primordial (always already lost?) union in twoness that is beyond conceptual knowledge, but it also points to the possibility of an elemental understanding of the path of enlightenment—as the tantric path of enlightenment is achieved by virtue of body radiation (and *prāṇa* as its essential subtle element). As we will see, this position is very close to Böhme's and Baader's mystical-elemental path to the supreme love encounter, as is related to the possibility of the highest co-breathing (*conspiratio*) and breath-kiss (the mutual exchange of *pneuma*).

Finally, regarding the logic of sexual difference in Buddhism, there are differences between earlier Pāli sources, Mahāyāna developments, and the tantric path in Vajrayāna. The question of whether women enjoy an equal position to men and can attain enlightenment, or whether they are only sexually exploited and appropriated as a means to the enlightenment of men, is not beyond the scope of these traditions. Yael Bentor argues that, in the literature of the Pāli and Mahāyāna, "we can find very clear statements which negate the possibility that women as such can attain enlightenment."[10] On the other hand, both traditions still struggle with this theme and propose either that women could attain enlightenment if they would change into a man in another life, or that women can indeed achieve enlightenment but again only regarded as nāginis or goddesses. The third path is related to the attempts in both traditions to surpass this problem by going beyond the distinction between male and female by the rise of an idea of emptiness. In Vajrayāna, to which *The Great Tantra of the Lion's Perfected Display-Energy* belongs, women are endowed with wisdom (*prajñā*) and men with compassion (or means; *upāya*): "When two practitioners unite, they engage in the Bodhisattva path to enlightenment in which emptiness and means are equal. Therefore, the wisdom here—the female practitioner—must be equal to the means, the male practitioner."[11] In the tantric sexual embrace of Samantabhadrī and Samantabhadra—as highest and sublime loving encounter of two *archaic-pure bodies*—there is nothing to contemplate but contemplation itself. This encounter is a pure gift to all buddhas and all sentient beings. We will be able to reflect upon the interbodily elemental dynamics of this encounter (exchange and sharing of subtle bodily energies—*prāṇa*) after looking at our next example.

Now, we wish to focus on some rich Christian analogies to the tantric way of a higher love and the loving encounter itself. As Hermann Spreckelmeyer succinctly observes in his dense and rich elaboration on Baader (which is closely related to our elaborations on the tantric practices), "the order of the transcendent relationship of humanity and love stand in close connection" and "shows that primordial guilt as non-love casts its shadow upon the inward- and the between-human realms of love."[12] But, what is the meaning of this phrase? The primordial Love has always been lost, concealed, and forgotten. Humanity, in whatever epoch of its history, and in whatever capacity of the uncovering of the mystery of love, was always already caught in the amnesia of this primeval and sacred bond of love. Here, Baader is strongly influenced by Böhme, whose philosophy of the primordial couple represents one of the peaks of the erotico-sexuate theology of love and develops on this trace his own philosophical theology of love.

Apart from Baader, Böhme also strongly influenced Schelling and Feuerbach and his thoughts on the feminine Matrix (understood as Sophia and Mary) represent a unique trait of the Western mystical philosophy—presented by Böhme as the mystico-elemental intertwining of the feminine and masculine tinctures of Being and resulting in the idea of the androgyne

Christ—as related to the *Brautmystik* of the Middle Ages.[13] According to Böhme, the androgyne Christ is "for every sex what (s)he lacks in her/his unity and wholeness."[14] In this aspect, Christ fulfills the role of a pure (and sexuate) being, beyond divided or contested sexual and conceptual dichotomies, such as Ādibuddha in Buddhism. It is in this light that, for Böhme, Christ and Sophia can represent the ultimate heavenly couple—as a paradigm of supreme love and harmony—in themselves, but also as a symbol of our perfection as humans: *"darum sie Sophia heißt / als die Braut Christi."*[15] For Böhme and his metaphysics of two sexes in the domain of the human being, Adam as the first (androgyne!) being (*Urmensch*) fell asleep and thus lost his paradisiacal unity with God. As a consequence, two sexes are created from Adam, and, from this moment on, the highest desire of humankind is to regain this primeval unity: to become united one more time with the lost oneness and unity in the very core of our being. Man and woman now aim at rejoining their separated elemental tinctures (subtle elements of fire and light) of two disembodied halves into the oneness—higher erotic love could prepare the new place of this reunion, and, as Baader will now show, the exchange of subtle bodily pneumatic energies in the breath-kiss will be the highest symbol of this encounter.[16]

Franz von Baader (1765–1841) was a contemporary of both Schelling and Feuerbach. In his mystical works, linked to the Catholic tradition, Baader elaborated on the *Paradise Couple-in-Union* of Böhme; he took the motif of the lost union and presented it as a creative relationship and a magical oneness, visible in our immanent desire for the transformative *dwelling-with*. In line with his predecessors (such as Paracelsus and Böhme), Baader argues that every living creature is endowed with the sidereal and elemental life forms: he explains them as the "electricity and sexual or erotic energy."[17] From this initial stage, both genders (as in the tantric path), for Baader, strive toward the return to the original and lost *twofold-being*. As argued by Spreckelmeyer, the Adamic-Being was supposed to bring its masculine and feminine elements: "After his creation, these elements found themselves in temperature and in the possibility of non-union. The essence of the Androgyne-being is thus the concept of the human Idea-relationship regarded in its wholeness or integralness, because this relationship guaranteed the immediacy of its existence before the Face of God, the eternal duration of the *imago Dei in homine*."[18] This primordial Adam-Being—as a fe/male-being-in-unity—is the all-present germ of creation. The ability of this being is to procreate itself through the conjunction of both intragendered beings. But, once this unity was broken due to original sin, sexual intercourse without the libido was not possible anymore, and the tertiary entity was needed to assist humanity: "the primordial image of this process is the three-in-one God."[19] Among human beings, the third factor of this yawning gap of the *in-between* is the Holy Spirit, or the Holy Breath. The spiritual exchange of this pneumatico-somatic energy now incarnates in the breath-kiss: Baader here recalls "the lovely legend of the East, according to which the *Paradisiacal Humanity* could have been able to digest with the mouth and procreate itself from the heart through a kiss [*breath-kiss* or *spirit-embrace*: hearts or spirits embracing or breathing together]. . . . The two that kiss truly breathe together, and that which comes into being through the union of both breaths works and weaves in both of them."[20] The breath-kiss materializes in the so-called and higher *heart-region* (Baader adds *breast-region* as another antipode to the *belly*-related lower region of the instinct) of the human being, to which are linked *the embrace, the tender hug*, and the *breath-kiss*—all of them as expressions of love. The embrace and breath-kiss therefore represent the highest possibility of a reunification into the forgotten and lost *twofold-being*. Baader now reflects on this as follows: "*Breathing-together* or the Spirit requires a mutual embrace; for not only Father and Son (but also man and woman) find themselves to be one or in union again in or through the *breathing-together*; rather, both of them, with the Spirit are three in one, out of which they then immediately separate in differentiation."[21] The in-breathing of the Spirit into ourselves is beautifully described in Hippolytus's *Commentary on the Song of Songs* (which may be the earliest extant Christian commentary on the *Song of Songs*, before 235 CE):

> 2.1 Now come and let us see this proposition of it [him/the book], in which he says. "Kiss me with the kisses of his mouth, because your breasts are lovelier than wine, and [the] aroma of your anointing oil greater than all incense, and as aroma of anointing oil poured out is your name."

> 2.2 What is the will of the Spirit, for what [is its] force, or what might be the interpretation (*lit.* indication, sign) of this mystery? We must proclaim to those who will hear, for it is the representation (*lit.* type) of the people that entreats the heavenly Word to kiss them, because *[the people] wish to join [together] mouth to mouth*. For [the people] wishes to join the power of the Spirit to itself.

2.3 And it says, "Let him kiss me with the kisses of his own mouth," which is this very thing: through the commandment that he commands let it be applied to me, since from this mouth comes love—[Lord,] make me worthy.[22]

In Keller's essay on the theology of the eros, the *kiss* appears in the context of the *Gospel of Philip* in which Mary Magdalene is called Jesus's companion or *koinonos*—which could mean "spouse," "wife," or "spiritual consort." Now, in the scene from the Gospel, we find the following words: "And the companion (*koinonos*) of the [S]aviour is . . . Mary Magdalene. [But Christ loved] her more than [all] the disciples [and used to] kiss her [often] on her."[23] As there is a lacuna in the original manuscript, Keller joins the interpreters in thinking that the body part in question of this kiss is most probably the mouth. While kissing often stood for sexual intercourse, Keller agrees with Robert Price that even if a kiss implies sexual intercourse, the gesture still is spiritual and metaphoric in nature.[24] But there might be another explanation of the kiss between Jesus and Mary Magdalene: it symbolizes their unique spiritual encounter toward sharing their breaths in the *breath-kiss*. In *Antigone's Sisters*, we have already indicated that the resurrected Jesus first appeared to Mary Magdalene, *and only later breathed* the reserve of his divine Breath back onto His disciples (Jn 20:22—"When he had said this, he breathed on them and said to them, Receive the Holy Spirit"). According to our understanding of this event of His resurrection, Jesus is now exchanging the Holy Breath with Mary Magdalene first (as she is the first apostle and his spiritual companion), and only then breathes it to the apostles. In the Gospel according to John, we witness the moment in the Trinitarian crisis when Jesus says to Mary Magdalene not to hold on to him (*me mou haptou*) because he "has not yet ascended to Father" (Jn 20:17[25]). The prohibition of the touching of Jesus in this particular moment relates to an idiosyncratic *pneumatic* meaning; it is namely the touching within an *ethico-pneumatic interval* between two autonomous bodies and two autonomous breaths that we are witnessing: an encounter of a purely divine character, an announcement of a new spiritual bond or conspiracy—the coming of love to this world, when men and women will become respiratory brothers and sisters in love by compassionately sharing their spiritual breaths in the community-to-come. *But Christ loved her more than all the disciples and used to kiss her often*—this bond between them (Mary Magdalene as the *koinonos* of Jesus) was an announcement of the resurrection mystery still to come. In this light, Jesus's apparition to Mary Magdalene entails this now ultimate *breath-kiss* to her as a prerequisite for sharing his divine Breath with the disciples and humanity: Jesus and Mary Magdalene are the Ultimate Couple.

Let us return to Baader. John Trinick succinctly states that a loving encounter arises from "the independent and separate self-offering of the two distinct carnalities *as having been previously effected*, that the two psyches may rise together to the proper plane of their own true union."[26] For Baader, two *carnalities* preeminently meet in the embrace and kiss. *Per analogiam* to St. Bernard's teaching of the holy Spirit as a *kiss* of the Father and the Son, for Trinick, "[t]wo beings who embrace are truly united in a breath common to them both. . . . Baader speaks of the possibility of a union between two souls by the 'inspiration' of the one into the other. . . . There is, in other words, a 'conspiration' of beings, a union in respiration."[27] This somatico-pneumatic *conspiracy of love*—as an exchange of spiritual(-breath) energies (*pneuma* and *prāṇa*)—is, thus, the highest act of the loving encounter and is as such analogous to the highest forms of sexual embrace between the Buddhas in the Tantras, or in the breath-kiss between Jesus and Mary Magdalene.

This somatico-pneumatic *conspiracy of love* needs now to be taken literally: in both Tantric and Christian contexts, the pneumatic or pranic aspects of the body represent the subtle materially energetic layers of our being. Spiritual here means "carnal-energetic": the bond of love gestures toward the exchange of our internal breath-energies. This description coincides with the thinking of energy in Catherine Keller as she points to William Blake, who was deconstructing the Western soul-body (and apathetic God) binary with a stunning reintroduction of the notion of energy, in his words:

> Energy is the only life and is from the Body and Reason is the bound
> or outward circumference of Energy.
> Energy is Eternal Delight.[28]

Energy as delight does not relate to the banality of egoistic sensual pleasure or hedonistic commodities; it is much more than this and extends toward the cosmologico-ontological plane of being. Namely, it is already Whitehead who, as early as in the 1920s, contends that "[a]ll flow of energy obeys 'quantum' conditions"[29] and, as various quantum physicists and Keller observe, the experiments associated with Bell's theorem have suggested that "once connected in any elemental sense, two particles—once separated—actually do not cease to be connected."[30] This mysterious yet *material/elemental* entanglement of particles—if translated into our carnal-energetic being—suggests that two beings subsist on this body of mysterious energy (quantum field), as beautifully expressed by Keller when she states that our bodies are woven of subtle intercommunicating energies and questions whether God is the "One Who *energizes* all in all . . . is that energy of our intimate/infinite entanglement?"[31]

In light of the problem of an alleged exclusive heteronormativity as visible both in the Tibetan Tantras and Christian mysticism of Böhme, and especially in the thought of Baader, we need to affirm that gestures of embrace, the loving encounter, a oneness through sexual encounters, and breath-kiss are all signs of *one humanity* in desire—of women, men, and individuals beyond duality of (sexual, or any) identities—all aiming at the once lost place of pure relationality, mutual devotion, and enhanced love. Amy Hollywood writes about this as she elaborates on women mystics: "When women mystics write about eagerly kissing the sacred wound [represented as vulva], then, their relationship with Christ is queered, for the body they desire and with which they identify is both male and female."[32] Furthermore, as these mystics use intensely erotic language and imagery, they often challenge the prescriptive heterosexuality of Christian culture and faith. For some of them, "gender becomes so radically fluid that it is not clear *what* kind of sexuality—within the heterosexual/homosexual dichotomy most readily available to modern readers—is being metaphorically deployed to evoke the relationship between humans and the divine. . . . [T]he intensity of divine desire forces sexual language into new, unheard-of configurations. Hence the emergence in the later Middle Ages of what Lochrie aptly calls the 'mystical queer.'"[33] A beautiful example of this is Mechtild of Magdeburg, where, in her, as it were, tantra-*related* work *Flowering Light of the Godhead*, she testifies in an eroticized manner about her experience of divine encounter. These words express a most subtle testament of a humanely divine loving encounter:

> the bride of all delights goes to the Fairest of lovers in the secret chamber of the invisible Godhead. There she finds the bed and the abode of love prepared by God in a manner beyond what is human.

> Our Lord speaks:
> "Stay, Lady Soul."
> "What do you bid me, Lord?"
> "Take off your clothes."
> "Lord, what will happen to me then?"
> "Lady Soul, you are so utterly ennatured in me
> That not the slightest thing can be between you and me . . ."[34]
> Then a blessed stillness
> That both desire comes over them.
> He surrenders himself to her,
> And she surrenders herself to him.
> What happens to her then—she knows—
> And that is fine with me.
> But this cannot last long.
> When two lovers meet secretly,
> They must often part from one another inseparably.[35]

This encounter is normative in nature, but the roles of lovers are still interchangeable: the encounter here does not imply only heterosexually defined proximity but—as the above verses show, it rather testifies for the supremely pure experience of the twoness-becoming-as-one mode: *That not the slightest thing can be between you and me . . . / Then a blessed stillness . . .* This nicely resonates with the following verses on the interval of dualis as based on two breaths joined in love from one of Niko Grafenauer's poems:

> over the garden table breath-and-breath.
> eternity leaning against nothing
> between us.[36]

Finally, we may now align this observation of ours with a remark of Hollywood, namely that with another mystic—Hadewijch—the proximity of an individual with the divine "undermines any stable distinction between male and female and . . . the association of masculinity with the divine and of femininity with the human."[37] But we can also relate this wonderful and sublime exposition of love as it appears within the Tantric way of the couple in union, appearing purely within an encounter, lacking any sign of permanence or nihility.

As we are always searching for proximity and touch, any encounter between two human beings—as will be revealed later—is a meeting and intimacy of the two in promise of a union of two still-mysteriously entangled lives. Upon our meetings and encounters, especially when we are sharing the spaces of our sexuate identities, we are exchanging our energies (tinctures of being), but also hopes, fears, and memories that we inherited from our predecessors. The ultimate couple as represented both in Tantric as well as Christian contexts is thus the highest symbol of this meta humanly and divinely love: a bond of twoness sealed by an embrace and enthroned beyond any conceptual, sexual, or ontological dichotomies and hindrances—in this view, any loving couple is the ultimate couple.

The Shell of Intimacy

> A lip breath to another breath, an eye to an eye
>
> —Niko Grafenauer, *Dihindih*[38]

What is the logic of the loving couple then? What longing and intertwining of the two is implied in the conspiracy of the encounter, the oneness—as Binswanger would argue—as a primordial form or "we" (the dualis mode)? Toward what ontological layer gestures *stillness* of the peak moment of such an encounter—as exemplified in Buddhist, Christian, and Binswanger's elaborations on love when two carnalities meet in the embrace and kiss, and, for this infinitesimally small moment of time, hold their breaths in expectation of a coming miracle of love? Love indwells the mysterious silence of this moment. In the breath-upholding moment of the dualis, we become one and, as in Mechtilde's encounter, the *blessed stillness comes over us* ("atemlose Stille" in Binswanger[39]) and envelops us into a delicate cocoon of twoness: a replica, as it were, of the primordial wombing-forth or emanating of love from the First Breath.

We wish to delve further into the carnal logic of loving encounter. The modalities of meeting with the other that we have encountered in the first part of this postlude have given us theologico-mystical and related carnal-energetic dimensions of the forms of encounters. Now, we wish to address the intimacy of this encounter: as a horizon of love, now emanating from the meeting of two carnal and sensible subjectivities. *The Way of Love* by Irigaray is without doubt the most elaborate meditation on this intimacy;[40] it is our opinion that, in the chapter "Wandering to the Source of the Intimate," we can find the most elaborate presentation of the logic of between-two as related to our questioning of loving encounter. This chapter is dedicated to speech "in order to uncover still mute domains of Being."[41] Through this work, Irigaray aims to look at the modalities of one being meeting with the other: gestures that need to be invented to fulfill the promise of a meeting—and of a new and still unknown domain of our cobeing. Here, a divine sphere enters this meeting; for Irigaray, it is "in a new listening to oneself and to the other that they [i.e., new words of an encounter] will be discovered, pronounced."[42] And it is here that a new horizon for this meeting is required—as another revelation of the divine:

> And it is not certain that old gods or goddesses could serve us here as guides. We are perhaps confronted with the unveiling of another relation with the divine than the one that we already know, a divine not only living with humans but in them, and to be greeted and listened to between us. . . . Sky and gods, in what is most divine in them, are related to breathing and, through the breath, they can communicate with the earth and mortals, dwell in them and among them.[43]

This revelation of the divine is presented by Mayra Rivera in her beautiful essay on the theology of relational transcendence. In this essay, Rivera explores "the interpenetration of transcendence in the flesh and between persons as well as its broader cosmic dimensions, where transcendence appears as erotic cosmological incarnation."[44] Rivera rightly asserts that a Levinasian face-to-face encounter needs a theologico-ethical extension into the sexual or erotic body-to-body (skin-to-skin) encounter. Working with Irigarayan horizontal transcendence, Rivera affirms that an erotic encounter "demands an imaginary that can accommodate bodily transcendence—as bodies in touch and *within each other*."[45] Within her imaginary of the sexual encounter, there is a need for a dynamic interval, a space between two bodies, that can safeguard and protect the two of the dualis. Rivera posits the following question here: "May we imagine God as the living and dynamic envelope that links us while protecting the space between us? An envelope that subtends the 'space' of difference and opens creatures to a relational infinity that is transformed as a result of the relations across difference?"[46]

Now, although Irigaray does not acknowledge this explicitly in her works, a key predecessor of hers in this way of love *as a horizontally divinely encounter* is, without doubt, Ludwig Feuerbach. Feuerbach was often regarded as a proponent of a materialist philosophy of religion, and, from a theological point of view, his thought was simply regarded as atheist. As a solitary thinker in the age of giants such as Hegel, Feuerbach was not willing to follow vertical theological modes of revelation and related ontological schemes. The anthropological core of religion in Feuerbach was thus negatively judged and dismissed. But, if we listen to the most sensitive and most elementally infused passages from his works, we already hear Irigaray: for Feuerbach, the searching for a divine means that God now is *not only living with humans but in them, and is to be greeted and listened to between us:* "Whatever is God to a man, that is his heart and soul; and conversely, God is the manifested inward nature, the expressed self of man—religion the solemn unveiling of a man's hidden treasures the revelation of his intimate thoughts, the open confession of his love-secrets."[47]

God reveals in the intimacy of our being and its secrets—of being, which, as Feuerbach has shown, is always already intersubjective, dialectical, and relational. And it is this mysterious bond of love (love as energy) that acts between us when the self is limited through its inherent sense of relationality and dependence. "Only in feeling and love has the demonstrative *this*—this person, this thing, that is, the particular—absolute value; only then is the *finite infinite*. In this and this alone does the infinite depth, divinity and truth of love consist. . . . The *true* dialectic is not a *monologue of the solitary thinker with himself.* It is a *dialogue between 'I' and 'Thou.'*"[48] Love is the mystery of transforming the finite into the infinite; my own self, first encapsulated in its own boundaries, opens itself toward Nature, as its real and inherent elemental (and, as we will see, energetic) core. Two beings meet in an intimacy of the encounter.

Feuerbach bases his entire philosophy of sensibility on the elements of Nature, among them preeminently on water and air (thus his entire teaching was called by him as "pneumatic water therapy"; *pneumatische Wasserheilkunde*[49]). To these elements he adjoins the human being as an element of Nature, along with the organs or body parts (eyes, head, heart, stomach, sexual organ), where, in the preeminent position (as the fundamental organ of perception), appears none other than the *skin*: ethically, skin can thus be regarded as an organ of touch, embrace, hug, and various carnal encounters, including sexuality. The philosophy of sensibility thus begins in the body as it is enveloped by porous skin—and for Feuerbach, the body is fully transparent and radiates through skin. As related to sexual encounter and breath-kiss from our previous elaborations, skin now represents the threshold of our incarnated self, a shell of our carnal being. Skin is the bodily intention and limit of our subjectivity toward the human and divine other, or with Feuerbach:

> Through the body, the Self is not the Self, but rather an object. Being-in-the-body means being-in-the-world. So many senses—so many pores. The self is nothing other than the *porous self*. . . . However, the most essential, original, inevitable contradiction associated with the Self is the Body, the Flesh, the conflict between the Spirit and the Flesh, which is, my gentlemen, the highest principium metaphysicum, nothing less than the secret of Creation, the foundation of the World. Yes, the Flesh, or if you prefer, the Body, does not have only a natural-historical or empirico-psychological, but also an essentially speculative and metaphysical meaning.[50]

A human being is a creature of nature, but divinity is now also thought of in these terms by Feuerbach: God is nothing but Nature. From this perspective, in a radicalized manner and as related to the divine person of Jesus Christ, "the Incarnation was a tear of the divine compassion, and it was only the visible advent of a Being having human feelings, and therefore essentially human."[51] For Feuerbach, therefore, human and divine realms are closely connected as they both can be understood as nature: "The Divine Being which is revealed in Nature, is nothing but Nature herself."[52] In this relation to nature, speculation is replaced by sensitivity—which is a gesture wholly contrary to Kant, Hegel, or speculative theology. Intersubjectivity as relationality is only conceivable through this newly acquired sensitivity, which is grounded in the elemental sources of nature—seen as water, air, earth, food, and light. The sense perception (skin) is now literally "the organ of the Divine and True Being."[53] Finally, in § 60 of *Principles of Philosophy of the Future*, for Feuerbach our intersubjective being is defined as follows: "Solitude means being *finite and limited,* community means being *free and infinite. For himself* alone, man is just man (in the ordinary sense); but *man with man*—the unity of 'I' and "You'—that is *God*."[54]

Will we be finally willing to greet and host this God among ourselves—in an encounter and intimacy of this Dualis?

Dualis—a Quantum Encounter?

It is with the help of nature that we can seek love. But we now need to recall what Whitehead describes about the energy of this nature when he contends that *all flow of energy obeys quantum conditions*. Earlier in this book, in our chapter on *Interstellar*, we have seen that analogously to the "mysterious" or scientifically still-undisclosed relationality of brane and bulk (and its hypothetical "beings" in each category), the same relationality appears between two temporal moments. We have affirmed that, under quantum conditions, our time must be related in a yet unknown manner to the temporality of a "God," who, as it were, interferes with our "ordinary" worlds through the effects that we have learned to understand as "miracles" (such as a meeting event, love, or telepathy). We have also assumed that—in an analogous manner—it might now be so that God exists as a supreme bulk being: if He (Jesus) does, and if it somehow (mysteriously) *passes* through our worlds, we could be affected by this "gravity" in ways we do not yet know to apprehend or describe. The basis for this conjecture is the following hypothesis:

> It's a reasonable, half-educated guess that, if bulk forces and fields and particles do exist, we will never be able to feel them or see them. When a bulk being passes through our brane, we will not see the stuff of which the being is made. The being's cross sections will be transparent. . . . On the other hand, we *will* feel and see the being's gravity and its warping of space and time. For example, a hyperspherical bulk being appears in my stomach and has a strong enough gravitational pull, my stomach may begin to cramp as my muscles tighten, trying to resist getting sucked to the center of the being's spherical cross section.[55]

But is this not a bit of an unpolished explanation of what actually happens when one is attracted by someone's *gravitational pull* when being in love? Let us now suppose, with Feuerbach, that we are actually nothing other than the *porous* self, a carnal being, enveloped by skin—upon feeling, thinking, or meeting a person that we love, our skin is excited as it suddenly begins to shiver. The transcendence of the other encompasses me—it subtly tackles my porous self as in an annunciation of a loving encounter in which a couple will be formed. The body feels the excitement and vibrates itself; this gravitational pull in my stomach, as it were, now becomes what is known as a phenomenon of *butterflies in one's stomach*: a sign of the presence of love in someone, now taken literally. Translated into the language of quantum physics we may describe this excitement of a loving encounter as an attraction (or excitation), closely related to the "subtle pressure that the quantum vacuum exerts on each."[56]

The void—or perhaps the *breath of love*? As we have already seen in our previous elaborations on telepathic coupling, the quantum vacuum and the energy behind does not exert an arbitrary pressure upon us. The entrance of the other into me is an effect of the energy of love, of a higher and more sublime manifestation of gravity. We may now also suppose that, when we become excited by the pull of another kind (which we only sense and cannot explain for now yet), then, analogously to the still unexplained and mysterious *dark matter*, we may call the effect feeling of love in one's stomach as a mysterious—yet sensible—presence of *dark love* in my body. For Arthur Schopenhauer, the bodily feeling when we have wronged someone appears as *felt* pain in our inside/womb (stomach) as a result of our bad conscience; it is this inner feeling that inaugurates the *correspondence* between beings through the *nexus*, called "Will," which is related to the phenomenon of telepathy. The entanglement *with-in* telepathy can be further understood as a mode of still-undisclosed synchronicity within the logic of the psyche itself—a disclosure of the correspondence in which the *breath of (dark) love* would be the connecting nexus. This unexplained and subtle breath-energy will now finally reveal as the cosmic bond: a stillness of the divine field from which an intimacy of the two emanates. A breath-energy weaving the cocoon of love.[57]

Our entangled lives must somehow subsist on one common *resonating* field and—in those rare but enhanced moments of the emanating matrix of love—we, as human beings, are capable of connecting to a kind of divine or cosmic matrix in ways we cannot foresee or explain rationally. For Irigaray, "[a]ir is the medium of our natural and spiritual life, of our relation to ourselves, to speaking, to the other. And this medium imperceptibly crosses the limits of different worlds or universes, sometimes giving the illusion of a gained intimacy while we are only sharing a common element."[58] The loving encounter subsists on this matrix, and it mysteriously and unexplainably incarnates into a simultaneous and mutual telepathic understanding, loving speech, proximity of the touch, and sharing of fragrances—all encapsulated into a mindfulness of love, an intimacy of the couple, confined by respect and dignity: the transcendence of love. With this breath of love, God subtly transpires through ourselves—from within and from inside the heart, stomach, and so forth. God is an organ of Love, the sacrament of intersubjectivity.

Two bodies transpire through each other, like two spectral selves touching invisibly through the air. Love inhabits our bodies: it enters and ignites the desire. . . . I love you and I love the invisible and visible scars and wounds in you. The radiance of your delicate being has now conspired with my body and our lips are joined in a breath-kiss. You are the Chosen One. You are divine. Dualis is the highest bliss.

elemental resonance

Notes

Introduction

1. David Abram, *The Spell of the Sensuous: Perception and Language in a More-Than-Human World* (New York: Vintage Books, 1997), 156.

2. Among the key books that have a particular strong bearing on the post-Christianity is without doubt Gianni Vattimo's *After Christianity*, trans. Luka D'Isanto (New York: Columbia University Press, 2002), especially chap. 2 "The Teachings of Joachim of Fiore."

3. In the German context, we find the term "post-Christianity" already in Franz von Baader's essay "Sätze aus der erotischen Philosophie" from 1828: "zeigt sich in den vorchristlichen, in den christlichen und in unserem zum Teil nachchristlichen Zeiten derselbe unverkennbare Unterschied." Cited from Franz von Baader, *Erotische Philosophie*, ed. von Gerd-Klaus Kaltenbrunner (Frankfurt am Main: Insel Verlag, 1991), 135. In his writings, Von Baader also mentions the three eras ("die drei Weltepochen," 133) that will be important for our discussion of the post-Christianity. For our German thinker, the third epoch actually indicates the last emanation of God into humanity as a sign of a coming and final natural eschatology of which the loving couple (see this book's postlude "God in Dualis") will be the highest manifestation.

4. See Ludwig Feuerbach, *Kritiken und Abhandlungen*, vol, 3 (Frankfurt am Main: Suhrkamp, 1975), 1: "die plastische Persönlichkeit ist nur Christus."

5. Giorgio Agamben, *The Coming Community*, trans. Michael Hardt (Minneapolis: University of Minnesota Press, 2009), 52.

Prologue

1. Niko Grafenauer, *Dihindih* (Ljubljana: Mladinska knjiga, 2000), 125. This collection of poems by one of the greatest living Slovenian poets is titled "dihindih," which translates as "breathandbreath." I thank Ana Jelnikar for the translation.

2. John D. Caputo, *Cross and Cosmos: A Theology of Difficult Glory* (Bloomington: Indiana University Press, 2019), 183. In this book, Caputo addresses another problem of the so-called cosmic mystery, namely that from what we know from science today, "the entire universe is doomed by virtue of its accelerating expansion. . . . the bad news is that all things are headed for extinction." For Caputo this view opens a perspective of cosmic nihilism, indeed "a cosmological Good Friday" (185).

3. See Alexandra Pleshoyano, "Etty Hillesum: For God and with God," *The Way* 44, no. 1 (January 2005): 14. https://www.theway.org.uk/back/441Pleshoyano.pdf.

4. Maurice Merleau-Ponty, *Nature: Course Notes from the Collège de France*, trans. Robert Vallier (Evanston, IL: Northwestern University Press, 1995), 38.

5. See Vattimo, *After Christianity*, 26: "Joachim of Fiore offers us a model for living postmodern religious experience on the basis of the specific content of his teaching on the age of spirit and of his general theological tendency to understand salvation history as the story of the transformation in which the Scripture's meaning is spiritualized."

6. Luce Irigaray, *Key Writings* (New York: Continuum, 2004), 165–70 (chap. "The Age of the Breath").

7. Irigaray, *Key Writings*, 167–68.

8. See Joel P. Brereton and Stephanie W. Jamison, *The Rigveda: A Guide* (Oxford: Oxford University Press, 2020), 120–21. See on this also Patrick Olivelle, *Upaniṣads* (Oxford: Oxford University Press, 1996), liii–liv.

9. Brereton and Jamison, *The Rigveda: A Guide*, 125. The most important Vedic connections were between Sun and the eye, cosmic Wind and breath, and Moon and mind. Ultimately, the highest correspondence or equation was between Brahman (as an expression of truth and reality) and Ātman (as the essential self), paving the way toward later major developments in Indian philosophical and theological traditions.

10. *The Rigveda: The Earliest Religious Poetry of India*, vol. 3, trans. Stephanie W. Jamison and Joel P. Brereton (Oxford: Oxford University Press, 2014), 1608–9. All references to the hymn are from this translation.

11. Catherine Keller, *Face of the Deep: A Theology of Becoming* (London: Routledge, 2007), 10.

12. *The Holy Bible—New Revised Standard Version* (Nashville, TN: Thomas Nelson Publishers, 1990).

13. Keller, *Face of the Deep*, 22; the quotes are from Ivone Gebara's *Longing for Running Water: Ecofeminism and Liberation*, trans. David Mollineaux (Minneapolis: Fortress Press, 1999), 47.

14. Keller, *Face of the Deep*, 22.

15. Keller, *Face of the Deep*, 22, 34.

16. Jason Wirth, *The Conspiracy of Life: Meditations on Schelling and His Time* (Albany: State University of New York Press, 2003), 2.

17. Friedrich Wilhelm Joseph Schelling, *Philosophical Inquiries into the Nature of Human Freedom*, trans. J. Gutman (La Salle, IL: Open Court, 1989), 88–89. On

more on this, see Lennart Škof, *Antigone's Sisters: On the Matrix of Love* (Albany: State University of New York Press, 2021), chap. 4.

18. The word for (non-)being is "(a)sát," which is etymologically related to Gr. "to eón" and originates from the Indo-European "*$h_1$sent-,$" which comes from the root "*$h_1$es-" (see also the related Lat. "essens" and "essentia"). Translation of the verse was modified.

19. Keller, *Face of the Deep*, 12. In full the passage reads: "If we discern a third space of beginning, neither pure origin nor nihilist flux—its difference translated into another interstitial space: that between the self-presence of a changeless Being who somehow suddenly (back then) created; and the pure Nonbeing out of which that creation was summoned, and toward which its fluency falls. That alternative milieu, neither being nor nonbeing, will signify the site of becoming as *genesis*: the topos of the Deep."

20. The translation was modified here: the genitive absolute structure in the 4a verse namely allows for both interpretations and we stand with the interpreters who affirm the priority of desire (*kāma*; love) over thought (*manas*)—see, for example, Ralph T. H. Griffith, *The Hymns of the Ṛgveda* (Delhi: Motilal Banarsidass, 1995), 633 (cf. also the cosmogonical role of *éros* in Hesiodus).

21. Schelling, *Philosophical Inquiries into the Nature of Human Freedom*, 79.

22. In a passage on *The Holy Trinity Icon* painted in 1411 by Andrei Rublev, Richard Kearney argues that the empty chalice appearing in the center of the icon actually represents the "womb-heart" of Mary itself as *khora*. See Richard Kearney, *Anatheism: Returning to God after God* (New York: Columbia University Press, 2010), 25: "And this empty receptacle at the core of the circle is, arguably, none other than the womb-heart of Mary itself (*khora*)." According to Kearney, *khora* also appears as an empty center, around which the persons of the Trinity are moving endlessly in the movement of *perichoresis*. More on this in part II of this book.

23. See *Cosmology, Ecology, and The Energy of God*, ed. Donna Bowman and Clayton Crockett (New York: Fordham University Press, 2012): "As for dark energy . . . the term doesn't mean nothing. It might not be dark. It might not be energy. The whole name is a placeholder for the description that there's something funny that was discovered twelve years ago now that we don't understand" (29).

24. *The Rigveda*, 1609.

25. Our addition. Patrick Burke, "Creativity and Unconscious in Merleau-Ponty and Schelling," in *Schelling Now: Contemporary Readings*, ed. Jason M. Wirth (Bloomington: Indiana University Press, 2005), 196.

26. Burke, "Creativity and Unconscious in Merleau-Ponty and Schelling," 198.

27. Jacob Denz, "Rigorous Mediacy: Addressing Mother in Hölderlin's 'Am Quell der Donau,' 'Die Wanderung,' and 'An die Madonna,'" *MLN* 130, no. 3 (April 2015): 554–79.

28. Immanuel Kant, *Critique of Judgement*, trans. P. Guyer and E. Matthews (Cambridge: Cambridge University Press, 2000), 288. Cf. original: "Hier steht es nun dem Archäologen der Natur frei, aus den übriggebliebenen Spuren ihrer ältesten

Revolutionen, nach allem ihm bekannten oder gemutmaßten Mechanism derselben, jene große Familie von Geschöpfen (den so *müßte* man sie sich vorstellen, wenn die genannte durchgänzig zusammengehende Verwandtschaft einen Grund haben soll) entspringen zu lassen. Es kann den Mutterschoß der Erde, die eben aus ihrem chaotischen Zustande herausging (gleichsam als ein großes Tier), anfänglich Geschöpfe von minder-zweckmäßiger Form, diese wiederum andere, welche angemessener ihrem Zeugungsplatze und ihrem Verhältnisse unter einander sich ausbildeten, gebären lassen; bis diese Gebärmutter selbst, erstarrt, sich verknöchert, ihre Geburten auf bestimmte fernhin nicht ausartende Spezies eingeschränkt hätte, und die Mannigfaltigkeit so bliebe, wie sie am Ende der Operation jener fruchtbaren Bildungskraft ausgefallen war." See *Kritik der Urteilskraft*, Werkausgabe, Band X, ed. von Wilhelm Weischedel (Frankfurt am Main: Suhrkamp: 1996), 374–75 (§ 80).

29. Denz, "Rigorous Mediacy," 557.

30. Friedrich Hölderlin, *Poems and Fragments*, trans. Michael Hamburger (London: Anvil Press Poetry, 2005), 617.

31. Burke, "Creativity and Unconscious in Merleau-Ponty and Schelling," 196.

32. Hölderlin, *Poems and Fragments*, 617.

33. Hölderlin, *Poems and Fragments*, 621.

34. Denz, "Rigorous Mediacy," 578. Or, with Holderlin: "Do / Not perplex the nurse / Who gives the birth to day" ("To the Virgin Mary," *Poems and Fragments*, 623).

35. Hölderlin, *Poems and Fragments*, 697 ("Greece," second version). In German the verses read as follows: "Gott an hat ein Gewand. / Und Erkenntnissen verberget sich sein Angesicht / Und deket die Lüfte mit Kunst. / Und Luft und Zeit dekt."

36. Martin Heidegger, *Elucidations of Hölderlin's Poetry*, trans. K. Hoeller (New York: Humanity Books, 2000), 188. On this plane, Heidegger adds: "In-finite means that the ends and the sides, the regions of the relation, do not stand by themselves cut-off and one-sidedly; rather, freed of onesidedness and finitude, they belong in-finitely to one another in the relation which 'thoroughly' holds them together from its center" (188).

37. For the poem we are using, https://hopkinspoetry.com/poem/the-blessed-virgin/.

38. Pierre Teilhard de Chardin, *The Future of Man*, trans. Norman Denny (New York: Image Books, 1964), 307.

39. Pierre Teilhard de Chardin, "The Eternal Feminine," in *Writings in Time of War*, trans. René Hague (New York: Harper and Row, 1968), 192, 202.

40. John O'Donnell, "The Trinitarian Panentheism of Sergej Bulgakov," *Gregorianum* 76, no. 1 (1995): 32–33. For more on Russian Sophiology and Mary, see the chapter "Sophia" in Škof, *Antigone's Sisters*, 64–69.

41. Christopher Pramuk, *At Play in Creation: Merton's Awakening to the Feminine Divine* (Collegeville, MI: Liturgical Press, 2015), 32.

42. Keller, *Face of the Deep*, 22.

43. See Judith Simmer-Brown, *Dakini's Warm Breath: The Feminine Principle in Tibetan Buddhism* (Boulder, CO: Shambala, 2002), 68.

44. Simmer-Brown, *Dakini's Warm Breath*, 92.

45. "The ḍākinī in her most profound level of meaning is beyond form, gender and expression, but 'she' gives rise to bountiful forms and expressions, which sometimes take the female gender as a way to express 'her' essence" (Simmer-Brown, *Dakini's Warm Breath*, 30).

46. Keller, *Face of the Deep*, 34.

47. Simmer-Brown, *Dakini's Warm Breath*, 73, 102, and 112.

48. See our chapter on telepathy, where we cite the following excerpt from Stephen H. Webb's *Mormon Christianity*: "The Higgs field permeates all of space, and thus space is not really empty, although the Higgs field represents the lowest state of energy in the universe, and thus space is as empty as you can get. . . . The Higgs field, which is really a form of quantum energy, is more basic than the Higgs boson, so perhaps it should be called 'God's field,' since the image of a divinely saturated matrix more accurately conveys the way in which everything that exists does so because of its relationship to something else." Stephen H. Webb, *Mormon Christianity* (Oxford: Oxford University Press, 2013), 77–78.

49. Simmer-Brown, *Dakini's Warm Breath*, 290.

50. Simmer-Brown, *Dakini's Warm Breath*, 291.

51. Cited from B. E. Whalen, *Dominion of God: Christendom and Apocalypse in the Middle Ages* (Cambridge: Harvard University Press, 2009), 100. The passage is from Joachim of Fiore's *Liber de concordia novi et veteris testamenti*. "Spiritual" must here necessarily be understood in its etymological meaning as related to breath/ing (from Proto-Indo-European [s]peys- ("to blow, breathe").

Chapter 1

1. France Bevk, *Umirajoči bog Triglav: Zgodovinska povest* (Kobarid: Turistično društvo; Notranje Gorice: Društvo Slovenski staroverci, 2018), 5. I am thankful to Andrej Pleterski and Cirila Toplak for all their comments on my work on the Slovenian Indigenous religion of Staroverstvo. We keep this excerpt in its original tone, although the gender pronouns could of course be changed to "woman," "she," "her," etc.

2. Vine Deloria Jr. and Daniel Wildcat, *Power and Place: Indian Education in America* (Golden, CO: American Indian Graduate Center and Fulcrum Resources, 2001), 12.

3. Caputo, *Cross and Cosmos*, 191.

4. In "The Entangled Cosmos: An Experiment in Physical Theopoetics," *Journal of Cosmology* 20 (September 2012): 8648–66, Catherine Keller explains the phenomenon of entanglement of cosmos as follows: "The maximum has and

yet might be called 'God.' But the physics of entanglement will not witness to the existence of a classical deity. It may however offer material evidence of a universe so mysteriously entangled as to escape the rival classicisms that pit science and theology against each other in the first place. What I want to share today belongs to the wider and polydoxical investigation of what I call 'apophatic entanglement.'" Thus, all phenomena in nature are ontologically entangled.

5. Staroverstvo as used in this chapter is an exonym—namely, the members of this tradition have referred to themselves for the most of the time simply with the designations "us" and "ours." As "Old Faith" was also often derogatorily employed toward them by the members of the Catholic Church, in this chapter we will rather refer to their believers as "Nature Worshippers." See on this in Cirila Toplak, "Družbeno-politični vidiki zahodnoslovenske naravoverske skupnosti" [Sociopolitical aspects of western Slovenian nature worshippers' community], in *Staroverstvo v Sloveniji med religijo in znanostjo* [The Old Faith between religion and science], edited by Saša Babič and Mateja Belak, *Studia mythologica Slavica*, Supplementa 17 (Ljubljana: Založba ZRC, 2022), 53–54.

6. For an official statement on this, see the United Nations Declaration on the Rights of Indigenous Peoples, adopted by the General Assembly on September 13, 2007.

7. John Grim, "Indigenous Lifeways and Knowing of the World," in *The Oxford Handbook of Religion and Science*, ed. Philip Clayton and Zachary Simpson (Oxford: Oxford University Press, 2006), 87–88. Cf. here *Maori Philosophy* by Georgina Tuari Stewart (London: Bloomsbury, 2021), 3, which defines the fundamental characteristics of "Māori philosophy" as follows: "Past events do not lose their significance, and ancestors can collapse the space-time continuum to be co-present with their descendants" and "knowledge in Māori terms is not restricted to the physical senses, but includes knowledge obtained through intuition and dreams."

8. Pavel Medvešček-Klančar was from the Posočje region of Slovenia (i.e., the area of the Soča River Valley in western Slovenia). Apart from working as a teacher, writer, and graphic designer, Medvešček was also one of the most devoted collectors of Slovenian oral folk tradition. For over thirty years, he has been collecting oral testimonies from numerous informants. In this chapter, we refer to the oral testimonies of Janez Strgar, his main and most important source and an authority of the tradition (and also Jože Pangerc, Jože Blažev, Toni Javor, Valentin Šmončev, and Valentin Hvalica). Cirila Toplak writes about Medvešček's ethnographic work as presented in his seminal book from 2015, *Iz nevidne strani neba: Razkrite skrivnosti staroverstva* [From the invisible side of the sky: Revealed secrets of the old belief] (Ljubljana: ZRC SAZU, 2015) as follows: "On almost 600 pages, Pavel Medvešček revealed exclusive and well documented ethnographic records, mainly composed of interviews conducted with residents of remote hilly areas of Western Slovenia in the period from 1950 to 1978. The contents of these interviews could not be revealed earlier due to the oath of secrecy required of Pavel Medvešček by his interviewees after

they had confided in him and partially co-opted him into their secret community." About the tradition, Toplak also explains: "When discovered by Pavel Medvešček in mid-20th century, the Nature Worshippers' community had been reduced to a few dozen elderly single male members, called uncles. According to their oral tradition, however, prior to the First World War at least several hundred people all together may still have been part of it in the Soča River valley. The existence of the community was concealed due to constant persecution perpetrated by the clergy and intolerant members of the Catholic majority. It was this utmost secrecy and geographic isolation in very remote subalpine and Dinaric areas of Western Slovenia as well as efficient leadership and organised defence against outer threats that decisively contributed to the survival of the community which, again according to their tradition, lasted centuries" (Cirila Toplak, "Tales in Social Practices of Nature Worshippers of Western Slovenia," *Acta histriae* 30, no. 3 [2022], 628). For more on the Nature Worshippers' community and tradition, see Toplak's insightful paper.

9. Pavel Medvešček-Klančar, *Iz nevidne strani neba: Razkrite skrivnosti staroverstva* [From the invisible side of the sky: Revealed secrets of the old belief] (Ljubljana: ZRC SAZU, 2015). This invaluable work was edited by Andrej Pleterski in Mateja Belak, with a scientific-critical study contributed by Andrej Pleterski. The volume was published in the collection Studia mythologica Slavica—Supplementa. In 2012, a testimony by Boris Čok titled *V siju mesečine: Ustno izročilo Lokve, Prelož in bližnje okolice* [In the glow of the moon: Oral heritage of the villages of Lokev, Prelože and the surrounding areas] (Ljubljana: ZRC SAZU, 2012) was published in the same collection, describing the rich lore of the last representatives of Slovenian Nature Worshippers from the Kras region, another extraordinarily valuable cultural document about Slovenian Indigenous religion (Kras is a limestone borderline plateau region in southwestern Slovenia).

10. For a reconstruction of "African philosophy" (here in the broader sense of a set of mythological, religious, philosophical, and ethnographic traditions) as ethnophilosophy, see Henry Odera Oruka, *Sage Philosophy: Indigenous Thinkers and Modern Debate on African Philosophy* (Leiden: Brill, 1990) and his essay "Four Trends in Current African Philosophy," in *The African Philosophy Reader*, ed. P. H. Coetzee and A. P. J. Roux (London: Routledge, 2003), 120–36. More on this in Lenart Škof, "Do Rta dobrega upanja in nazaj: Tri vprašanja o afriški filozofiji," *Filozofski vestnik* 26, no. 3 (2005): 171–85, which, together with the related thematic block about African philosophy, raises questions about the relationship between the oral and written traditions, about relationships between the ethnographically centered and rationalizing (or analytical) currents in the studies of world traditions, and, ultimately, about the long-standing monocultural trend in the history of both Western philosophy and Christian theology.

11. David Abram, "The Commonwealth of Breath," in *Atmospheres of Breathing*, ed. Lenart Škof and Petri Berndtson (New York: State University of New York Press, 2018), 269.

12. Vrhovčev Avguštin, 1962, as quoted in Medvešček-Klančar, *Iz nevidne strani neba*, 365 (emphasis added).

13. See chapter 6 titled "Verovanje host v sklopu staroverstva na Slovenskem in verovanja starih Slovanov" [The belief of "hoste" in the context of Old Belief in Slovenia and the belief of the ancient Slavs] by Andrej Pleterski, in *Staroverstvo v Sloveniji med religijo in znanostjo*, ed. S. Babič and M. Belak, Studia mythologica Slavia, Supplementum 17 (Ljubljana: Založba ZRC, 2022), 117. For the hypothesis by Nikolai Mikhailov, see *Zgodovina slovanske mitologije v XX. stoletju* [The history of Slovenian mythology in the 20th century] (Ljubljana: ZRC SAZU, 2021), 182. See in this regard also Andrej Pleterski, *Kulturni genom: Prostor in njegovi ideogrami mitične zgodbe* [The cultural genome: Space and its ideograms of the mythical story] (Ljubljana: ZRC SAZU, 2014), 76–85.

14. The question whether it could be argued for the understanding of the indigeneity of Slovenian Nature Worshippers shall remain open here, although Staroverstvo as a cultural, ethnic, and religious tradition would hardly be able to pertain to its original scope: due to the sociopolitical, economic, and environmental causes, the meritocratic succession (as based on their political and religious leaders—called *dehnars*) was critically interrupted already after the World War II and at least since the '80s or '90s Slovenian Nature Worshippers could be regarded as historical (I would still restrain from calling this tradition as extinct as we cannot know for certain whether some rites were still being preserved by the remaining members in secrecy until now). As argued by Toplak: "During the 20th century, the Nature Worshippers' community gradually disintegrated due to environmental destruction and human loss, especially that of their leaders dehnars, caused by both World Wars. Modernization processes (infrastructure construction, industrialization, and urbanization) severed the inter-generational ties and depopulated remote rural areas" (Toplak, "Tales in Social Practices of Nature Worshippers of Western Slovenia," 631). As Medvešček (who unfortunately passed away in 2020) was admitted to the tradition (still, he was not a *dehnar*), he could then be regarded as (one of the) last Nature Worshipper(s). I thank Cirila Toplak for her clarifications of some of my conjectures.

15. Medvešček-Klančar, *Iz nevidne strani neba*, 15. On the basis of the exceptionally close connection of this religion with nature, Pleterski also refers to it with the equivalent term "Naturalism." In the conclusion to his introductory study he writes: "It is precisely this 'inner voice' with its deep ethics and infinite respect for nature and its balance that gives this book its incommensurable, unique and significant value, especially in this rampant globalized world that only cares about profit." Medvešček-Klančar, *Iz nevidne strani neba*, 31.

16. Cf. Čok, *V siju mesečine*, 12–13.

17. See Škof, *Antigone's Sisters*. The exceptions are some parts of Hinduism and Buddhism (particularly in the framework of Tantrism), the tradition of Sophia/Wisdom within the Judeo-Christian tradition, and, of course, the currents of contemporary

feminist theology. Another example where the feminine principle is also considered would definitely be philosophical Daoism in the context of Chinese tradition.

18. Jan Assmann, "Monotheismus und Kosmotheismus: Ägyptische Formen eines 'Denkens des Einen' und ihre europäische Rezeptionsgeschichte" (Heidelberg: Universitätsverlag Winter, 1993). This was a lecture given by Assmann on April 24, 1993.

19. Assmann, "Monotheismus und Kosmotheismus," 8.

20. For more on this, see the ninth brāhmaṇa of *Bṛhadāraṇyakopaniṣad* (BAU 3.9), in which Vidagdha Śākalya asks the wise Yājñavalkya how many gods there are in this world. Yājñavalkya first answers there are 3,303, then continues with thirty-three gods, six gods, three gods, two, one and a half, and, finally, one—which is Breath (*prāṇa*), also referred to as *bráhman* or *tyad*. These gods inhabit the elemental world of earth, fire/light/heat, water, breath/air, and, as we shall see, the ancient Indian Vedic and the Slovenian pre-Christian thoughts are quite close in this elemental conception of the world.

21. Assman rightly points to another important dimension when he states: "Es handelt sich bei dem Begriff 'Monotheismus' ja auch lediglich um eine neuzeitliche Etikettierung und keineswegs um eine antike, quellensprachliche Prägung" (12). The term "monotheism" first appeared in 1680 (and polytheism in 1630); the British philosopher and theologian Henry More (1614–1687) introduced this term not as an expression to be used against the religions of the New World, but rather to separate his own position from the Unitarian position within Christianity. Particularly in the nineteenth century, this concept, together with that of polytheism, was used to classify religions into more or less developed, more or less original, and so forth. For more about the differences in the language of violence within polytheisms and Jewish monotheism dating to the period of Josiah's religious reform described in 2 Ki, see Jan Assmann, *Totale Religion: Ursprünge und Formen puritanischer Verschärfung* (Vienna: Picus Verlag, 2016). For so-termed Slavic monotheism, see Mikhailov, *Zgodovina slovanske mitologije*, 22 and 133. This book seeks to distance itself as much as possible from any trend or mode of totality within the fields of religious studies and theology. See on this a study by Stathis Gourgouris, *The Perils of the One* (New York: Columbia University Press, 2019); see the chapter "Every Religion Is Idolatry." Gourgouris addresses and analyzes the historical and contemporary narratives of what since Carl Schmitt is known as "political theology."

22. Wilhelm Schmidt, *The Origin and Growth of Religion: Facts and Theories*, trans. H. J. Rose (London: Methuen & Co., 1935; repr., Proctorville, OH: Wythe-North Publishing, 2014). For more about his life and work, see Hans Waldenfels, "Wilhelm Schmidt," in Axel Michaels, ed., *Klassiker der Religionswissenschaft: Von Friedrich Schleiermacher bis Mircea Eliade* (Munich: C. H. Beck, 1997). At the beginning of his treatise, Waldenfels identifies Schmidt as an ethnologist and religious studies expert, and the inclusion of the latter among key classics of religious studies in Michaels's exceptional volume is logical and befitting. After completing

his theological studies, Schmidt devoted himself to Oriental (as they were called at the time) and Islamic studies. He developed an interest in cultures outside the so-called standard Western World–Asia cultural axis when his order engaged in a mission in Papua New Guinea. Although he did not work as a proper ethnologist (in the field), his missionary work was strongly informed by the empirical data of the ethnological and religious studies of the time, and he considered a comparison between languages to be very important as well. What critically distinguished Schmidt, as Waldenfels also notes, was that he may have been the first theologian ever to deprecate the humiliation of the reputedly "uncivilised cultures" in relation to Christianity, thereby shifting these cultures from the utter periphery toward the center of religious studies and early theology of religion (borrowing here from the theological jargon of W. C. Smith). In conclusion, Waldenfels raises the key point that in the late nineteenth and early twentieth centuries it was not at all self-evident to adopt the point of view of the "other" or "foreign" (aside from relations to the Indian and Chinese religions, which were already presented as such) and that Schmidt's attempt was thus an invaluable gesture of respect and appreciation of other cultures and religions *as partners* (Waldenfels, "Wilhelm Schmidt," 195).

23. In this book, the designations "god/dess," "supreme being," "(primal) force," and "nature" are equal but applied with regard to context and the various traditions.

24. A basis for a break with previous hypotheses on religion is Smith's belief in *a personal quality* intrinsic to all religious activity. His method involves, in a first phase, the accumulation of material (from textual materials to individual things that can be observed in the environment of each individual religion under study), and in a second phase, the essential reflection on the role that these data or facts have for *the people living in this faith*. An expression of this methodological credo is the dictate: "No statement involving persons is valid, I propose, unless theoretically its validity can be verified both by the persons involved and critical observers not involved" (*Wilfred Cantwell Smith: A Reader*, ed. Kenneth Cracknell [Oxford: Oneworld, 2001], 216). A third and final phase of research consists of understanding the meaning and importance of these facts, both in relation to the universal human situation and to the effort to find the truth, to which we are all committed.

25. Schmidt, *The Origin and Growth of Religion*, 188. For example, with regard to African religions he argues the same for the "religion of the Pygmy tribes" and their highest God. Quite interesting is, in terms of religious studies, the sequence of chapters in this part of Schmidt's book: (a) Indo-Europeans; (b) Amerindians; (c) Pygmy Peoples; (d) Semites (chapter 8, "The Progressive Recognition of the Primitive High God, during the Twentieth Century"). Among the examples related to Slavic cultures, Schmidt mentions the word "Bog" [God] and cites Perun as the chief Slavic god and Wolos (Veles) as his hypostasis (see 46 and 53).

26. Laurel C. Schneider, *Beyond Monotheism: A Theology of Multiplicity* (London: Routledge, 2008).

27. Schneider, *Beyond Monotheism*, ix.

28. Slovenian Natural Worshippers were teritorially organized in units called "hosta" (= forest).

29. See the testimony by Marija Rajceva (b. 1922) about Triglav, in Boris Čok, "Naš Triglav," *Studia mythologica Slavica* 23 (2020): 255–58: "His very name intimates that this god of ours had three heads, meaning three gods in one! The right head was the god Kres [Fire], who protected the sky and would punish people who treated nature badly by casting lightning bolts onto the earth! Wherever the bolt hit the ground, the god's flower, the iris, would spring up. This ancient god was the most feared one as his lightning bolts were unpredictable! The left head was the god Vilež, protector of the underworld, of the souls of the dead and the fairies, and of domestic animals in the upper world. He also watched over people, observed what they did during their lifetime, and when they sinned against nature and animals, he caused earthquakes. But wait till you hear this: the middle head, a little taller, was a female god, she [alternately] protected and harmed nature. During spring and summer time she was Živa [signifying alive, live, living], Kres's lover, but on the full moon in August she would turn into Mora [signifying death] and become Vilež's lover for the autumn and winter. See, and this is also how nature works! When there is thunder and lightning and fog rolls out from caves, the two male gods are fighting over power and the two goddesses over nature. One goddess does good, making the nature turn green and alive, hence her name. The other does ill, killing nature, and therefrom she gets her name, too. Our ancestors did not worship this other goddess, they hated her. This is how our ancestors saw and believed in this god, and some others too!" (256).

30. Pleterski, "Verovanje host," 135. There is no consensus, yet, among researchers of the Natural Worshippers concerning the origin of the name of this goddess. On the possibility of the androgynous first being see the concluding chapter of this book.

31. Deloria and Wildcat, *Power and Place*, 1.

32. Deloria and Wildcat, *Power and Place*, 5.

33. The term "spiritual" used in this book refers to the elemental presence of life energy in us, which, unlike the classical metaphysical and scientific views of "spirituality," is not understood as a Platonist-Cartesian antipode to the body, but quite the opposite, as a vital force (i.e., *spiritual matter*) that is in its nature connected to air, breath, and the related vital bodily energies of the (meso)cosmos, nature, and mankind. See Lenart Škof, *Breath of Proximity: Intersubjectivity, Ethics and Peace* (Dordrecht: Springer, 2015).

34. Catherine Keller, "Tingles of Matter, Tangles of Theology," in *Entangled Worlds: Religion, Science, and New Materialism*, ed. Catherine Keller and Mary-Jane Rubenstein (New York: Fordham University Press, 2017), 118–19.

An interesting analogy with regard to the mineral core and stones can be found in a work by Ernst Haeckel, a German zoologist and philosopher of biology. In his final work, titled *Kristallseelen: Studien über das anorganische Leben* (accessible in a

1917 edition by Pranava Books of New Delhi), Haeckel developed an idiosyncratic and at the time utterly uncomprehended theory of the "psyche" of minerals, stating the following: "Alle Substanz besitzt Leben, anorganische ebenso wie organische; alle Dinge sind beseelt, Kristalle so gut wie Organismen." (viii) Cf. also his penultimate work *Gott-Natur (Theophysis)* (Leipzig: Alfred Kröner Verlag, 1914), in which he put forth a monistic interpretation of God, that is, as expressing itself through all nature. Lamentably, it should also be pointed out that Haeckel, as an evolutionist, defended extremist eugenic and racist positions, thereby simultaneously and inherently refuting his own theory about the theological-ontological intertwinement of all living beings.

35. All page number references for the cited passages are from Medveščék-Klančar, *Iz nevidne strani neba*.

36. Jože Pangerc thus says that unlike "teachers and preachers, who punish children by making them kneel on hard grain for hours," their members do not subject their children to corporal punishment; they follow nature in this too, for animals never torture their young (Medveščék-Klančar, *Iz nevidne strani neba*, 463). This remarkable note reflects the respect for children, which has been absent throughout histories of philosophical thought and theology. On the other hand, the symptom of the Christian attitude toward children and of a lacking ontology of the child manifests in the uncountable instances of sexual abuse of children and adolescents in the Catholic Church.

37. Medveščék-Klančar, *Iz nevidne strani neba*, 23 (introduction by A. Pleterski). For the dragon motif, see Vladimir Yakovlevich Propp, *Zgodovinske korenine čarobne pravljice* [The historical roots of fairy-tales] (Ljubljana: ZRC SAZU: Inštitut za slovensko narodopisje, 2013), 191–246. Initially, Propp links the dragon motif to the elements—particularly fire and water. Later he also refers to ancient Babylonian tradition: "In the Babylonian creation myth it is said: 'When Tiamat opened her mouth to its full extent, he [Marduk] let in the Evil Wind [Imhullu] so that she close not her lips" (Propp, *Zgodovinske korenine čarobne pravljice*, 213).

38. In the words of W. C. Smith: "If Christians take seriously the revelation of God in Christ—if we really mean what we say when we affirm that his life, and his death on the cross, and his final triumph out of the very midst of self-sacrifice, embody the ultimate truth and power and glory of the universe—then two kinds of consequence follow, two orders of inference. On the moral level, there follows an imperative toward reconciliation, unity, harmony, and fellowship. At this level, all humanity is included: we strive to break down barriers, to bridge gulfs; *we recognize all people everywhere as neighbors, as friends, as loved of God as we are*. . . . On the other hand, there is another level, the intellectual, the order of ideas. . . . At this level, the doctrines that most Christians have traditionally derived have tended to affirm a Christian exclusivism, a separation between those who believe and those who do not, a division of humanity into a 'we' and a "they,' a gulf between Christendom and the rest of the world: a gulf profound, ultimate, cosmic" (W. C.

Smith, *Patterns of Faith around the World* [Oxford: Oneworld, 1998], 134; emphasis added).

39. Agamben, *The Coming Community*, 14–15. This refers to the passage 1 Cor 15:28: "But when all things have been placed under Christ's rule, then he himself, the Son, will place himself under God, who placed all things under him; and God will rule completely over all."

40. John D. Caputo, *The Insistence of God: A Theology of Perhaps* (Bloomington: Indiana University Press, 2013), 250 and 251–52. This thought reminds us of a distant yet subtle *material* link between Christ, humans (or, various *homo* species), and the rest of creation—*including minerals and stones*. Cf. also the following statement from Niels Henrik Gregersen: "Already in the creation story, we hear that the body of Adam was taken from the dust of the Earth. (Gen 2:7). The very name of Adam is derived from the Hebrew *adamah*, meaning 'ground,' 'earth,' or 'land.' " See the chapter "The Extended Body of Christ: Three Dimensions of Deep Incarnation," in *Incarnation: On the Scope and Depth of* Christology, ed. Neils Henrik Gregerson (Minneapolis: Fortress Press, 2015), 229.

41. Caputo, *Insistence of God*, 251. Caputo also mentions Jesus's stay in the desert, as described at the beginning of the *Gospel of Mark* (Mk 1:12–14): Jesus is taken into the desert by the Spirit (Gr. *pneûma*, so instead of Spirit it would be more accurate to say "Breath" as in the ancient divinity), where he coexists with wild animals and is ministered to by angels: all of this points to a new "interspecies" proximity that traverses the usual dichotomies or ontological caesurae between beings in the world in bilateral direction—from the animal toward the divine and vice versa.

42. Keller, "The Entangled Cosmos," 8654. And more: "Entangled particles apparently coordinate instantly, precisely and at any distance whatsoever—even across the galaxy . . . the events far apart seem to 'feel' each other" (8655 and 8856).

Chapter 2

1. Srečko Kosovel, "Cosmic Life," in *Open: Selected Poems and Thoughts / Srečko Kosovel*, selected and ed. Mateja Kralj, trans. Ana Jelnikar and Barbara Siegel Carlson (Sežana: Društvo Konstruktivist, 2018), 1. Slovenian poet Srečko Kosovel (1904–1926) is considered one of central Europe's major modernist poets.

2. Athanasius, *De Incarnatione* 16. Cited from Niels Henrik Gregersen, ed., *Incarnation: On the Scope and Depth of Christology* (Minneapolis: Fortress Press, 2015), 225.

3. Such as Denisovan, Neanderthal, Sapiens—cf. on this aspect Kennan Ferguson, "What Was Politics to the Denisovan?," in *Political Theory* 42, no. 2 (2014): 167-87: "What does it mean that humans were not the only hominin? Or, more importantly, what does it mean that other hominins held cultural, biological, and perhaps even linguistic equivalence to human beings?" (167). We may add

"early religious equivalence" to this list; as it will be argued later, deep history must accompany deep incarnation within a search for a new environmental theology.

4. Cf. Rosi Braidotti on the "Spinozist indicator of raw cosmic energy," in *The Posthuman* (Cambridge: Polity, 2017), 55–56: "Vitalist materialism is a concept that helps us make sense of that external dimension, which in fact enfolds within the subject as the internalized score of cosmic vibrations. . . . It also constitutes the core of a posthuman sensibility that aims at overcoming anthropocentrism."

5. Marko Pogačnik, *Christ's Power and Earth Wisdom: Searching for the Fifth Gospel* (W. Sussex: Clairview, 2019), 60. The book was originally published in 1999 and its contents are fully in line with similar works, such as Matthew Fox's *The Coming of the Cosmic Christ: The Healing of Mother Earth and the Birth of a Global Renaissance* (New York: Harper, 1989). Cf. also Sally McFague's seminal book *The Body of God: An Ecological Theology* (Minneapolis: Fortress Press, 1993).

6. Karl Marx, "Theses on Feuerbach," in *The Marx-Engels Reader*, ed. Robert C. Tucker, 2nd ed. (New York: W. W. Norton, 1978). For another misunderstanding or criticism of Feuerbach's thought, see also Friedrich Engels, *Ludwig Feuerbach and the Outcome of Classical German Philosophy* (New York: International Publishers, 1941). Engels's view in taking Feuerbach to be just the latter phase of German classical philosophy was mistaken since, in his reductionist and highly limited historicist and materialistic critique, Engels could not (fore)see the philosophical and theological core of Feuerbach's epistemology and his understanding of religion. For both Marx and Engels, this kind of criticism was an obvious and necessary consequence. In the twenty-first century, marked by the climate crisis and related environmental concerns, Feuerbach's philosophy of religion again grows in importance.

7. Cf. Jeffrey W. Robbins, "Necessity as Virtue: On Religious Materialism from Feuerbach to Žižek," in *The Future of Continental Philosophy of Religion*, ed. Clayton B. Crockett, B. Keith Putt, and Jeffrey W. Robbins (Bloomington: Indiana University Press, 2014), 230.

8. For more on Feuerbach's philosophy of intersubjectivity, see Škof, *Breath of Proximity*, chap. 5. For Feuerbach as transitional philosopher, see 67.

9. Ludwig Feuerbach, *The Essence of Christianity*, trans. George Eliot (New York: Harper & Row, 1957), 95. For German original citations, we are referring to *Das Wesen des Christentums* (1841), Theorie Werkausgabe (Frankfurt am Main: Suhrkamp), 1976.

10. Feuerbach, *The Essence of Christianity*, 89.

11. Feuerbach, *The Essence of Christianity*, 94.

12. Feuerbach, *The Essence of Christianity*, 94, emphasis added. In German: "[D]ie haben ihren Ursprung, wo der Blitz des Lichtes in der Liebe auffgangen ist. Dann derselbe Blitz wird in der Sanftmut geboren und ist das Herze im Centro der Quellgeister, darum seind dieselben Steine auch sanfte, kräftig und lieblich" (Feuerbach, *Das Wesen des Christentums*, 112). The original citation is from the early collection of the works of Böhme, *Kernhafter Auszug aller Jacob Böhme'schen Schriften*

(Amsterdam, 1718), 58. Cf. also about flowers: "The heavenly powers gave birth to to heavenly joy-giving fruits and colours, to all sorts of trees and shrubs . . . [L]ook diligently at this world, at the varieties of fruits and plants that grow upon the earth—trees, shrubs, vegetables, roots, flowers, oils, wines, corn, and everything that is there, and that thy heart can search out" (94–95). This is fully in line with Irigaray's new vegetal philosophy as presented in Luce Irigaray and Michael Marder, *Through Vegetal Being* (New York: Columbia University Press), 2016 (cf. for example chapter 1: 'Seeking Refuge in the Vegetal World').

13. Feuerbach, *The Essence of Christianity*, 96.
14. Feuerbach, *The Essence of Christianity*, 50.
15. Feuerbach, *The Essence of Christianity*, 53. We can recall a similar passage on the ontological primacy of love from Schelling (who, besides Böhme, also was an important reference point to Feuerbach), who states in his *Freedom Essay* from 1809 the following: "For not even spirit itself is supreme; it is but spirit, or the breath of love [*der Hauch der Liebe*]. But love is supreme. It is that which was before there were the depths and before existence (as separate entities), but it was not there as love, rather—how shall we designate it?" (Schelling, *Philosophical Inquiries into the Nature of Human Freedom*, 86). More on this later.
16. Feuerbach, *The Essence of Christianity*, 62.
17. Feuerbach, *Das Wesen des Christentums*, 176.
18. Feuerbach, *The Essence of Religion*. For the German original, we refer to *Kritiken und Abhandlungen III, 1844–1866*, vol. 4 of *Werke in sechs Bänden*, 81–153, Theorie Werkausgabe (Frankfurt am Main: Suhrkamp, 1975), here 1.
19. Feuerbach, *The Essence of Religion*, 2.
20. Feuerbach, *The Essence of Religion*, 2.
21. Feuerbach, *The Essence of Religion*, 6. With Van A. Harvey we may observe, that, first of all, "Liberal Christian theologians and rationalists, Feuerbach argued, do not sufficiently understand the emotional power inherent in the Christian notion of the God-man. To Feuerbach, therefore, any notion of God must relate to this constellation. The figure of Jesus is not merely a model of ethics and an assurance of God's love but the guarantee that God has indissolubly joined His divine nature with human nature. The Christian finds in this doctrine the veritable identity of the divine and the human, the human elevated to the divine and the divine embodied in the human. Moreover, Jesus Christ as model is the pledge not just of the divinity and immortality of the reason but of the embodied person" (Van Austin Harvey, *Feuerbach and the Interpretation of Religion* [Cambridge: Cambridge University Press, 1995], 224).
22. Feuerbach, *The Essence of Religion*, 26.
23. Feuerbach, *Das Wesen des Christentums*, 14.
24. Feuerbach, *The Essence of Christianity*, 275. Cf. the elaboration on this topic in Škof, *Breath of Proximity*: Thus, water is paradigmatic for entry into the field of the mesocosm as an intermediate or mediating substance while also serving as a

ritual space for a new epistemology and ethics. In some senses water is even more primary than breath since it is the element that surrounds humans in the womb, thereby conferring their being on them. In this sense, according to Feuerbach, water is "the element of natural equality and freedom, the mirror of the golden age" (69). Accordingly, any rehabilitation of sensibility must first acknowledge water as the most primary of all elements of Nature.

25. And *not* the mystical, celestial, or heavenly body—as in Paul, early Church fathers, or early Christologies; cf. Caputo, *The Insistence of God*, 252.

26. Caputo, *The Insistence of God*, 253–54.

27. Richard Bauckham, "The Incarnation and the Cosmic Christ," in Gregersen, *Incarnation*, 35. See also Elizabeth Johnson, "Deep Resurrection," *Modern Believing* 64, no. 2 (Spring 2023): 152–61. Johnson argues: "The immense task facing theology in our day is to seek understandings of the beliefs and practices of faith that include the whole planet, indeed the whole cosmos, in what is religiously important" (Johnson, "Deep Resurrection," 153). For other important recent works in ecological theology, see Elizabeth Johnson, *Ask the Beasts: Darwin and the God of Love* (London: Bloomsbury, 2014); Pope Francis, *Laudato Si'/ Praise Be to You: On Care for Our Common Home* (Vatican: Libreria Editrice Vaticana, 2015); Denis Edwards, *The Natural World and God: Theological Explorations* (Adelaide: ATF Press, 2017); Mark L. Wallace, *When God Was a Bird: Christianity, Animism, and the Re-Enchantment of the World* (New York: Fordham University Press, 2019); Adam Pryor, *Living with Tiny Aliens: The Image of God in the Anthropocene* (New York: Fordham University Press, 2020).

28. Bonaventure's excerpt cited from Bauckham, "The Incarnation and the Cosmic Christ," in Gregersen, *Incarnation*, 38.

29. Cf. Arthur Peacocke, *All That Is: A Naturalist Faith for the Twenty-First Century* (Minneapolis: Fortress Press, 2007).

30. Cf. Jakob Klapwijk, *Purpose in the Living World? Creation and Emergent Evolution*, ed. and trans. Harry Cook (Cambridge: Cambridge University Press, 2008).

31. Cf. Gregory S. Engel, Tessa R. Calhoun, Elizabeth L. Read, Tae-Kyu Ahn, Tomáš Mančal, Yuan-Chung Cheng, Robert E. Blankenship, and Graham R., Fleming, "Evidence for Wavelike Energy Transfer through Quantum Coherence in Photosynthetic Systems," *Nature* 446 (2007): 782–86.

32. Ina Wunn, "Beginning of Religion," *Numen* 47, no. 4 (2000): 417–52, here 431.

33. Cf. Ferguson, "What Was Politics to the Denisovan?," 173, for both DNA similarities and his citation.

34. Peter S. Alterman, "Aliens in Golding's 'The Inheritors,'" *Science Fiction Studies* 5, no. 1 (1978), cited from 3, 7, and 10 (our emphasis).

35. Niels Henrik Gregersen, "The Cross of Christ in an Evolutionary World," *Dialog: A Journal of Theology* 40, no. 3 (2001): 192–207, here 205.

36. Denis Edwards, *Ecology at the Heart of Faith* (Maryknoll; NY: Orbis, 2006), 60.

37. Elizabeth Johnson, "Jesus and the Cosmos: Soundings in Deep Christology," in Gregersen, *Incarnation*, 133–56, here 134.

38. This vegetal comparison also includes an elemental presence of the breath (*ruaḥ*) of God: "All people are grass, / their constancy is like the / flower of the field. / The grass withers, the flower / fades, / when the breath of the LORD / blows upon it." (*The Holy Bible, NRSV* [Nashville, TN: Thomas Nelson, 1989]).

39. Johnson, "Jesus and the Cosmos," 137 and 138. Also, Johnson clearly contends that, as already explained by Peacocke ("Every atom of iron in our blood would not be there had it not been produced in some galactic explosion billions of years ago and eventually condensed to form the iron in the crust of the earth") that human beings "are made of the stuff of the cosmos" (137).

40. Pierre Teilhard de Chardin, *Hymn of the Universe* (New York: Harper & Row, 1961). For criticism, see McFague, *The Body of God*: "What was special about his work and why in spite of continuing criticisms of it from both scientific and theological circles it continues to draw attention is that he felt deeply the need to reimagine Christian doctrine in terms of twentieth-century science and to see the new scientific story in Christian terms. . . . Our point is not that Teilhard's remythologizing of the new creation story was entirely successful; rather, it is that he attempted it at all" (82).

41. Teilhard de Chardin, *Hymn of the Universe*, 17.

42. Teilhard de Chardin, *Hymn of the Universe*, 38.

43. Teilhard de Chardin, *Hymn of the Universe*, 44.

44. *Upaniṣads*, trans. Patrick Olivelle (Oxford: Oxford University Press, 1996), 32 (2.5.15). The excerpt comes from the *Bṛhadāraṇyaka Upaniṣad*, the earliest of all Upanishads (from the seventh to sixth centuries BCE). On an idiosyncratic, even more ancient Vedic teaching on *food* (as a material *hypokeimenon* of all creation), see Lenart Škof, "Food in Ancient Indian Philosophy," in *Encyclopedia of Food and Agricultural Ethics*, ed. P. B. Thompson, D. M. Kaplan, K. Millar, L. Heldke, and R. Bawden (Dordrecht: Springer, 2014).

45. Teilhard de Chardin, *Hymn of the Universe*, 56. We have changed the masculine gender in this passage into the feminine.

46. Teilhard de Chardin, *Hymn of the Universe*, 137.

47. Schelling, *Philosophical Inquiries*, 79. For more on this, see Škof, *Breath of Proximity*, chap. 3 ("Schelling, or from the Abyss of Ethics").

48. Schelling, *Philosophical Inquiries*, 89.

49. Petri Berndtson, "Phenomenological Ontology of Breathing: The Phenomenologico-Ontological Interpretation of the Barbaric Conviction of We Breathe Air and a New Philosophical Principle of Silence of Breath, Abyss of Air," PhD diss., University of Jyväskylä, 2018, 222. For an explication of this, see his *Phenomeno-*

logical Ontology of Breathing: The Respiratory Primacy of Being (London: Routledge, 2023).

50. Maurice Merleau-Ponty, *Themes from the Lectures at the Collège de France (1952–1960)*, trans. John O'Neill, in *In Praise of Philosophy and Other Essays*, trans. John Wild and James Edie John (Evanston, IL: Northwestern University Press, 1988), 134.

51. Merleau-Ponty, *Themes from the Lectures at the Collège de France*, 143.

52. Merleau-Ponty, *Nature*, 204.

53. Simpson, *Merleau-Ponty and Theology*, 111.

54. Simpson, *Merleau-Ponty and Theology*, 112.

55. Merleau-Ponty, *Sense and Non-Sense*, 174.

56. Caputo, *The Insistence of God*, 253.

57. Caputo, *The Insistence of God*, 254.

58. Cf. Teilhard de Chardin, *Hymn of the Universe*, 137.

59. Merleau-Ponty, *Themes from the Lectures*, 143.

60. Cf. Feuerbach, *The Essence of Christianity*, 94.

61. Maurice Merleau-Ponty, *The Visible and the Invisible*, trans. Alphonso Lingis (Evanston, IL: Northwestern University Press, 1968), 139–40.

62. Merleau-Ponty, *The Visible and the Invisible*, 142.

63. Cf. Simpson, *Merleau-Ponty and Theology*, 38–39.

64. Cf. Feuerbach, *The Essence of Christianity*, 94.

Chapter 3

1. Adam S. Miller, *Future Mormon: Essays in Mormon Theology* (Salt Lake City: Greg Kofford Books, 2016), 114.

2. See, for example, Douglas J. Davies, *An Introduction to Mormonism* (Cambridge: Cambridge University Press, 2003); Adam S. Miller, *Badiou, Marion and St Paul: Immanent Grace* (London: Bloomsbury, 2008); Webb, *Mormon Christianity*; Terryl L. Givens, *Wrestling the Angel* (Oxford: Oxford University Press, 2015).

3. Miller, *Badiou, Marion and St Paul*.

4. Simon Critchley, "Why I Love Mormonism," *New York Times*, September 16, 2012, https://opinionator.blogs.nytimes.com/2012/09/16/why-i-love-mormonism/.

5. Or also called "The Age of the Breath." See, on this, Luce Irigaray, "The Age of the Breath," in Irigaray, *Key Writings*, 165-70. Irigaray writes: "[T]he age of the Spirit, rather corresponds to the age of cultivation, by man and woman, of the divine breath they received as human beings—if I trust the narrative of Genesis as a basic myth of our tradition. The God-Father creates humanity by sending his breath into matter, into earth, the text tells us. Then sin occurs, the loss of divinity for man and for woman, and the necessity of the second age, the age of the redemption through the generation of a woman—Mary—and of man—Jesus—who

are both inhabited by the breath of the Spirit. In the third age of the history of Judeo-Christianity, after the age of the world's redemption, thanks to Mary and to Jesus, the task of humanity will be to become itself divine breath." Irigaray, "The Age of the Breath," 168.

6. See Luce Irigaray, *Sharing the World* (London: Continuum, 2008); Luce Irigaray, *In the Beginning, She Was* (London: Bloomsbury, 2013); Luce Irigaray, *To Be Born* (New York: Palgrave Macmillan, 2017).

7. See Richard Rorty and Gianni Vattimo, *The Future of Religion*, ed. Santiago Zabala (New York: Columbia University Press, 2005); Richard Rorty, *An Ethics for Today: Finding Common Ground between Philosophy and Religion* (New York: Columbia University Press, 2011).

8. Rorty, *An Ethics for Today*, xix.

9. Rorty, *An Ethics for Today*, 14.

10. Stephen T. Cranney, "Divine Darwinism, Comprehensible Christianity, and the Atheist's Wager: Richard Rorty on Mormonism—an Interview with Mary V. Rorty and Patricia Rorty," *Dialogue: A Journal on Mormon Thought* 43, no. 2 (2010): 109–30.

11. Jean-Luc Marion, *L'Idole et la distance: Cinq études* (Paris: Bernard Grasset, 1977), 80–81.

12. Jean-Luc Marion, *The Idol and Distance: Five Studies*, trans. Thomas A. Carlson (New York: Fordham University Press, 2001), 55.

13. Marion, *L'Idole et la distance*, 86 (emphasis added).

14. Marion, *The Idol and Distance*, 60–61 (emphasis added).

15. Marion, *L'Idole et la distance*, 104.

16. Friedrich Nietzsche, *Thus Spoke Zarathustra*, ed. A. Del Caro and R. Pippin, trans. A. Del Caro (Cambridge: Cambridge University Press, 2006), 16.

17. Nietzsche, *Thus Spoke Zarathustra*, 17.

18. Nietzsche, *Thus Spoke Zarathustra*, 108.

19. Marion, *The Idol and Distance*, 139.

20. See Škof, *Antigone's Sisters*, 120–28.

21. Irigaray, *To Be Born*, v.

22. Irigaray, *To Be Born*, 1.

23. "Through its autonomous breathing and its sexuation, the little human gives birth to itself, it brings into the world a singular living being of which it will have to cultivate life, a life irreducible to any other, towards its achievement for itself and for the world into which it takes place" (Irigaray, *To Be Born*, 5).

24. Marion, *The Idol and Distance*, 139.

25. Marion, *The Idol and Distance*, 225.

26. Marion, *The Idol and Distance*, 225.

27. Marion, *The Idol and Distance*, 231.

28. Martin Heidegger, *On Time and Being*, trans. Joan Stambaugh (New York: Harper and Row, 1972), 6, 8, 19.

29. Martin Heidegger, *Pathmarks*, ed. W. McNeill (Cambridge: Cambridge University Press, 2007), 277.

30. Martin Heidegger, *Poetry, Language, Thought*, trans. A. Hofstadter (New York: Harper and Row, 1971), 147–48.

31. Martin Heidegger, *Überlegungen II–VI: Schwarze Hefte 1931–1938*, GA94, ed P. Trawny (Frankfurt am Main: Kostermann, 2014), 231.

32. Marion, *The Idol and Distance*, 246.

33. Marion, *The Idol and Distance*, 252–53.

34. Cf. for example Luce Irigaray's *The Forgetting of Air in Martin Heidegger*, trans. Mary Beth Mader (Austin: University of Texas Press, 1999), and also Škof, *Breath of Proximity*, which is entirely dedicated to this forgotten but sacred element.

35. See Cranney, "Divine Darwinism, Comprehensible Christianity, and the Atheist's Wager."

36. Richard Rorty, *Philosophy and Social Hope* (London: Penguin, 1999), 171.

37. We learn from Mary Rorty that in his personal life, he was never opposed to raising his two children as Mormons. He also often accompanied his mother-in-law, Vivian Varney, of whom he was extremely fond, to church (see Cranney, "Divine Darwinism," 111).

38. Rorty and Vattimo, *The Future of Religion*, 40. As also testified by Mary Rorty, the religious wager for him simply was: "If there is God, and if He is good, He will not judge me on the basis of whether I believed in Him of not. He will judge me on the basis of my life, my choices, my decisions, and the responsibility that I've accepted for them. And if He does not, I don't regret not having believed in Him." See Cranney, "Divine Darwinism," 123.

39. We recognize that, in *The American Religion: The Emergence of the Post-Christian Nation* (New York: Simon and Schuster, 1993), Harold Bloom takes Baptists and Mormons as his main case studies.

40. The Mormon scriptures (four primary texts, also called Standard Works) consist of *The Bible* (KJV), *Book of Mormon* (1830), *Doctrine and Covenants* (1835), and *Pearl of the Great Price* (1851). If not otherwise indicated, the citations from the scriptures are from the official LDS Church website at https://history.lds.org/article/web-resources?lang=eng. This citation from D&C goes as follows:

32 And every man whose spirit receiveth not the light is under condemnation.

33 For man is spirit. The elements are eternal, and spirit and element, inseparably connected, receive a fulness of joy;

34 And when separated, man cannot receive a fulness of joy.

35 The elements are the tabernacle of God; yea, man is the tabernacle of God, even temples; and whatsoever temple is defiled, God shall destroy that temple.

41. John Durham Peters, "Reflections on Mormon Materialism," *Sunstone* (March 1993): 47–52.

42. Peters, "Reflections on Mormon Materialism," 47. Cf. full citation from D&C 130:22: "The Father has a body of flesh and bones as tangible as man's; the Son also; but the Holy Ghost has not a body of flesh and bones, but is a personage of Spirit. Were it not so, the Holy Ghost could not dwell in us."

43. Givens, *Wrestling the Angel*, 122.

44. Davies, *An Introduction to Mormonism*, 68.

45. Givens, *Wrestling the Angel*, 45.

46. Givens, *Wrestling the Angel*, 205.

47. See on these teachings about Mother in Heaven by various Mormon theologians and thinkers: since the 1854 revelation of Sister Eliza R. Snow about Mother in Heaven in "O My Father" hymn, this topic developed into an (un)official doctrine of the LDS. On this, and related dogmatic controversies over the decades, see David L. Paulsen and Martin Pulido, " 'A Mother There': A Survey of Historical Teachings about Mother in Heaven," *BYU Studies* 50, no. 1 (2011): 71–97, and an excellent study written by Taylor G. Petrey, "Rethinking Mormonism's Heavenly Mother," *Harvard Theological Review* 109, no. 3 (2016): 315–41.

48. Rosalynde Welch, "The New Mormon Theology of Matter," *Mormon Studies Review* 4, no. 1 (2017): 69.

49. *The King Follet Discourse* is regarded by many as Smith's greatest sermon. It was delivered in front of a large audience (estimated at 8,000) on April 7, 1844 (a few months before his death). On that day, Smith spoke for more than two hours while three men took official notes, and, by adding the fourth source—and with comparisons of various versions—the sermon was completed and composed into its current version. On this and more details on the historical setting of the sermon, see Donald Q. Cannon, "The King Follet Discourse: Joseph Smith's Greatest Sermon in Historical Perspective," *BYU Studies* 18, no. 2 (1978): 179–92.

50. Joseph Smith, "The King Follett Discourse," *Times and Seasons* 5 (1844): 612–17, http://mldb.byu.edu/follett.htm (accessed April 20, 2022).

51. See, on the ethical relevance of "lungs" in Levinas's thought, in Škof, *Breath of Proximity*: "That the subject could be a lung at the bottom of its substance—all this signifies a subjectivity that suffers and offers itself before taking a foothold in being. . . . It is the longest breath there is, spirit. Is man not the living being, capable of the longest breath in inspiration, without the stopping point, and in expiration, without return?" Škof, *Breath of Proximity*, 137–38. Also, Merleau-Ponty mentions "some immense external lung" as a cosmico-ethical organ in his *Phenomenology of Perception*, trans. Donald A. Landes (London: Routledge, 2012), 219. See, on this, Petri Berndtson's chapter "The Possibility of a New Respiratory Ontology," in *Atmospheres of Breathing*, ed. Lenart Škof and Petri Berndtson (New York: State University of New York Press, 2018), 44n.

52. See, here, an excellent interpretation of Mormon theology and materialism in the chapter "What's Up with Mormons and Matter" in Webb, *Mormon Christianity*. Webb presents a fascinating comparative analysis of contemporary quantum physics

and Mormon theology and calls the Higgs field (which is more basic than the Higgs boson) "God's field" or a "divinely saturated matrix" (Webb, *Mormon Christianity*, 78). See also the following thoughts of Webb's: "As we have seen, however, some bosons do not have mass, and space is hard to define as matter. . . . Then there is the fact that most of the matter in the universe consists of dark matter and dark energy, and nobody knows what these substances are. And what do you do with antimatter, which destroys regular matter if the two come into contact?" (Webb, *Mormon Christianity*, 79).

53. Heidegger, *Elucidations of Hölderlin's Poetry*, 109.

54. For more on problems related to respiratory thinking, see Škof and Berndtson, *Atmospheres of Breathing*. We may mention Descartes here, who undoubtedly is one of Marion's philosophical heroes. In Derrida's *Writing and Difference*, we have this passage on Descartes's relation to respiration: "Concerning 'Being' and 'respiration,' let us permit ourselves a juxtaposition which does not only have the value of a historical curiosity. In a letter to X . . . , dated March 1638, Descartes explains that the proposition " 'I breathe therefore I am' concludes nothing, if it has not been proven previously that one exists, or if one does not imply: *I think that* I breathe (even if I am mistaken in this), therefore I am; and it is nothing other to state in this sense *I breathe therefore I am* than *I think, therefore I am*." Which means—in terms of what concerns us here—that the *meaning* of respiration is always but a dependent and particular determination of my thought and of Being in general. Supposing that the word 'Being' is derived from a word meaning 'respiration' (or any other determined thing), no etymology of philology—as such, and as determined sciences—will be able to account for the thought for which 'respiration' (or any other determined thing) becomes a determination of Being among others." Jacques Derrida, *Writing and Difference*, trans. Alan Bass (London: Routledge, 2009), 174. This remark positions Derrida into the lineage of Western respiratory thinkers and poets (Hölderlin, Feuerbach, Schelling, Paul Claudel, Paul Celan, Merleau-Ponty, Irigaray, Peter Sloterdijk).

55. Mormons usually refer to the Holy Ghost rather than to the Holy Spirit, although both designations are used.

56. Petri Berndtson, "The Temple of the Holy Breath as the Place of Conspiracy between the Respiratory Body and the Space of Open Air," in *Art and Common Space*, ed. Anne-Karin Furunes, Simon Harvey, and Maaretta Jaukkuri (Trondheim: Norwegian University of Science and Technology, 2013), 39–47.

57. Berndtson argues on this basis, and in using a new respiratory vocabulary, that "the Holy Breath is the most valuable treasure that is given to us." Berndtson, "The Temple of the Holy Breath," 43.

58. Marion, *The Idol and Distance*, 252.

59. Jean-Luc Marion, *Givenness and Revelation*, trans. Stephen E. Lewis (Oxford: Oxford University Press, 2016).

60. Marion, *Givenness and Revelation*, viii.

61. Marion, *Givenness and Revelation*, ix.

62. One cannot stop wondering about this *insensitivity* to sexual difference in Marion, and similarly, in the major philosophical traditions of Western thinkers (with some rare exceptions, such as Feuerbach in the nineteenth century and among more contemporary philosophers Derrida and Alain Badiou, and—of course—Simone de Beauvoir and Irigaray. See also Shé M. Hawke, "The Exile of Greek Metis: Recovering a Maternal Divine Ontology," in "Ontologies of Asylum," *Poligrafi* 23, no. 91/92 (2018): 41–75, who, taking her lead from Irigaray, does consider this insensitivity in the way cosmic worlds have been written up without acknowledgment of the "theological exile" of female deities, sexual difference, and an "ontology of maternal asylum" (Hawke, "The Exile of Greek Metis," 42, 44).

63. Marion, *Givenness and Revelation*, 114.

64. Marion, *Givenness and Revelation*, 57.

65. Webb, *Mormon Christianity*, 29.

66. Webb, *Mormon Christianity*, 33.

67. Webb, *Mormon Christianity*, 37.

68. Another version of the Eucharist is to be found in Irigaray's *Sharing the World*, where she states beautifully: "It is perhaps to her, as living nature, that I have to abandon myself in order to preserve my own life, its growth, and what they bear of the life and growth of the other. Such a hospitality is so subtle and intimate that I have to seek help in nature for my survival and my becoming, notably through being attentive to the abundance that she gives to be contemplated, heard, breathed, touched, felt. It suffices to agree to receive, in silence, this eucharist that she unsparingly offers—often without any visible object or symbol but as a communion with the real presence of the living. No transubstantiation is needed here—life itself is there, giving itself through all that surrounds me" (Irigaray, *Sharing the World*, 42).

Chapter 4

1. Cited from Arthur Schopenhauer, *The World as Will and Representation*, vol. 1, trans. E. F. J. Payne (New York: Dover, 1958), 129.

2. For the classical work on visions of God and other (divine) beings within Christian religiosity, see Ernst Benz, *Die Vision: Erfahrungsformen und Bilderwelt* (Stuttgart: Ernst Klett Verlag, 1969).

3. The expression "theological" is, here, broadly used in a sense of an intellectual activity dealing with the realm of divinities and gods and thus including cosmological and philosophical approaches.

4. See Michael Witzel, *Kaṭha Āraṇyaka: Critical Edition with a Translation into German and an Introduction* (Cambridge: Harvard University Press, 2004), xxxiv. The paleological of magical thinking (*magische Weltanschauung*) is here modeled after

Silvano Arieti's *The Intrapsychic Self: Feeling, Cognition, and Creativity in Health and Mental Illness* (New York: Basic Books, 1967).

    5. Psi phenomena are defined as "the aggregate of parapsychological functions of the mind including extrasensory perception, precognition, and psychokinesis." (*Merriam-Webster.com Dictionary*, "psi phenomena," https://www.merriam-webster.com/dictionary/psi%20phenomena) (accessed September 9, 2022). For an exhaustive source on psi phenomena, see *The Psi Encyclopedia*, https://psi-encyclopedia.spr.ac.uk/.

    6. See David E. Cartwright, "Schopenhauer's Haunted World: The Use of Weird and Paranormal Phenomena to Corroborate His Metaphysics," in *The Oxford Handbook of Schopenhauer*, ed. Robert L. Wicks (Oxford: Oxford University Press, 2020), 175–92.

    7. Schopenhauer, The World as Will and Representation, 128–29.

    8. Schopenhauer, *The World as Will and Representation*, 126.

    9. Agamben, *The Coming Community*, 13–14.

    10. Schopenhauer, *The World as Will and Representation*, 111.

    11. Schopenhauer, *The World as Will and Representation*, 112. For the elaboration of the *body*, see § 6 of *The World as Will and Representation*: "the body is immediately *known*, is *immediate object*" (20).

    12. Schopenhauer, *The World as Will and Representation*, 365. Schopenhauer describes this suffering in ourselves as "pain" (364).

    13. Bracha L. Ettinger, "Transgressing With-In-To the Feminine," in *Feminist Readings of Antigone*, ed. by Fanny Söderbäck (Albany: State University of New York Press, 2010), 198 and 199. "Matrixial" is related to the concept of matrix as understood both philosophico-cosmically and philosophico-feministically. Both understandings lead us back to the original meaning of *khora* in Plato (*Timaeus* 49a and 52a)—that is, as a cosmic matrix, the primal ontological receptacle, and, as it were, cosmic wetnurse. See also Richard Kearney's interpretation of the *Holy Trinity Icon* painted in 1411 by Andrei Rublev, in which he argues that the empty chalice appearing in the center of the icon actually represents the womb-heart of Mary. See Kearney, *Anatheism*, 25: "And this empty receptacle at the core of the circle is, arguably, none other than the womb-heart of Mary itself (*khora*)."

    14. Giordano Bruno, *The Expulsion of the Triumphant Beast*, trans. Arthur D. Imerti (Lincoln: University of Nebraska Press, 2004), 125 and 129.

    15. Bruno, *Cause, Principle and Unity / Essays on Magic*, trans. Robert de Lucca (Cambridge: Cambridge University Press, 1998), 170–71.

    16. Arthur Schopenhauer, *On the Will in Nature*, trans. Madame Karl Hillenbrand (London: G. Bell and Sons, 1903), 64.

    17. For various somatic expressions for this pain within the Semitic and Asian religions, see Lenart Škof, "Metaphysical Ethics Reconsidered: Schopenhauer, Compassion and World Religions," *Schopenhauer Jahrbuch* 87 (2006): 101–17.

    18. Schopenhauer, *The World as Will and Representation*, 403 and 374.

    19. Schopenhauer, *The World as Will and Representation*, 404.

20. Arthur Schopenhauer, "Versuch über das Geistersehn," in *Parerga und Paralipomena I—Kleinere philosophische Schriften* (*Sämtliche Werke, Bd. IV*, ed. von Wolfgang Frhr. von Löhneysen [Frankfurt am Main: Suhrkamp, 1986]), 323: "Es ist wirklich die praktische Metaphysik, wie schon Baco von Verulam die Magie definiert—er ist gewissermaßen eine Experimental-metaphysik: den die ersten und allgemeinsten Gesetze der Natur werden von ihm beseitigt; daher es das sogar a priori für unmöglich Erachtete möglich macht."

21. Schopenhauer, "Versuch über das Geistersehn," 348. We can add a personal account of such an experience, communicated to us by S. Š. The event of telepathy happened in the early morning when she was suddenly wakened from her sleep by a voice (i.e., the phenomenon was entirely acoustic), calling her by her child's name. The person communicating with her was her grandmother who was 700 km away at that moment; they were very closely connected during her entire life. Immediately after this, S. Š. made a phone call and she was informed by her parents that her grandmother had experienced a serious brain stroke precisely in the early morning. We have two options here: to ascribe such an event to mere chance, or, alternatively, to take it as an example of what Schopenhauer would call a subterranean connection—or what Jung would later refer to as a proof or synchronicity, an example of an underlying cosmico-interpsychic connection of the world. On Freud and the analysis of a telepathic dream, see below.

22. Schopenhauer, "Versuch über das Geistersehn," 364.

23. See Schopenhauer, "Versuch über das Geistersehn," 367: "Da nun andererseits für uns feststeht, daß der *Wille*, sofern er Ding an sich ist, durch den Tod nicht zerstört und vernichtet wird; so läßt sich a priori nicht geradezu die Möglichkeit ableugnen, daß eine magische Wirkung der oben beschriebenen Art nicht auch sollte von einem bereits Gestorbenem ausgehn können." Schopenhauer is not alone in this thought—see for example Shelling's *Clara* and his philosophical account of communication with the dead: "Clara, remembering and mourning the loss of her husband Albert, argues that there must be a link, or a *communication* between this world and the next world—the spiritual world of the dead. This ontological temporality of Clara's main question and concern emerge from her devotion to her late husband, and from her love for him. Clara's question leads us to the very un-Kantian line of argument that, somehow, and in a way still to be revealed to us, a spiritual world (of deceased others) lives in us and is thus accessible to us." This excerpt is from Škof, *Antigone's Sisters*, 91. See Friedrich Wilhelm Joseph Schelling, *Clara, or, On Nature's Connection to the Spirit World*, trans. Fiona Steinkamp (Albany: State University of New York Press, 2002).

24. See a truly excellent book on the history of ideas as related to the myth of disenchantment (including the rich Western reception of occult and psi phenomena) by Jason Ā. Josephson-Storm, *The Myth of Disenchantment: Magic, Modernity, and the Birth of the Human Sciences* (Chicago: University of Chicago Press, 2017).

25. See Gottlieb Florschütz, "Schopenhauer und die Magie—die praktische Metaphysik," *Schopenhauer Jahrbuch* 93 (2012): 471–84.

26. Hartmut Rosa refers to Mesmer and affirms that magnetic radiation as presented in his writings and practices could be relevant for his sociology of human relationships to the world, and that such ideas indeed could represent "a pure relation of resonance." See Hartmut Rosa, *Resonance: A Sociology of Our Relationship to the World*, trans. James C. Wagner (Cambridge: Polity Press, 2019), 67–68.

27. Schopenhauer, *On the Will in Nature*, 203–4.

28. See C. F. Emmons and J. Sobal, "Paranormal Beliefs: Functional Alternatives to Mainstream Religion?," *Review of Religious Research* 22, no. 4 (1981): 301–12; A. Orenstein, "Religion and Paranormal Belief," *Journal for the Scientific Study of Religion* 41, no. 2 (2002): 301–11; T. W. Rice, "Believe It or Not: Religious and Other Paranormal Beliefs in the United States," *Journal for the Scientific Study of Religion* 42, no. 1 (2003): 95–106; and M. Weeks, K. P. Weeks, and M. R. Daniel, "The Implicit Relationship between Religious and Paranormal Constructs," *Journal for the Scientific Study of Religion* 47, no. 4 (2008): 599–611. These studies show the pattern of correlation between belief in religious beliefs and belief in paranormal phenomena. Especially Orenstein (2002) concludes that "[p]aranormal belief is strongly influenced by both religious belief and religious participation" (306). Weeks, Weeks, and Daniel (2008), on the other hand, are much more cautious in their conclusions but still affirm that their results "show a strong schematic association between religious and paranormal constructs, though variability certainly exists in the strength of this association" (606). Weeks et al. categorize both fields under "supernatural beliefs" (600).

29. Cartwright, "Schopenhauer's Haunted World," n. 29 (bibliographic references omitted).

30. Schopenhauer, *On the Will in Nature*, excerpts from 214–16.

31. Florschütz, "Schopenhauer und die Magie—die praktische Metaphysik," 483. Florschütz quotes Walter von Lucadou, *Dimension Psi—Fakten zur Parapsychologie* (Leipzig: Ullstein-List Verlag, 2003) here: "Die nichtlokale Korrelation zwischen Ereignissen, ohne dass es zu einer Informationsübertragung kommt. Dieser Zusammenhang ist flüchtig—wie das Grinsen der Katze aus 'Alice im Wunderland,' das noch blieb, nachdem die Katze bereits verschwunden war. . . . Robert G. Jahn betonte, dass insbesondere die mögliche Verwundbarkeit dieser Geräte und Prozesse durch den Einfluss des menschlichen Beobachters und seines Bewusstseins eine Reihe von pragmatischen Konstruktionsfragen aufwirft und das Auftreten von quantenphysikalischen Phänomenen in makroskopischen Bereichen zu erzwingen scheint. Kann sich eine hochtechnisierte Gesellschaft wie unsere auf Dauer erlauben, solche Zusammenhänge zu ignorieren?" (12–13).

32. Cartwright, "Schopenhauer's Haunted World," 186.

33. See on this Cartwright, "Schopenhauer's Haunted World," 186 n. 11. Cartwright refers to Diethard Sawicki, *Leben mit den Toten: Geisterglauben und*

die Entstehung des Spiritismus in Deutschland 1770–1900 (Paderborn: Ferdinand Schöningh, 2002), and Stefan Andriopoulos, *Ghostly Apparitions: German Idealism, the Gothic Novel, and Optical Media* (New York: Zone Books, 2013), 49–71. See on this Josephson-Storm's *The Myth of Disenchantment*, which represents a full history of Western reception of paranormal phenomena. This rich book spans from the thought of René Descartes and Francis Bacon to Ludwig Wittgenstein and the Frankfurt School.

34. David Ray Griffin, *Parapsychology, Philosophy, and Spirituality: A Postmodern Exploration* (New York: State University of New York Press, 1997).

35. Griffin, *Parapsychology, Philosophy, and Spirituality*, 38. The citation is from Alfred North Whitehead, *Essays in Science and Philosophy* (New York: Philosophical Library, 1948), 227.

36. See Griffin, *Parapsychology, Philosophy, and Spirituality*, 276–283. For telepathy see also his *Reenchantment without Supernaturalism: A Process Philosophy of Religion* (Ithaca: Cornell University Press, 2001), 73–76. Here, Griffin argues: "Most directly relevant to this objection is process philosophy's endorsement of, along with the empirical evidence for, the reality of telepathic experience, meaning the direct feeling of one mind by another" (73) It is vital to add here that telepathy was also endorsed by thinkers such as William James and Alfred North Whitehead.

37. *Entangled Worlds: Religion, Science, and New Materialisms*, ed. Catherine Keller and Mary-Jane Rubenstein (New York: Fordham University Press, 2017), 5.

38. Karen Barad, *Meeting the Universe Halfway: Quantum Physics and the Entanglement of Matter and Meaning* (Durham: Duke University Press, 2007), 396. Interestingly enough, Barad employs the Schopenhauerian term "experimental metaphysics" here: "During the past decade, technological progress in experimental physics has opened up an entirely new empirical domain: the world of 'experimental metaphysics.' That is, questions previously thought to be a matter solely for philosophical debate have been brought into the orbit of empirical inquiry" (35).

39. See on this Sigmund Freud, *The Standard Edition of the Compete Psychological Works*, vols. 18 and 19, ed. and trans. J. Strachey (London: Vintage, 2001). The essays on the topic of the paranormal phenomena are "Psychoanalysis and Telepathy," "Dreams and Telepathy," and "The Occult Significance of Dreams." On Freud's confession on telepathy, see Ernst Jones, *Sigmund Freud: Life and Work*, 3 vols. (London: Hogarth Press, 1953–1957). Freud writes in a letter to Jones: "Our friend Jones seems to me to be too unhappy about the sensation that my conversion to telepathy has made in English periodicals" (3:422). Let us here add our own case for prophetic dreams or dreams and telepathy: a few years ago, we had an extremely vivid and clear dream (such as we rarely experience) in which our good friend from our youth (he was like my brother as we spent our entire childhood together—he was a foster child of our grandmother) appeared in front of us dressed entirely in black, with his face and hands and all his skin painted black, and his shoes were shining as they were just polished with a black shoe polish. In the morning,

immediately after we woke up, we received a telephone call informing us that our friend's mother has died last night. We knew she was unwell and sick for some time, but we hadn't had any previous knowledge (nor had any bad wishes for her, of course; Freud mentions a possibility of the wish-fulfilling elements is similar dreams; actually, we were very fond of her as she was a very honest person; finally, this was our first dream of our childhood friend) about an illness or worsening condition of hers that might result in her death. See Freud (19:198) for the explanation of his own death-dreams and dreams and telepathy. Despite being very skeptical in his writings and analyses of so-called occult phenomena, Freud contends: "One arrives at a provisional opinion that it may well be that telepathy really exists and that it provides the kernel of truth in many other hypotheses that would otherwise be incredible" (19:136). Cf. also his contention on the transfer of thought during his own psychoanalytic processes and experiments: "On the basis of a number of experiences I am inclined to draw the conclusion that thought-transference of this kind comes about particularly easily at the moment at which an idea emerges from the unconscious, or, in theoretical terms, as it passes over from the 'primary process' to the 'secondary process'" (19:138).

40. Jacques Derrida, *Psyche: Inventions of the Other*, part I, ed. P. Kamuf and E. Rottenberg (Stanford: Stanford University Press, 2007), chap. 9 ("Telepathy"), 236 and 244 (brackets removed from the last citation). For telepathy and clairvoyance, see also Walter Benjamin's two pieces: "Surrealism: The Last Snapshot of the European Intelligentsia," in *One-Way Street and Other Essays*, trans. Edmund Japhcott and Kingsley Shorter (London: New Left Books, 1979), 225–39, and "Doctrine of the Similar," *New German Critique* 17 (Spring 1979): 65–69. According to him, it is "to writing and language that clairvoyance has, over the course of history, yielded its old powers" (Benjamin, "Doctrine of the Similar," 68).

41. See an excellent essay on telepathy written by Steve Pile, "Distant Feelings: Telepathy and the Problem of Affect Transfer over Distance," *Transactions of the Institute of British Geographers*, n.s., 37, no. 1 (2012): 44–59. As a human geographer, Pile begins his essay with the notion of an "atmosphere" that enables us to feel the effects of other people. For Pile, after dealing with psychological, late nineteenth-century spiritistic, as well as experimental, cases (such as the experiments on remote sensing and remote viewing conducted by the CIA in the 1970s), concludes telepathy "is not occult but a (neglected) capacity of the mind and body" (54) adding, importantly, that telepathy is "'supernormal' not 'supernatural'" (49). Finally, telepathy is explained with quantum interconnectedness and thus also grounded in physics. For an early scientific approach to telepathy, see "What Is 'Telepathy,'" *Scientific American* 148, no. 4 (April 1933): 214–15. On the most recent scientific experiments on brain-to-brain communication, having rich potential for the future studies of telepathy, see Carles Grau et al., "Conscious Brain-to-Brain Communication in Humans Using Non-Invasive Technologies," *Plos One* (2014), https://doi.org/10.1371/journal.pone.0105225.

42. John Durham Peters, *Speaking into the Air* (Chicago: University of Chicago Press, 1999).

43. Elisa Marder, "Mourning, Magic and Telepathy," *Oxford Literary Review* 30, no. 2 (2008): 191–200, n. 25.

44. For more on *trinitarian pneumatics*, see chapter 6 of Škof, *Antigone's Sisters*: "We have seen that in Trinity we have an exhalation and inhalation as a mysterious logic of the trinitarian co-relationality and co-breathing (conspiratio) of the three divine persons: in Schelling this is visible in the primordial and anarchic exhalation and inhalation of the Ground itself, the pulsation of its archetypal life" (157).

45. Ernest L. Simmons, *The Entangled Trinity: Quantum Physics and Theology* (Minneapolis: Fortress Press, 2014), 151.

46. Simmons, *The Entangled Trinity*, 151. And Simmons continues: "So, too, the persons of the Trinity flow in and out of one another in a continuous, dynamic energy exchange of becoming. They are entangled in their mutual becoming, and as the external creation relates to them they manifest in one of the three expressions of the divine mystery" (151–52).

47. Simmons, *The Entangled Trinity*, 153. As we are working with the philosophical concepts of correspondence and synchronicity, in his interpretation, Simmons works with complementarity and superposition—as explanatory ideas from quantum physics.

48. Julian of Norwich, *Revelations of Divine Love*, trans. E. Spearing (London: Penguin, 1998), 16–17: "[T]he only pain I felt was the pain of Christ . . . for when he was in pain, we were in pain. And all creatures who were capable of suffering, suffered with him."

49. Caputo, *Cross and Cosmos*, 203. The example offered by both Keller and Caputo is the following: "In classical physics, a causal connection requires contiguity and disappears over distance ('local realism'). But in quantum mechanics, when a single particle is split in two, the two continue to act in tandem, no matter at how great a distance. As Brian Greene says, they behave as two dice, one being rolled in Las Vegas and the other in Atlantic City, but always coming up the same. If one is measured to have a clockwise spin, the other seems to 'know' this and exactly the same time is found to have a counter spin" (Caputo, *Cross and Cosmos*, 202).

50. Caputo, *Cross and Cosmos*, 203.

51. Caputo, *Cross and Cosmos*, 209.

52. In 1958, Jung reported to his assistant Aniela Jaffé: "Der große Fund meiner Nachforschung aber war Schopenhauer." See, on this, an excellent and in-depth study on psi phenomena and philosophy by Andrea Kropf, *Philosophie und Parapscyhologie: Zur Rezeptionsgeschichte parapsychologischer Phänomene am Beispiel Kants, Schopenhauers und C.G. Jungs* (Munster: LIT Verlag, 2000), 182.

53. Webb, *Mormon Christianity*, 77–78.

54. Webb, *Mormon Christianity*, 108.

55. Cf. *Jung on Synchronicity and the Paranormal*, selected and introduced by R. Man (London: Routledge, 1997; "Introduction"). The doctoral dissertation of Jung from 1902 was titled "On the Psychology and Pathology of the So-Called Occult Phenomena."

56. *Jung on Synchronicity and the Paranormal*, 15 (the excerpt is from Jung's essay "Synchronicity: An Acausal Connecting Principle" from 1952).

57. *Jung on Synchronicity and the Paranormal*, 22.

58. *Jung on Synchronicity and the Paranormal*, 127 ("On the Nature of the Psyche").

59. *Jung on Synchronicity and the Paranormal*, 101 ("The Theory of Synchronicity").

60. Kropf, *Philosophie und Parapscyhologie*, 200.

61. See Kropf, *Philosophie und Parapscyhologie*, 212.

62. Keller, "The Entangled Cosmos."

63. For the elaboration of the futurity of God, see the next chapter.

64. *Yoga Powers: Extraordinary Capacities Attained through Meditation and Concentration*, ed. Knut A. Jacobsen (Leiden: Brill, 2012), 1.

65. "Iddhi," in *Buddhism and Jainism* (Encyclopaedia of Indian Religions), ed. K. T. S. Sato and Jeffery D. Long (Dordrecht: Springer, 2017), 573.

66. See Bradley S. Clough, "The Cultivation of Yogic Powers in the Pāli Path Manuals of Theravāda Buddhism," in *Yoga Powers*, 77 (chap. 3).

67. Clough, "The Cultivation of Yogic Powers," 575.

68. Clough, "The Cultivation of Yogic Powers," 575.

69. See, on this, Škof, "Metaphysical Ethics Reconsidered, 101–17. Cf. also *Schopenhauer's Encounter with Indian Thought: Representation and Will and Their Indian Parallels*, ed. Stephen Cross (Honolulu: University of Hawai'i Press, 2013).

70. See, the entry *Tattvārtha-Sūtra*, in *Buddhism and Jainism*, 1188–91. We are using the following edition of *Tattvārtha-Sūtra*: *Ācārya* Umāsvāmī's *Tattvārthasūtra*—with Explanation in English from *Ācārya* Pūjyapāda's *Sarvārthasiddhi*, ed. Vijay K. Jain (Dehradun: Vikalp Printers, 2018).

71. *Tattvārtha-Sūtra* 1.9 and 1.23.

72. Piotr Balcerowicz, "Extrasensory Perception (*Yogi-Pratyakṣa*) in Jainism, Proofs of Its Existence and Its Soteriological Implications," in *Yoga in Jainism*, ed. Christopher Key Chapple (London: Routledge, 2016), 57.

73. Balcerowicz, "Extrasensory Perception (*Yogi-Pratyakṣa*) in Jainism," 57.

74. Balcerowicz, "Extrasensory Perception (*Yogi-Pratyakṣa*) in Jainism," 58.

75. See, on this, Paul Dundas, *The Jains* (London: Routledge, 2002), 86–88.

76. Cf. Schopenhauer, *The World as Will and Representation*: "[It] is Māyā, the veil of deception, which covers the eyes of mortals, and causes them to see a world of which one cannot say either that it is or that it is not" (8); and "The *Vedas* and Puranas know no better simile for the whole knowledge of the actual world, called by them the web of Māyā, than the dream, and they use none more frequently" (17).

77. Balcerowicz, "Extrasensory Perception (*yogi-pratyakṣa*) in Jainism," 58.
78. Balcerowicz, "Extrasensory Perception (*yogi-pratyakṣa*) in Jainism," 58.
79. Kristi L. Wiley, "Extrasensory Perception and Knowledge in Jainism," in *Essays in Jaina Philosophy and Religion*, ed. Piotr Balcerowicz (Delhi: Motilal Banarsidass, 2003), 91.
80. *Tattvārtha-Sūtra* 1.26.
81. Wiley, "Extrasensory Perception and Knowledge in Jainism," 98.

Chapter 5

1. Raymond Ruyer, "The Status of the Future and the Invisible World," trans. R. Scott Walker, *Diogenes* 36 (1980): 43.
2. D. R. Anderson, "Awakening in the Everyday," in *Pragmatism and Religion*, ed. S. Rosenbaum (Urbana: University of Illinois Press, 2003), 142–52.
3. Richard Rorty, *Philosophy as Cultural Politics* (Cambridge: Cambridge University Press, 2007), 29.
4. A passage from J. Dewey's letter to Charles E. Witzell (see Anderson's "Awakening in the Everyday," 148).
5. John Dewey, *A Common Faith* (New Haven: Yale University Press, 1934), 50.
6. Dewey, *A Common Faith*, 50.
7. Dewey, *A Common Faith*, 50 (emphasis added).
8. Dewey, *A Common Faith*, 51.
9. Dewey, *A Common Faith*, 48. Dewey adds: "We need no external criterion and guarantee for their goodness. They are had, they exist as good, and out of them we frame our ideal ends" (48).
10. See, on this, an excellent presentation and analysis of his work in Elizabeth Grosz, *The Incorporeal: Ontology, Ethics, and the Limits of Materialism* (New York: Columbia University Press, 2018), chap. 6 ("Ruyer and Embryogenesis of the World"). On Tao-God, see "The Status of the Future and the Invisible World" and "Person-God and Tao-God," trans. K. Pender, *Revue de Métaphysique et de Morale* 52, no. 2 (1947): 1–11.
11. Ruyer, "The Status of the Future and the Invisible World," 42.
12. Ruyer, "The Status of the Future and the Invisible World," 43 (emphasis added).
13. Ruyer, "The Status of the Future and the Invisible World," 53.
14. Grosz, *The Incorporeal*, 211.
15. Grosz, *The Incorporeal*, 212. Secondary forms are composites and aggregates—such as a house, a car, or a bridge, which are all planned, and they are also not self-repairing in themselves. What they have is the ability of decomposition or recomposition, but they do not possess autoaffection or consciousness such as do primary forms.

16. Grosz, *The Incorporeal*, 213 (emphasis added).
17. Grosz, *The Incorporeal*, 216.
18. Grosz, *The Incorporeal*, 229.
19. Ruyer, "The Status of the Future," 46.
20. Ruyer, "The Status of the Future," 46.
21. Caputo, *The Insistence of God*, 8–9.
22. Caputo, *The Insistence of God*, 5.
23. Caputo, *The Insistence of God*, 5 (emphasis added).
24. Caputo, *The Insistence of God*, 4.
25. Caputo, *The Insistence of God*, 259.
26. Caputo, *The Insistence of God*, 261.
27. These are originally the words of Lorenzo Snow, recorded in Eliza R. Snow's *Biography and Family Record of Lorenzo Snow* (Salt Lake City: Deseret News Co., 1884), see 46–47.
28. Cf. Critchley, "Why I Love Mormonism."
29. Davies, *An Introduction to Mormonism*, 80.
30. Smith, "The King Follett Discourse."
31. Smith, "The King Follett Discourse." A short review of Mormon teachings of God could be presented here: Mormonism differs radically from other Christian Trinitarian doctrines in its teaching that there are God, the Eternal Father (and, sometimes, also Mother), His Son, Jesus Christ, and the Holy Ghost, but with an important distinction, namely, that Jesus is identified with Jehovah (according to the teachings of Joseph Smith, Jesus Christ only *became* divine at some point in the distant pre-Earth past). God the Father (and, sometimes, Mother) is now identified with *Elohim* in its original plural meaning, and thus represents the "Gods" in their plurality rather than being one and the only God. If both God the Father and Son have tangible bodies, finally, the Holy Ghost is more purely spiritual although still enigmatically subtly material in its ontological character. Although some Mormons think that it also must possess a certain kind of spiritual bodily substance, it usually will be recognized in the form of unembodied cosmic ether, being able to "dwell in us" (cf. *Doctrine & Covenants*, 130:22).
32. Cf. here is an excellent account on Mormon materialism by Peters, "Reflections on Mormon Materialism."
33. See Lenart Škof, "The Third Age: Reflections on Our Hidden Material Core," *Sophia* 59, no. 1 (2020): 83–94.
34. We refer here to Ward Blanton, Clayton Crockett, Jeffrey W. Robbins, and Noëlle Vahanian, *An Insurrectionist Manifesto: Four New Gospels for a Radical Politics* (New York: Columbia University Press, 2016).
35. F. W. J. Schelling, *Briefe und Dokumente, Bd. 3* (Bonn: Bouvier u. Co., 1975), 222.
36. F. W. J. Schelling, *Bruno, or On the Natural and the Divine Principle of Things*, trans. Michael G. Vater (New York: State University of New York Press,

1984), 221 (emphasis added). For the Fichte-Schelling controversy, see the introduction by Michael G. Vater.

37. Schelling, *Bruno*, 222.

38. For more on this aspect, cf. our reading of Schelling's *Clara* in Škof, *Antigone's Sisters*, with *material* markers as related to an ontology of mourning.

39. Bruno, *Cause, Principle and Unity*.

40. Bruno, *Cause, Principle and Unity*, 7.

41. Bruno, *Cause, Principle and Unity*, editor's introduction, xviii.

42. See Bruno, *Cause, Principle and Unity*, 80 (for Averroes) and 44 (for spiritual substance).

43. Witzel, *Kaṭha Āraṇyaka*, xxxiii. The paleological thinking is modeled after Arieti's *The Intrapsychic Self*.

44. Frits Staal specializes in the study of Vedic ritual and mantras and an Indological scholar and comparative philosopher of high esteem who once said of the Upanishads: "That the Upanishads are full of absurdities and contradictions is not something we did not know before." See his chapter "Is There Philosophy in Asia?," in *Interpreting across Boundaries: New Essays in Comparative Philosophy*, ed. G. J. Larson and E. Deutsch (Princeton: Princeton University Press, 1988), 221.

45. On the triadic thinking as linked to this constellation and mesocosm, see Witzel, *Kaṭha Āraṇyaka*, n. 129 on xl. Witzel writes how curious it is that "the term has not been used in this context before." He refers to its first usage in a book on Newar religion authored by Robert I. Levy and Kedar Rāj Rājopādhyāya and titled *Mesocosm: Hinduism and the Organization of a Traditional Newar City of Nepal* (Berkeley: University of California Press, 1990). This Vedic way of thinking uses different mystic correlations and equivalents, some obvious (such as between Sun and the eye or Wind and breath), and some more hidden and esoteric (between Moon and mind). But there always exists a nexus or a connection between two beings (called *bandhu* and *upaniṣad*). See also Michael Witzel, "Macrocosm, Mesocosm, and Microcosm: The Persistent Nature of 'Hindu' Beliefs and Symbolic Forms," *International Journal of Hindu Studies* 1, no. 3 (December 1997): 501–39.

46. See Olivelle, *Upaniṣads*, liii–lvi (chap. "Cosmic Connections"). Citation on lvi.

47. See Webb, *Mormon Christianity*, 46–76.

48. Gary A. Anderson, *Sacrifices and Offerings in Ancient Israel: Studies in Their Social and Political Importance* (Atlanta: Scholars Press, 1987), 10.

49. Webb, *Mormon Christianity*, 48.

50. Webb, *Mormon Christianity*, 49.

51. Danah Zohar and Ian Marshall, *SQ: Connecting with Our Spiritual Intelligence* (London: Bloomsbury, 2000), 9.

52. Zohar and Marshall, *SQ*, 69–70. This is known in physics as "the Casimir Effect."

53. Webb, *Mormon Christianity*, 57.

54. Webb, *Mormon Christianity*, 58. Also, note the following: "Matter, according to Mormonism, exists according to gradations of spiritual refinement, so that even spiritual entities like God, angels and the soul are composed of some kind of matter" (59).

55. Webb, *Mormon Christianity*, 60. Iamblichus, who, like Smith, was also accused of being an advocate for magical practices, teaches that "rituals reveal the fundamental forms that hold the cosmos together. The gods give us rituals so that we can participate with our bodies in the divine nature. . . . Rituals are knowledge-in-action, shaping us in quite literal ways in preparation for the soul's ascent to the beyond by initiating the transformation of matter into spirit" (64).

56. Webb, *Mormon Christianity*, 70.

57. Ingrid D. Rowland, *Giordano Bruno: Philosopher / Heretic* (Chicago: University of Chicago Press, 2009), see chap. 15. For those of a more skeptical character, let us only mention the existing practice of exorcism in the Catholic Church. For rites of exorcism, see the document *Of Exorcisms and Certain Supplications* (*De Exorcismis et Supplicationibus Quibusdam*); revised in 1999.

58. Rowland, *Giordano Bruno*, 120.

59. Bruno, *Cause, Principle and Unity*, xxviii (introduction).

60. Bruno, *Cause, Principle and Unity*, xxix (introduction).

61. Bruno, *The Expulsion of the Triumphant Beast*, 31 (editor's introduction).

62. Bruno, *The Expulsion of the Triumphant Beast*, 31.

63. Bruno, *Cause, Principle and Unity*, 125 and 129.

64. See Kip Thorne, *The Science of Interstellar* (New York: W. W. Norton, 2014), 22–26.

65. Bruno, *Cause, Principle and Unity*, 170–71.

66. Bruno, *Cause, Principle and Unity*, 171.

67. Merleau-Ponty, *Nature*, 204.

68. Simpson, *Merleau-Ponty and Theology*, 111.

69. Timothy Egan, *The Worst Hard Time* (Boston: Mariner Books, 2006), 147.

70. Caputo, *The Insistence of God*, 5.

71. Jacqueline Furby, "About Time Too: From *Interstellar* to *Following*, Christopher Nolan's Continuing Preoccupation with Time-Travel," in *The Cinema of Christopher Nolan: Imagining the Impossible*, ed. Jacqueline Furby and Stuart Joy (London: Columbia University Press, 2015), 247–67. See 249 for the citation.

72. Egan, *The Worst Hard Time*, 9. On the history of the Dust Bowl, see Dayton Duncan, *The Dust Bowl: An Illustrated History* (San Francisco: Chronicle Books, 2012). Cf. the following excerpts on this ecological disaster from Egan, *The Worst Hard Time*: "In parts of Nebraska, Kansas, Colorado, New Mexico, Oklahoma, and Texas, it seemed on many days as if a curtain were being drawn across a vast stage at world's end. . . . Cattle went blind and suffocated. When farmers cut them open, they found stomachs stuffed with fine sand. . . . Children

coughed and gagged, dying of something the doctors called 'dust pneumonia.' In desperation, some families gave away their children. The instinctive act of hugging a loved one or shaking someone's hand could knock two people down, for the static electricity from the dusters was so strong. . . . As the black wall approached, car radios clicked off, overwhelmed by the static. . . . Nothing compares to the black dusters of the 1930s, he says, a time when the simplest thing in life—taking a breath—was a threat" (2 and 5–6).

73. See Thorne, *The Science of Interstellar*, on the quest of many physicists to understand the so-called singularities: "That quest produced superstring theory, which in turn led to a belief that our universe must be a brane residing in a higher dimensional bulk" (227). And for the explanation of brane and bulk: "Throughout this book I visualize warped space by picturing our universe as a two-dimensional warped membrane, or brane, that resides in a bulk with three space dimensions" (186).

74. Furby, "About Time Too," 250–51. See also about the full plot and other details about "*Interstellar* (film)" from https://en.wikipedia.org/wiki/Science_fiction_film (accessed June 28, 2020).

75. Thorne, *The Science of Interstellar*, 263.

76. In episode four of the second season of *The Expanse*, we witness the launch of the giant spaceship *Nauvoo*, which has been designed by the Latter-day Saints: "The Nauvoo was originally commissioned by the Mormons to take thousands of their members on a generations-long trip to Tau Ceti, a G-class star located approximately twelve light-years from our solar system." See, on this, Kevin Murnane, "Science and Tech in Syfy's 'The Expanse': The Spectacular Launch of the 'Nauvoo,'" *Forbes* (March 1, 2017). https://www.forbes.com/sites/kevinmurnane/2017/03/01/science-and-tech-in-syfys-the-expanse-the-spectacular-launch-of-the-nauvoo/ (accessed June 5, 2021). *The Pearl of Great Price*—one of the sacred texts of Mormonism—describes the planet Kolob as a location that is geographically closest to God while also being the planet which Latter-day Saints head to in their afterlife (see *The Pearl of Great Price*, Abraham 3:2–16). The creator of the postapocalyptic series *Battlestar Galactica* (1978–79), Glen A. Larson, was himself a member of the Church of Jesus Christ of Latter-day Saints, and he has incorporated Mormon elements into the series—most notably by introducing a planet called Kobol (i.e., Kolob) as the dwelling place of gods. The very idea of an intergalactic trip is unusual for Christianity because of its skepticism toward critical or technological posthumanism. But it "should [also] not be forgotten that in the depths of Christian history, remote settlements such as monasteries preserved civilization during dark times" (B. P. Green, "The Catholic Church and Technological Progress: Past, Present, and Future," in *Religion and the New Technologies*, ed. N. Herzfeld [Basel: MDPI 2017], 25), and that, from the very beginning of the history of the Church, exploration—both physical and intellectual—was encouraged. See also Barry H. Downing's *The Bible and Flying Saucers* (New York: Avon 1970) in which he links UFOs with angels, as well as defends the possibility that life could have been brought to Earth by extraterrestrials.

Similarly, we can find thoughts on UFOs as being a part of God's angelic host in Billy Graham's *Angels: God's Secret Agents* (Garden City, NJ: Doubleday, 1975).

77. Thorne, *The Science of Interstellar*, 22. There are three options here: (A) Bulk beings are our descendants, caught in a disastrous and slowly closing time-loop due to an impending catastrophe awaiting them if they are not able to communicate vital data to us. They can travel back in time but they are restrained by the rule that they can never travel to their own past. (B) Bulk beings are gods, or a god, which, as intellectually, materially, and technologically evolved supreme being(s), communicate(s) back in time from the hyperspace between two singularities. They act like Buddhist Bodhisattvas, refusing to enter their final enlightenment (i.e., a point beyond the singularity's edge) due to their highest ethical vow not to reach *nirvāṇa* until someone else is able to achieve enlightenment. (C) Bulk beings are extraterrestrials with advanced technology, communicating with us through tesseract.

78. Thorne, *The Science of Interstellar*, 192–93.

79. Zohar and Marshall, *SQ*, 17.

80. Bruno, *Cause, Principle and Unity*, 70–71.

81. Zohar and Marshall, *SQ*, 89–90. The notion of 40 Hz oscillations comes from the research of Rodolfo Llinas and his team, as well as Wolf Singer and Charles Gray on the *binding problem* showed that "bundles of neurons all over the brain oscillate simultaneously at similar frequencies (about 40 Hz) if they perceive the same object" (see 67–68). This theory might represent the microcosmic answer to the riddle of the unity of a bonding agent, connecting the three cosmic spheres (macrocosmic, microcosmic, and mesocosmic).

82. Webb, *Mormon Christianity*, 77–78.

83. Thorne, *The Science of Interstellar*, 32. Interestingly enough, the possibility of a hyperspace as related to psi phenomena was already mentioned as early as in 1926 by Zoë Countess Wassilko-Serecki in her elaboration of the case of the Romanian girl Eleonore Zugin (attributed with psychokinetic phenomena and other paranormal capabilities), where "Wassilko suggested, for example, that the movement of objects was a kind of telekinesis, produced by what appeared to a 'hole in the world,' which she proposed might indicate that Eleonora was somehow causing objects to pass in and out of 'hyperspace.'" For the citation, see Josephson-Storm, *The Myth of Disenchantment*, 262.

84. M. B. Green and J. H. Schwarz, "Anomaly Cancellations in Supersymmetric D = 10 Gauge Theory and Superstring Theory," *Physics Letters B* 149, nos. 1–3 (1984): 117–22. For more about the superstring theory, see Brian Greene, *The Elegant Universe: Superstrings, Hidden Dimensions, and the Quest for the Ultimate Theory*, 2nd ed. (New York: W. W. Norton, 2010). We do not yet possess available means for the scientific experiments that could prove the validity of this theory.

85. Caputo, *The Insistence of God*, 8–9.

86. In their elaboration of a field of the *ethic of astrobiology*, Richard O. Randolph and Christopher P. McKay ("Protecting and Expanding the Richness

and Diversity of Life, an Ethic for Astrobiology Research and Space Exploration," *International Journal of Astrobiology* 13, no. 1 [2014]: 28–34) argue for the following scenario: since human beings may most likely find, in the future, nonintelligent or nonsentient organisms somewhere in the solar system, this would pose problems similar to our "obligations" toward the microbes or "microbial community." If, on the contrary, humans found new extraterrestrial life, or a sign of the "second genesis," being completely different from the unity of life on the Earth, then important new ethical questions would arise. Now, these questions are subsumed by these authors under the label of the so-called Cosmic Golden Rule, stating: "Never impose on others what you would not choose for yourself" (32). But, there is a third possibility, *perhaps*, when species with vastly superior intelligence and technology were discovered or encountered, and, similarly to Nolan's *Interstellar*, our astrobiologists proposed to shift our focus in time and reflect upon the following scenario: "Instead of imagining what our expectations would be for superior extraterrestrials visiting Earth in the present, imagine our expectations if these superior extraterrestrials had visited Earth several billion years ago, just as life was first emerging from the primordial soup of Earth" (32). It holds that, by imagining this scenario, if extraterrestrials (having godlike power over humans) were observing the rules of an ethics of astrobiology and the cosmic Golden Rule, then evolution would not have been disturbed.

87. Cited after Thorne, *The Science of Interstellar*, 193.

88. Cf. Luce Irigaray, *To Be Two* (New York: Routledge, 2001), 34: "a woman gives birth to a woman."

89. Bruno, *Cause, Principle and Unity*, xxix.

90. See Peters, *God—The World's Future*, 699–734. The term "Astro-Theology" was originally coined by William Derham (1657–1735).

91. Peters, *God—The World's Future*, 733–34. (emphasis added). Cf. also: "Because God is the world's future, the eyes of faith can foresee a better world coming. This vision includes a new creation, a harmonious whole, a home of healthy interconnectedness. . . . In short, we do not have a whole until the eschaton. Yet the power of the eschatological whole is effective in the present. It is effective proleptically. It is the power of God's grace calling us forward and empowering us to center our existence through trust in the future that will be God's" (336–37 and 338–39). This is how God exists as our future within Peters's systematic theology.

92. See Dewey, *A Common Faith*, 50. The idea of God, in Dewey's view, stands for the unification of ideal values, with imagination intervening into the very core of our beliefs and values, and unifying our attitudes and conduct into a signifying whole.

93. Keller, "The Entangled Cosmos," 8.

94. Keller, "The Entangled Cosmos," 11.

95. Catherine Keller, "The Energy We Are: A Meditation in Seven Pulsations," in *Cosmology, Ecology, and the Energy of God*, ed. Donna Bowman and Clayton Crockett (New York: Fordham University Press, 2012), 23.

Chapter 6

1. Agamben, *The Coming Community*, 52.
2. Marjorie Reeves, "The Originality and Influence of Joachim of Fiore," *Traditio* 36 (1980): 271.
3. Cf. Reeves, "The Originality and Influence of Joachim of Fiore," 272n15.
4. Cf. Reeves, "The Originality and Influence of Joachim of Fiore," 277–78. Interestingly enough, Reeves does not mention Amalric and his school in her otherwise excellent study.
5. Cf. Reeves, "The Originality and Influence of Joachim of Fiore," 285–86.
6. *The Babylonian Talmud*, trans. Michael L. Rodkinson, book 9 (Tract Abuda Zara), vol. 1 (Boston: Boston New Talmud Publishing Company, 1918), chap. 1, 16.
7. For these ideas, Joachim of Fiore was of course regarded in his time as being "a prophet of the Antichrist." See Gary Dickson, "Joachism and the Amalricians," *Florensia* 1 (1987): 35. Joachim of Fiore's movement, and related movements in the twelfth century (Amalricians, among others), have indeed been called the "Antichurch" by Ernest Bloch. See E. Bloch, *Avicenna and the Aristotelian Left* (New York: Columbia University Press, 2019), 29–33.
8. Irigaray, *Key Writings*, 168.
9. We need to add that in her writings (as usual) Irigaray does not mention either Joachim of Fiore or Amalric of Bène.
10. Peter Sloterdijk, *You Must Change Your Life: On Anthropocentrics*, trans. W. Hoban (Cambridge: Polity, 2013), 1.
11. Sloterdijk, *You Must Change Your Life*, 2.
12. Sloterdijk, *You Must Change Your Life*, 4.
13. The idea that, in the era of post-Enlightenment, the strongest narrative left to us would rest entirely either on the idea of a death of God or, alternatively, on some form of a secular or atheist response to the crisis of religion in the modern world becomes untenable quickly as we realize that this talk, even if it is largely true and historically perfectly just, still remains tied to a certain understanding of the crisis of religion—one that does not allow us to think any more of any future salvation or possibility of divinization of humankind.
14. Vattimo, *After Christianity*, 29.
15. Vattimo, *After Christianity*, 29–30. The citation is taken from Vattimo. It's possible to detect here a parallel with Hasan Hanafi's "Heritage and Renewal" project, wherein he examines the Muslim attitudes toward (1) their own heritage (Islam, revolving around turning the foundations of Islamic law [*usul al-fiqh*] into a general philosophical method); (2) the heritage of the West (as Hasan Hanafi wrote a critique of the New Testament); and, (3) the current situation/reality (influenced by liberation theology and also very much directed toward the future).
16. Cited after Whalen, *Dominion of God*, 100. The passage is from Joachim of Fiore's *Liber de concordia novi et veteris testamenti*.

17. Cf. Whalen, *Dominion of God*, 116.
18. Vattimo, *After Christianity*, 31.
19. See Škof, *Breath of Proximity*, on breath as an elemental-material substratum of the spirit. See, for example, Jacques Derrida, *Of Spirit: Heidegger and the Question*, trans. G. Bennington (Chicago: University of Chicago Press, 1991), 74: "*Spirit/soul/life, pneûma/psyché/zoé* or *bíos, spiritus/anima/vita, Geist/Seele/Leben*—these are the triangles and squares in which we imprudently pretend to recognize stable semantic determinations, and then to circumscribe or skirt round the abysses of what we ingenuously call translation."
20. Derrida, *Of Spirit*, 52. See, on the history of this oblivion of the breath in the history of philosophy, two of my monographs, *Atmospheres of Breathing*, ed. L. Škof and P. Berndtson, and *Breath of Proximity*.
21. Agamben, *The Coming Community*, cited on 12 and 14.
22. Agamben, *The Coming Community*, 14.
23. Bloch, *Avicenna and the Aristotelian Left*, 30. Thomas Aquinas adds: "[He] most stupidly taught that God is prime matter" (*Summa Theologica* 1.3.8.; see Bloch, *Avicenna and the Aristotelian Left*, 84n133) Bruno refers in his *Cause, Principle, and Unity* (*De la causa, principio, et Uno*, from 1584) to David of Dinant and his sentence on the unity of God, matter, and spirit. For Bruno, as Bloch rightly and poignantly observes, "the eternal God-Nature weaves alone for itself the eternal garment of the world, natura naturata. . . . Bruno's glowing naturalism which brings Avicenna, Avicebron, and Averroës fully to the world, is so capricious that he even views the Aristotelian concept of the drive of matter toward form (as something molding its shape) as being inconsistent with the autarchy of matter (as an eternal womb of creation)" (Bloch, *Avicenna and the Aristotelian Left*, 31).
24. Hermann Ley, *Studie zur Geschichte des Materialismus im Mittelalter* (Berlin: VEB Deutscher Verlag der Wissenschaften, 1957), 214–25. Also, other religious sects of that time shared similar social messages, such as the Valdesians, Cathars, or Albigensians.
25. On these and related events in the beginning of the thirteenth century, see Gary Dickson, "The Burning of the Amalricians," *Journal of Ecclesiastical History* 40, no. 3 (July 1989): 347–69.
26. Cf. Dickson, "Joachism and the Amalricians," 38.
27. We think of Irigaray's thesis that if woman is "divine from birth" and thus more closely related to the spiritual breath, then it is logical that the neglect of the feminine aspects in almost all institutionalized religions is related to the need of the men for religious education, which he actually requires for himself to attain his redemption (see *Key Writings*, 165).
28. This label comes from Ernest Bloch; see his excellent *Avicenna and the Aristotelian Left*.
29. Bloch, *Avicenna and the Aristotelian Left*, 21.
30. Bloch, *Avicenna and the Aristotelian Left*, 13. It should be noted that Averroës was very critical of *Philosophia Orientalis*, regarding it as obscurantist.

31. Bloch, *Avicenna and the Aristotelian Left*, 8. Both Avicenna's and Averroës's books were later prohibited by propounders of orthodox Islam, and burned.

32. Ley, *Studie zur Geschichte des Materialismus im Mittelalter*, 132-44. As for Avicenna, also for Averroës, all becoming, change, and perishing in the world is rooted *in matter*. It is in these ontologies that we can search for one of the decisive influences for the "materialistic" developments within unorthodox Christian philosophy following Averroës.

33. See De Lacy O'Leary, "Al-Hallaj," *Philosophy of East and West* 1, no. 1 (1951): 56-62. There are other genealogies or early forms of *theōsis* that could be mentioned. For example, in Maximus the Confessor (580-662), another mystic, who was condemned as a heretic, we have a teaching on a theology of deification in which there is an exchange of natures between God and man: "if God becomes man by condescension, man becomes, and is called, God by grace." We find this mention in Roberto M. Unger's *The Religion of the Future* (Cambridge: Harvard University Press, 2014), 286, along with his own strong antinomian thoughts on the theology of deification and Christianity as the religion of the future. On Maximus the Confessor's *Mystagogia*, see A. Louth, *Maximus the Confessor* (New York: Routledge, 1996), 73-74; the original excerpt goes as follows: "For we believe that in this present life we already have a share in these gifts of the Holy Spirit through the love that is in faith, and in the future age after we have kept the commandments to the best of our ability we believe that we shall have a share in them in very truth in their concrete reality according to the steadfast hope of our faith and the solid and unchangeable promise to which God has committed himself" (*Mystagogia* 24:704D–705A).

34. See Herbert W. Mason, *Al-Hallaj* (London: Routledge, 2007), chap. 1. Al-Hallāj was the grandson of a Magian priest and the son of a convert. He was born in the village of Tur in southwestern Iran, in a Shi'ite milieu that was highly influenced by the Hellenistic and neognostic teachings. Among his contemporaries and friends were philosophers and theologians who shaped the unique atmosphere of "an eclectic mix of religious backgrounds and influences, including Nestorian Christian, Jewish, Zoroastrian, and, by the end of the 4th/10th century, quasi-Buddhist" (Mason, *Al-Hallaj*, 10). It was this cultural and intellectual "experimental" environment that produced some of the most advanced ideas and innovations of their time, including those of al-Hallāj. See, for example, the theosophy of Ibn al-'Arabī (1165-1240) and his unique synthesis of Hellenic, Persian, and Indian influences into a monistically designed pantheism, in which all beings are the manifestation of one Being.

35. O'Leary, "Al-Hallaj," 60 (emphasis added).

36. Agamben, *The Coming Community*, 23. This narrative rests upon an old story from one of the Haggadahs from the Talmud, in which "two places are reserved for each person, one in Eden and one in Gehenna. The just person, after being found innocent, receives a place in Eden plus that of a neighbor who was

damned. The unjust person, after being judged guilty, receives a place in hell plus that of a neighbor who was saved. . . . At the point when one reaches one's final state and fulfills one's own destiny, one finds oneself for that very reason in the place of the neighbor. What is most proper to every creature is thus its substitutability, its being in any case in the place of the other" (Agamben, *The Coming Community*, 22). The aim of the Badaliya is, clearly, the destruction of the wall dividing Eden from Gehenna—which would be to achieve a future "absolutely unrepresentable community" (Agamben, *The Coming Community*, 24). The society of the third age would mean, as it were, the *taking-name* of this community. But, it is also necessary to mention that for Louis Massignon, the aim of Badaliya is to pray and testify for the Christian truth within Islam, or as he has put it—"for, in their Muslim, imperfect, tradition, they preciously keep something like an imprint of the sacred face of Christ whom we adore"; see *Derrida and Religion: Other Testaments*, ed. Y. Sherwood and K. Hart (New York: Routledge, 2005), chap. 5 ("Mary, Maternity and Abrahamic Hospitality in Derrida's Reading of Massignon"), 85.

37. Unger, *The Religion of the Future*, 277 (emphasis added). Unger also mentions Aquinas's "Feast of Corpus Christi" sermon, in which we read the following: "Since it was the will of God's only-begotten Son that men should share in his divinity, he assumed our nature in order that by becoming man he might make men gods" (Unger, *The Religion of the Future*, 286). Unger rightly comments that, hearing this, we might indeed say that we are "reading from Feuerbach or Emerson rather than from Aquinas" (286).

38. For more on the literature and for an elaborate account on the very context of the suppression of the heresy, see J. M. M. H. Thijssen, "Master Amalric and the Amalricians: Inquisitional Procedure and the Suppression of Heresy at the University of Paris," *Speculum* 71 (1996): 43–65. Another important source is a book by G. C. Capelle, *Autour du Décret de 1210: Amaury de Bène. Etude sur son panthéisme formel* (Paris: J. Vrin, 1932).

39. Thijssen, "Master Amalric and the Amalricians," 46.

40. Karl Albert, "Amalrich von Bena und der mittelalterliche Pantheismus," in *Die Auseinandersetzungen an der Pariser Universität im XIII. Jahrhundert*, ed. A. Zimmermann (Berlin: Walter de Gruyter, 1976), 193–212, cited on 195.

41. Gilles Deleuze, *Expressionism in Philosophy: Spinoza* (New York: Zone Books, 1992), 16 and 99.

42. Deleuze, *Expressionism in Philosophy*, 321. The Church document against Amalricians from 1210 stated the "Omnia unum, quia quicquid est, esrt deus" as the principal sentence of Amalricians.

43. G. S. Kirk, J. E. Raven, and M. Schofield, *The Presocratic Philosophers* (Cambridge: Cambridge University Press, 1999), 95 (=Diels Kranz 11 A 22).

44. *The Early Upanishads*, trans. P. Olivelle (New York: Oxford University Press, 1998), 407 (I.1). The sentence means that the whole world is enveloped (*vāsyam*) in/by God.

45. See our chapter on God in matter. Cf. also Peters, "Reflections on Mormon Materialism"; Givens, *Wrestling the Angel*; Webb, *Mormon Christianity*; and Welch, "The New Mormon Theology of Matter." According to Peters, Mormon cosmology thus "is the story of humankind's increasing immersion in matter for the sake of progress and growth" (Peters, "Reflections on Mormon Materialism," 47).

46. Albert, "Amalrich von Bena und der mittelalterliche Pantheismus," 209: "Quicquid in deo est, deus est. Sed in deo sunt omnia, quia, quod factum est, in ipso vita erat. Ergo deus est omnia." Finally, for Albert, Amalricians are labeled as being idealistic and *not* materialistic, but this statement is to be counterweighted with his own strong Marxist view.

47. Dickson, "Joachism and the Amalricians," 41. The end of the Amalricians was caused by the ecclesiastical spy Richard of Namur who infiltered himself into the sect and brought it to its end.

48. Dickson, "The Burning of the Amalricians," 358-59.

49. Dickson, "The Burning of the Amalricians," 359.

50. Dickson, "The Burning of the Amalricians," 361. Note, also, that "[b]y the early thirteenth century the orthodox economy of salvation had moved away from Romanesque transcendence—with its stress upon the divine majesty—toward Gothic immanence and a corresponding emphasis upon divine proximity" (Dickson, "The Burning of the Amalricians," 367).

51. Nietzsche, *Thus Spoke Zarathustra*, 108.

52. Purushottama Bilimoria, "Philosophical Orientalism in Comparative Philosophy of Religion: Hegel to Habermas (& Žižek)," *Cultura Oriental* 2, no. 2 (July–December 2015): 49. The original paragraph appears in Hegel's *Vorlesungen über die Geschichte der Philosophie*, Werke 12 (Stuttgart: Suhrkamp, 1986), 417.

53. F. W. J. Schelling, *Philosophie der Offenbarung* (part II, book 4), 70. Cited from *Schellings Werke: Nach der Originalausgabe in neuer Anordnung*, ed. Manfred Schröter (Munich: C. H. Beck, 1927–1959 and 1962–1971): "Die dritte Zeit, die während der ganzen Schöpfung die *zukünftige* ist, in die alles gelangen soll, sey die Zeit des Geistes [. . . , as followed by] eine dritte Oekonomie, eine dritte Zeit bevorstehe, die Zeit des Geistes, welche das *ewige* Evangelium bringen solle." (II/4, 71 and 72; see 328 for the third age as an age of the religion of humanity when Christianity finally becomes "erst wahrhaft *öffentliche* Religion—nicht als *Staats*religion, nicht als Hochkirche, sondern als Religion des Menschengeschlechts, das in ihm zugleich die höchste Wissenschaft besitzt"). For Jn 7:39, see *The Holy Bible*, NRSV (Nashville, TN: Thomas Nelson Publishing, 1989).

54. Irigaray, *Key Writings*, 167.

55. Unger, *The Religion of the Future*, 261. On cosmic Jesus, see Caputo's *The Insistence of God*: "I treat Jesus as a Judeo-pagan prophet and healer, in tune with the animals and the elements, in whose body the elements dance their cosmic dance, supplying as it does a conduit through which the elements flow, and I treat the elements as a cosmic grace which is channeled by the body of Jesus" (251-52).

56. For the notion of self-affection, see Irigaray, *In the Beginning, She Was*, 161–62: "Self-affection today needs a return to our own body, our own breath, a care about our life in order not to become subjected to technologies, to money, to power, to neutralization in a universal 'someone,' to assimilation into an anonymous world, to the solitude of individualism. Self-affection needs faithfulness to oneself, respect for the other in their singularity, reciprocity in desire and love—more generally, in humanity. We have to rediscover and cultivate self-affection starting, at each time and in every situation, from two, two who respect their difference, in order to preserve the survival and the becoming of humanity, for each one and for all of us." More on this in Lenart Škof, "Breath as a Way of Self-Affection: On New Topologies of Transcendence and Self-Transcendence," *Bogoslovni vestnik* 77, no. 3/4 (2017): 577–87.

57. Gaston Bachelard, *Air and Dreams: An Essay on the Imagination of Movement*, trans. E. R. Farrell and C. F. Farrell (Dallas: Dallas Institute of Humanities and Culture, 2011), chap. 5, "Nietzsche and the Ascensional Psyche," 136–37.

58. Agamben, *The Coming Community*, 52.

59. Irigaray, *Key Writings*, 170. And also: "God is us, we are divine if we are woman and man in a perfect way" (169).

60. Rorty and Vattimo, *The Future of Religion*, 40.

Postlude

1. Verses by the author.

2. *The Great Tantra of the Lion's Perfected Display-Energy* (Tib.: *Senge rtsal rdzogs chen po'i rgyud*), trans. Janet Gyatso, in *Buddhist Scriptures*, ed. Donald S. Lopez Jr. (London: Penguin, 2004), 489.

3. *The Great Tantra of the Lion's Perfected Display-Energy*, 492 and 491.

4. See Škof, *Antigone's Sisters*, 116.

5. Dualis, or dual, is a grammatical number that, among the Indo-European languages, is rarely attested. It is fully preserved and used in the Slovenian language, and, in addition, it can be found also in the Lower and Upper Sorbian languages in the southeast of Germany and in the Lithuanian language. Among the non-Indo-European languages, it can be found in Arabic.

6. Schelling, *Philosophical Inquiries into the Nature of Human Freedom*, 79. For more on the topics of the Vedic creation and Schelling, see Škof, *Breath of Proximity*, chap. 3, and *Antigone's Sisters*, chap. 4.

7. *The Great Tantra of the Lion's Perfected Display-Energy*, 491 and 492.

8. In Tibetan Buddhism, Ādibuddha is the highest being and all buddhas are seen as aspects of his nature as *śūnyatā* (emptiness). Ādibuddha is the personification of the *Dharma*-body. In India, this buddha is known as Vajradhāra, while in Tibet it is known as Samantabhadra.

9. I thank Donald S. Lopez for his commentary on this beautiful tantra. Rnying-ma practice (known as Nyingma sect) involves sexual activity under controlled meditative conditions, in which its energy is transmuted into a form of wisdom.

10. Yael Bentor, "Can Women Attain Enlightenment through Vajrayāna Practices?," in *Karmic Practices: Israeli Scholarship on India*, ed. David Shulman and Shalva Weil (New Delhi: Oxford University Press, 2008), 132.

11. Bentor, "Can Women Attain Enlightenment through Vajrayāna Practices?," 133. Bentor adds: "The fourteenth Dalai Lama holds the same view: 'But the position of Highest Yoga Tantra is different [from that of the Vinaya, Abhidharma, and Mahāyāna]. . . . In Highest Yoga Tantra—for example, in the Guhyasamāja Root Tantra—the possibility of a female practitioner becoming fully enlightened in her lifetime in female form is stated explicitly and unambiguously'" (133).

12. Hermann Spreckelmeyer, *Die philosophische Deutung des Sundenfalls bei Franz Baader*, trans. Robert Faas (Würzburg: C. J. Becker Universitäts Druckerei, 1938), 262. I thank Robert Faas for sharing his unpublished translation of this work with me (I have slightly modified some portions of this translation). This chapter includes essential portions from Baader's erotic philosophy. For his erotic philosophy, see the following edition: Baader, *Erotische Philosophie*; the excerpts from both editions are based on the following collection: Franz von Baader, *Sämtliche Werke*, 16 vols., ed. von Franz Hoffman et al. (Leipzig: Christoph Schlüter, 1851–1860; new ed. in Aalen, 1963).

The following note needs to accompany our elaboration of the *sexuate theology*: we borrow "sexuate" from Irigaray, who affirms that "sexuate identity" must be distinguished from mere sexuality and thus only "sexual" aspects of the person. Regarding the elaboration of sexual difference in Baader, his eros-metaphysics might be labeled as being masculine-oriented. But we also need to add that during his stay in England (1792–1796), Baader had met Mary Wollstonecraft and wrote the following entry into his diary (dated from December 26, 1792): "Der Miss Mary Wollstoncraft Rights of Women haben mich sehr getroffen." (*Erotische Philosophie*, 71). Also, in his later erotic writings (*Sätze aus der erotischen Philosophie* from 1828) Baader writes: "Ich nenne das Weib darum die Bewahrenin der Liebe, weil bekanntlich beim Manne nicht die Liebe, sondern die Lust die inititive hat" (135). In this essay, and as based on his idea of original or ontological androgynity, Baader also affirms that a man assists woman to achieve the masculine part inside her, and a woman assists man to achieve the feminine part inside him.

Regarding the earliest testimony on sexual difference in the Indian context, we have in the *Bṛhadāraṇyaka Upaniṣad* the cosmologico-theological narrative of the creation of a woman and a man from the beginning of this world. According to this most ancient of all Upaniṣads, in the beginning this world was like one single body (*ātman*): there was nothing else around it. And then the creation of the two sexes happens as follows: "He found no pleasure at all; so one finds no pleasure when one is alone. He wanted to have a companion. Now he was as large as a man and a woman in close embrace. So he split (*pat*) his body into two, giving rise to husband (*pati*) and wife (*patni*). . . . He copulated with her, and from their union human beings were born" (*Upaniṣads*, trans. Patrick Olivelle (Oxford: Oxford University Press, 1996), 13–14; 1.4.3). As stated by Valerie J. Roebuck, "in Sanskrit, *ātman* remains masculine regardless of sex of the person to which it refers: 'himself,' 'herself,' itself etc." (*The Upaniṣads*, trans. and ed. Valerie J. Roebuck [London: Penguin Books, 2000, 396]). Ātman thus here takes on the role of the male creator-god.

13. For his influence on Schelling's thought, see Škof, *Antigone's Sisters*, chap. 4 ("Clara/The Matrix"). For his influence on Feuerbach, see chap. 3 on Mary and Sophia.

14. For Böhme, we are following the study of Ernst Benz, *Der Vollkommene Mensch nach Jacob Böhme* (Stuttgart: Kohlhammer, 1937), chap. 7: "Fall and Sex" ("Fall und Geschlecht"), see 117 for the citation.

15. Benz, *Der Vollkommene Mensch nach Jacob Böhme*, 119. It is interesting to observe that, both in Christianity and in Vajrayāna's symbolism, it is the feminine Sophia that represents wisdom.

16. For Feuerbach, being on a trace of this thought, alongside water, the pneumatic element represents the core of our being. See, on this, Škof, *Breath of Proximity*, chap. 5 ("Feuerbach's 'Pneumatische Wasserheillehre'").

17. Spreckelmeyer, *Die philosophische Deutung des Sundenfalls bei Franz Baader*, 265 ("Elektrizität und Geschlechtskraft").

18. Spreckelmeyer, *Die philosophische Deutung des Sundenfalls bei Franz Baader*, 267 (translation adjusted). Original: "Diese befanden sich nach seiner Schaffung in Temperatur und in der Möglichkeit: des posse der Nicht-union. Das Wesentliche der Androgyne ist somit der Gedanke des menschlichen Idea-bezugs von seiner Ganzheit her, weil dieser die Unmittelbarkeit seiner Existenz vor gott verbürgt, die ewige Dauer der imago Dei in homine."

19. Spreckelmeyer, *Die philosophische Deutung des Sundenfalls bei Franz Baader*, 270.

20. Spreckelmeyer, *Die philosophische Deutung des Sundenfalls bei Franz Baader*, 277–78.

21. Spreckelmeyer, *Die philosophische Deutung des Sundenfalls bei Franz Baader*, 279. Here Baader reflects on Bernard de Clairvaux's Sermon 81 of the *Song of Songs*.

22. Yancy Warren Smith, "Hippolytus' Commentary on the Song of Songs in Social and Critical Context," PhD diss., Texas Christian University, 2009, 268 (emphasis added).

23. *Gospel of Philip* (II.3), in *The Nag Hammadi Library*, ed. James M. Robinson (San Francisco: Harper & Row, 1977), 139. See, on this, Keller, "'She Talks Too Much': Magdalene Meditations," in *Toward a Theology of Eros: Transfiguring Passion at the Limits of Discipline*, ed. Virginia Burrus and Catherine Keller (New York: Fordham University Press, 2007), 240–41.

24. Keller, "'She Talks Too Much,'" 241.
25. *The Holy Bible—New Revised Standard Version* (Nashville, TN: Thomas Nelson, 1989).
26. John Trinick, *The Fire-Tried Stone* (Cornwall: Wordens of Cornwall, 1967), 101.
27. Trinick, *The Fire-Tried Stone*, 102.
28. Bowman and Crockett, *Cosmology, Ecology, and the Energy of God*, 14 (chap. 1 by Catherine Keller, "The Energy We Are: A Meditation in Seven Pulsations").
29. Bowman and Crockett, *Cosmology, Ecology, and the Energy of God*, 21.
30. Bowman and Crockett, *Cosmology, Ecology, and the Energy of God*, 22. See also: "If you interfere with particle **a**, its entangled particle **b**—even if it has gotten itself to a galaxy a billion light years aways—will respond as though you have interfered with it too. And it will respond instantaneously. Malin suggests that 'such a connection takes place because both events form a single creative act, a single actual entity, arising out of a common [energy] field of potentialities."
31. Bowman and Crockett, *Cosmology, Ecology, and the Energy of God*, 25.
32. Amy Hollywood, "Sexual Desire, Divine Desire; Or, Queering the Beguines," in Burrus and Keller, *Toward a Theology of Eros*, 120.
33. Hollywood, "Sexual Desire, Divine Desire," 122.
34. Ellipses in original.
35. Cited from Hollywood, "Sexual Desire, Divine Desire," 125–26.
36. Grafenauer, *Dihindih*, 125. Translated by Ana Jelnikar.
37. Hollywood, "Sexual Desire, Divine Desire," 128.
38. Grafenauer, *Dihindih*, 117. Translated by Ana Jelnikar.
39. Ludwig Binswanger, *Grundformen und Erkenntnis menschlichen Daseins* (Heidelberg: Roland Asanger Verlag, 1993), 179.
40. Luce Irigaray, *The Way of Love*, trans. Heidi Bostic and Stephen Pluháček (London: Continuum, 2002).
41. Irigaray, *The Way of Love*, 45.
42. Irigaray, *The Way of Love*, 50.
43. Irigaray, *The Way of Love*, 50 and 51.
44. Mayra Rivera, "Ethical Desires: Toward a Theology of Relational Transcendence," in Burrus and Keller, *Toward a Theology of Eros*, 256.
45. Rivera, "Ethical Desires," 260 (emphasis added).
46. Rivera, "Ethical Desires," 265. Rivera is critical of Irigaray's heteronormativity as well as of the forms of the flesh that Irigaray does not address—such as "skin color, the texture of the hair, the scars on the skin, one's body type marker of racial difference" (269)—all marking specific *memories* of these bodies. It remains a question whether Irigaray's thought really cannot accommodate and welcome these types of differences.
47. Feuerbach, *The Essence of Christianity*, 12–13.

48. Ludwig Feuerbach, *Principles of Philosophy of the Future*, trans. Zawar Hanfi (New York: Prism Key Press, 2013), 57 and 77. For more on this see my analysis of intersubjectivity in Feuerbach in *Breath of Proximity*, 78–82 (also as related to Fichte).

49. Feuerbach, *Das Wesen des Christentums*, viii–ix.

50. Ludwig Feuerbach, "Einige Bemerkungen über den 'Anfang der Philosophie' von Dr J. F. Reiff," in *Kritiken und Abhandlungen II, 1839–1843* (Frankfurt am Main: Suhrkamp, 1975),138 and 139.

51. Feuerbach, *The Essence of Christianity*, 50. In the first section of *The Essence of Religion*, he states: "That being, which is different from and independent of man, or, which is the same thing, of God, as represented in *The Essence of Christianity*, the being without human nature, without human qualities and without human individuality is in reality nothing but *Nature*" (Feuerbach, *The Essence of Religion*, 1).

52. Feuerbach, *The Essence of Religion*, 6–7.

53. Feuerbach, *Principles of Philosophy of the Future*, 62.

54. Feuerbach, *Principles of Philosophy of the Future*, 76.

55. Thorne, *The Science of Interstellar*, 192–93.

56. Zohar and Marshall, *SQ*, 70. See also: "At the beginning of this chapter I spoke of the quantum vacuum—the background energy state of the universe, the source of everything that exists. I pointed out that the vacuum is the ultimate transcendent reality describable within physics. It is the still, silent 'ocean' on which existence appears as 'waves' (oscillations of energy). The first thing to emerge from the vacuum is an energy field known as the Higgs Field. This is filled with very fast, coherent energy oscillations that are the origin of all fields and fundamental particles in the universe. It is in itself a huge Bose-Einstein condensate. If proto-consciousness *is* a fundamental property of the universe, then there is proto-consciousness in the Higgs Field, and the *quantum vacuum becomes very like what mystics have called the 'immanent God,' the God within all.* . . . 'God' is the true centre of the self." (89–90; emphasis added).

57. Cf. Caputo, *Cross and Cosmos*, 203: "Each thing is entangled with everything else in a common field of potentiality, a common (under)ground of being, a sea of entangled potentiality, a wavy undulating boundlessness, a *tehom*. Theologically, this resonates with a *Deus-sive-natura* panentheism."

58. Irigaray, *The Way of Love*, 67.

Bibliography

Abram, David. "The Commonwealth of Breath." In *Atmospheres of Breathing*, edited by Lenart Škof and Petri Berndtson. Albany: State University of New York Press, 2018.
Abram, David. *The Spell of the Sensuous: Perception and Language in a More-Than-Human World*. New York: Vintage Books, 1997.
Agamben, Giorgio. *The Coming Community*. Translated by Michael Hardt. Minneapolis: University of Minnesota Press, 2009.
Albert, Karl. "Amalrich von Bena und der mittelalterliche Pantheismus." In *Die Auseinandersetzungen an der Pariser Universität im XIII. Jahrundert*, edited by A. Zimmermann. Berlin: Walter de Gruyter, 1976.
Alterman, Peter S. "Aliens in Golding's 'The Inheritors.'" *Science Fiction Studies* 5, no. 1 (1978).
Anderson, D. R. "Awakening in the Everyday." In *Pragmatism and Religion*, edited by S. Rosenbaum, 142–52. Urbana: University of Illinois Press, 2003.
Anderson, Gary A. *Sacrifices and Offerings in Ancient Israel: Studies in Their Social and Political Importance*. Atlanta: Scholars Press, 1987.
Andriopoulos, Stefan. *Ghostly Apparitions: German Idealism, the Gothic Novel, and Optical Media*. New York: Zone Books, 2013.
Arieti, Silvano. *The Intrapsychic Self: Feeling, Cognition, Creativity in Health and Mental Illness*. New York: Basic Books, 1967.
Assmann, Jan. "Monotheismus und Kosmotheismus: Ägyptische Formen eines 'Denkens des Einen' und ihre europäische Rezeptionsgeschichte." Conference presentation. Heidelberg: Universitätsverlag Winter, 1993.
Athanasius. "De Incarnatione 16." In *Incarnation: On the Scope and Depth of Christology*, edited by Niels Henrik Gregersen. Minneapolis: Fortress Press, 2015.
Baader, Franz von. *Erotische Philosophie*. Aus den Schriften Franz von Baaders herausgegeben von Gerd-Klaus Kaltenbrunner. Frankfurt am Main: Insel Verlag, 1991.
The Babylonian Talmud, Book 9 (Tract Abuda Zara), vol. 1. Translated by Michael L. Rodkinson. Boston: Boston New Talmud Publishing Company, 1918.

Bachelard, Gaston. *Air and Dreams: An Essay on the Imagination of Movement*. Translated by E. R. Farrell and C. F. Farell. Dallas: Dallas Institute of Humanities and Culture, 2011.

Balcerowicz, Piotr. "Extrasensory Perception (Yogi-Pratyakṣa) in Jainism, Proofs of Its Existence and Its Soteriological Implications." In *Yoga in Jainism*, edited by Christopher Key Chapple. London: Routledge, 2016.

Barad, Karen. *Meeting the Universe Halfway: Quantum Physics and the Entanglement of Matter and Meaning*. Durham: Duke University Press, 2007.

Bauckham, Richard. "The Incarnation and the Cosmic Christ." In *Incarnation: On the Scope and Depth of Christology*, edited by Niels Henrik Gregersen. Minneapolis: Fortress Press, 2015.

Benjamin, Walter. "Doctrine of the Similar." *New German Critique* 17 (Spring 1979): 65–69.

Benjamin, Walter. "Surrealism: The Last Snapshot of the European Intelligentsia." In *One-Way Street and Other Writings*, translated by Edmund Japhcott and Kingsley Shorter, 225–39. London: New Left Books, 1979.

Bentor, Yael. "Can Women Attain Enlightenment through Vajrayāna Practices?" In *Karmic Practices: Israeli Scholarship on India*, edited by David Shulman and Shalva Weil. New Delhi: Oxford University Press, 2008.

Benz, Ernst. *Die Vision: Erfahrungsformen und Bilderwelt*. Stuttgart: Ernst Klett Verlag, 1969.

Berndtson, Petri. "Phenomenological Ontology of Breathing: The Phenomenologico-Ontological Interpretation of the Barbaric Conviction of We Breathe Air and a New Philosophical Principle of Silence of Breath, Abyss of Air." PhD diss., University of Jyväskylä, 2018.

Berndtson, Petri. *Phenomenological Ontology of Breathing: The Respiratory Primacy of Being*. London: Routledge 2023.

Berndtson, Petri. "The Possibility of a New Respiratory Ontology." In *Atmospheres of Breathing*, edited by Lenart Škof and Petri Berndtson. New York: State University of New York Press, 2018.

Berndtson, Petri. "The Temple of the Holy Breath as the Place of Conspiracy between the Respiratory Body and the Space of Open Air." In *Art and Common Space*, edited by Anne-Karin Furunes, Simon Harvey, and Maaretta Jaukkuri. Trondheim: Norwegian University of Science and Technology, 2013.

Bevk, France. *Umirajoči bog Triglav: Zgodovinska povest*. Kobarid: Turistično društvo; Notranje Gorice: Društvo Slovenski staroverci, 2018.

Bilimoria, Puruṣhottama. "Philosophical Orientalism in Comparative Philosophy of Religion: Hegel to Habermas (& Žižek)." *Cultura Oriental* 2, no. 2 (July-December 2015): 47–63.

Binswanger, Ludwig. *Grundformen und Erkenntnis menschlichen Daseins*. Heidelberg: Roland Asanger Verlag, 1993.

Blanton, Ward, Clayton Crockett, Jeffrey W. Robbins, and Noëlle Vahanian. *Insurrectionist Manifesto: Four New Gospels for a Radical Politics*. New York: Columbia University Press, 2016.
Bloch, Ernst. *Avicenna and the Aristotelian Left*. New York: Columbia University Press, 2019.
Bloom, Harold. *The American Religion: The Emergence of the Post-Christian Nation*. New York: Simon and Schuster, 1993.
Bowman, Donna, and Clayton Crockett, eds. *Cosmology, Ecology, and the Energy of God*. New York: Fordham University Press, 2012.
Braidotti, Rosi. *The Posthuman*. Cambridge: Polity, 2017.
Brereton, Joel P., and Stephanie W. Jamison. *The Rigveda: A Guide*. Oxford: Oxford University Press, 2020.
Bruno, Giordano. *Cause, Principle and Unity / Essays on Magic*. Translated by Robert de Lucca. Cambridge: Cambridge University Press, 1998.
Bruno, Giordano. *The Expulsion of the Triumphant Beast*. Translated by Arthur D. Imerti. Lincoln: University of Nebraska Press, 2004.
Buddhism and Jainism (Encyclopaedia of Indian Religions). Edited by K. T. S. Sato and Jeffrey D. Long. Dordecht: Springer, 2017.
Burke, Patrick. "Creativity and Unconscious in Merleau-Ponty and Schelling." In *Schelling Now: Contemporary Readings*, edited by Jason M. Wirth, 184–206. Bloomington: Indiana University Press, 2005.
Cannon, Donald Q. "The King Follet Discourse: Joseph Smith's Greatest Sermon in Historical Perspective." *BYU Studies* 18, no. 2 (1978): 179–92.
Capelle, G. C. *Autour du Décret de 1210: Amaury de Bène. Etude sur son panthéisme formel*. Paris, 1932.
Caputo, John D. *Cross and Cosmos: A Theology of Difficult Glory*. Bloomington: Indiana University Press, 2019.
Caputo, John D. *The Insistence of God: A Theology of Perhaps*. Bloomington: Indiana University Press, 2013.
Cartwright, David E. "Schopenhauer's Haunted World: The Use of Weird and Paranormal Phenomena to Corroborate His Metaphysics." In *The Oxford Handbook of Schopenhauer*, edited by Robert L. Wicks. Oxford: Oxford University Press, 2020.
Clough, Bradley S. "The Cultivation of Yogic Powers in the Pāli Path Manuals of Theravāda Buddhism." In *Yoga Powers: Extraordinary Capacities Attained through Meditation and Concentration*, edited by Knut A. Jacobsen. Leiden: Brill, 2012.
Čok, Boris. *V siju mesečine: Ustno izročilo Lokve, Prelož in bližnje okolice*. Ljubljana: ZRC SAZU, 2012.
Cranney, Stephen L. "Divine Darwinism, Comprehensible Christianity, and the Atheist's Wager: Richard Rorty on Mormonism—an Interview with Mary

V. Rorty and Patricia Rorty." *Dialogue: A Journal on Mormon Thought* 43, no. 2 (2010): 109–30.

Critchley, Simon. "Why I Love Mormonism." *New York Times* (September 16, 2012). https://archive.nytimes.com/opinionator.blogs.nytimes.com/2012/09/16/why-i-love-mormonism/.

Cross, Stephen. *Schopenhauer's Encounter with Indian Thought: Representation and Will and Their Indian Parallels.* Honolulu: University of Hawai'i Press, 2013.

Davies, Douglas J. *An Introduction to Mormonism.* Cambridge: Cambridge University Press, 2003.

Deleuze, Gilles. *Expressionism in Philosophy: Spinoza.* New York: Zone Books, 1992.

Deloria, Vine, Jr., and Daniel Wildcat. *Power and Place: Indian Education in America.* Golden, CO: American Indian Graduate Center and Fulcrum Resources, 2001.

Denz, Jacob. "Rigorous Mediacy: Addressing Mother in Hölderlin's 'Am Quell der Donau,' 'Die Wanderung,' and 'An die Madonna.'" *MLN* 130, no. 3 (April 2015).

Derrida, Jacques. *Of Spirit: Heidegger and the Question.* Translated by G. Berrington. Chicago: University of Chicago Press, 1991.

Derrida, Jacques. *Psyche: Inventions of the Other, Part 1.* Edited by P. Kamuf and E. Rottenberg. Stanford: Stanford University Press, 2007.

Derrida, Jacques. *Writing and Difference.* Translated by Alan Bass. London: Routledge, 2009.

Dewey, John. *A Common Faith.* New Haven: Yale University Press, 1934.

Dickson, Gary. "The Burning of the Amalricians." *Journal of Ecclesiastical History* 40, no. 3 (July 1989).

Dickson, Gary. "Joachism and the Amalricians." *Florensia* 1 (1987): 35.

Doctrine and Covenants. Church of Jesus Christ and the Latter Day Saints, 1835. https://www.churchofjesuschrist.org/study/scriptures/dc-testament?lang=eng.

Downing, Barry H. *The Bible and Flying Saucers.* New York: Avon, 1970.

Duncan, Dayton. *The Dust Bowl: An Illustrated History.* San Francisco: Chronicle Books, 2012.

Dundas, Paul. *The Jains.* London: Routledge, 2002.

Edwards, Denis. *Ecology at the Heart of Faith.* Maryknoll, NY: Orbis, 2006.

Edwards, Denis. *The Natural World and God: Theological Explorations.* Adelaide: ATF Press, 2017.

Egan, Timothy. *The Worst Hard Time.* Boston: Mariner Books, 2006.

Emmons, C. F., and J. Sobal. "Paranormal Beliefs: Functional Alternatives to Mainstream Religion?" *Review of Religious Research* 22, no. 4 (1981): 301–12.

Engel, Gregory S., Tessa R. Calhoun, Elizabeth L. Read, Tae-Kyu Ahn, Tomáš Mančal, Yuan-Chung Cheng, Robert E. Blankenship, and Graham R. Fleming. "Evidence for Wavelike Energy Transfer through Quantum Coherence in Photosynthetic Systems." *Nature* 446 (2007): 782–86.

Ettinger, Bracha L. "Transgressing With-In-To the Feminine." In *Feminist Readings of Antigone*, edited by Fanny Söderbäck. Albany: State University of New York Press, 2010.
Ferguson, Kennan. "What Was Politics to the Denisovan?" *Political Theory* 42, no. 2 (2014): 167–87.
Feuerbach, Ludwig. *Das Wesen des Christentums*. Leipzig: Otto Wigand, 1841.
Feuerbach, Ludwig. *The Essence of Christianity*. Translated by George Eliot. New York: Harper & Row, 1957.
Feuerbach, Ludwig. *The Essence of Religion*. Translated by Alexander Loos. New York: Prometheus Books, 2004.
Florschütz, Gottleib. "Schopenhauer und die Magie—die praktische Metaphysik." *Schopenhauer Jahrbuch* 93 (2012).
Fox, Matthew. *The Coming of Cosmic Christ: The Healing of Mother Earth and the Birth of a Global Renaissance*. New York: Harper, 1989.
Francis, Pope. *Laudato Si'/ Praise Be to You: On Care for Our Common Home*. Vatican: Libreria Editrice Vaticana, 2015.
Freud, Sigmund. *The Standard Edition of the Complete Psychological Works, Vols. 18 and 19*. Edited and translated by J. Strachey. London: Vintage, 2001.
Furby, Jacqueline. "About Time Too: From *Interstellar* to *Following*, Christopher Nolan's Continuing Preoccupation with Time-Travel." In *The Cinema of Christopher Nolan: Imagining the Impossible*, edited by Jacqueline Furby and Stuart Joy. New York: Columbia University Press, 2015.
Gebara, Ivonne. *Longing for Running Water: Ecofeminism and Liberation*. Translated by David Mollineaux. Minneapolis: Fortress Press, 1999.
Givens, Terryl L. *Wrestling the Angel*. Oxford: Oxford University Press, 2015.
Gourgouris, Statis. *The Perils of the One*. New York: Columbia University Pres, 2019.
Grafenauer, Niko. *Dihindih*. Ljubljana: Mladinska knjiga, 2000.
Graham, Billy. *Angels: God's Secret Agents*. Garden City, NJ: Doubleday, 1975.
Grau, Carles, Romuald Ginhoux, Alejandro Riera, Thanh Lam Nguyen, Hubert Chauvat, Michel Berg, Julià L. Amengual, Alvaro Pascual-Leone, and Giulio Ruffini. "Conscious Brain-to-Brain Communication in Humans Using Non-Invasive Technologies." *PLOS One*, 2014. https://journals.plos.org/plosone/article?id=10.1371/journal.pone.0105225.
The Great Tantra of the Lion's Perfected Display-Energy. Translated by Janet Gyatso. In *Buddhist Scriptures*, edited by Donald S. Lopez Jr. London: Penguin, 2004.
Green, B. P. "The Catholic Church and Technological Progress: Past, Present, and Future." In *Religion and the New Technologies*, edited by N. Herzfeld. Basel: MDPI, 2017.
Green, M. B., and J. H. Schwarz. "Anomaly Cancellations in Supersymmetric D = 10 Gauge Theory and Superstring Theory." *Physics Letters B* 149, nos. 1–3 (1984): 117–22.

Greene, Brian. *The Elegant Universe: Superstrings, Hidden Dimensions, and the Quest for the Ultimate Theory*. 2nd ed. New York: W. W. Norton, 2010.
Gregersen, Neils Henrik. "The Cross of Christ in an Evolutionary World." *Dialog: A Journal of Theology* 40, no. 3 (2001): 192–207.
Gregersen, Neils Henrik. "The Extended Body of Christ: Three Dimensions of Deep Incarnation." In *Incarnation: On the Scope and Depth of Christology*, edited by Neils Henrik Gregerson. Minneapolis: Fortress Press, 2015.
Griffin, David Ray. *Parapsychology, Philosophy, and Spirituality: A Postmodern Exploration*. New York: State University of New York Press, 1997.
Griffin, David Ray. *Reenchantment without Supernaturalism: A Process Philosophy of Religion*. Ithaca: Cornell University Press, 2001.
Griffith, Ralph T. H. *The Hymns of the Rgveda*. Delhi: Motilal Banarsidass, 1995.
Grim, John. "Indigenous Lifeways and Knowing of the World." In *The Oxford Handbook of Religion and Science*, edited by Philip Clayton and Zachary Simpson. Oxford: Oxford University Press, 2006.
Grosz, Elizabeth. *The Incorporeal: Ontology, Ethics, and the Limits of Materialism*. New York: Columbia University Press, 2018.
Haeckel, Ernst. *Gott-Natur (Theophysis)*. Leipzig: Alfred Kröner Verlag, 1914.
Haeckel, Ernst. *Kristallseelen: Studien über das anorganische Leben*. New Delhi: Pranava Books, 1917.
Harvey, Van Austin. *Feuerbach and the Interpretation of Religion*. Cambridge: Cambridge University Press, 1995.
Hawke, Shé M. "The Exile of Greek Metis: Recovering a Maternal Divine Ontology." In "Ontologies of Asylum," *Poligrafi* 23, no. 91/92 (2018): 41–75.
Hegel, G. W. F. *Vorlesungen über die Geschichte der Philosophie*. Werke 12. Stuttgart: Suhrkamp, 1986.
Heidegger, Martin. *Elucidations of Hölderlin's Poetry*. Translated by K. Hoeller. New York: Humanity Books, 2000.
Heidegger, Martin. *On Time and Being*. Translated by Joan Stambaugh. New York: Harper and Row, 1972.
Heidegger, Martin. *Pathmarks*. Edited by W. McNeill. Cambridge: Cambridge University Press, 2007.
Heidegger, Martin. *Poetry, Language, Thought*. Translated by A. Hofstadter. New York: Harper and Row, 1971.
Heidegger, Martin. *Überlegungen II–VI: Schwarze Hefte 1931–1938* (GA94). Edited by P. Trawny. Frankfurt am Main: Kostermann, 2014.
Hölderlin, Friedrich. *Poems and Fragments*. Translated by Michael Hamburger. London: Anvil Press Poetry, 2005.
Hollywood, Amy. "Sexual Desire, Divine Desire; Or, Queering the Beguines." In *Toward a Theology of Eros: Transfiguring Passion at the Limits of Discipline*, edited by Virginia Burrus and Catherine Keller. New York: Fordham University Press, 2007.

The Holy Bible—New Revised Standard Version. Nashville, TN: Thomas Nelson Publishers, 1990.
Hopkins, Gerard Manley. "The Blessed Virgin Compared to the Air We Breathe." *Hopkins Poetry.* http://hopkinspoetry.com/poem/the-blessed-virgin/.
Irigaray, Luce. *The Forgetting of Air in Martin Heidegger.* Translated by Mary Beth Mader. Austin: University of Texas, 1999.
Irigaray, Luce. *In the Beginning, She Was.* London: Bloomsbury, 2013.
Irigaray, Luce. *Key Writings.* London: Continuum, 2004.
Irigaray, Luce. *Sharing the World.* London: Continuum, 2008.
Irigaray, Luce. *To Be Born.* New York: Palgrave Macmillan, 2017.
Irigaray, Luce. *The Way of Love.* Translated by Heidi Bostic and Stephen Pluháček. London: Continuum, 2008.
Irigaray, Luce, and Michael Marder. *Through Vegetal Being.* New York: Columbia University Press, 2016.
Jacobsen, Knut A. *Yoga Powers: Extraordinary Capacities Attained through Meditation and Concentration.* Edited by Knut A. Jacobsen. Leiden: Brill, 2012.
Joachim of Fiore, *Liber figurarum: Il libro delle Figure dell'Abate Gioacchino da Fiore.* Edited by Leone Tondelli, Marjorie Reeves, and Beatrice Hirsch-Reich, 2 vols. Turin: Società editrice internazionale, 1953.
Johnson, Elizabeth. *Ask the Beasts: Darwin and the God of Love.* London: Bloomsbury, 2014.
Johnson, Elizabeth. "Deep Resurrection." *Modern Believing* 64, no. 2 (Spring 2023): 152-61.
Johnson, Elizabeth. "Jesus and the Cosmos: Soundings in Deep Christology." In *Incarnation: On the Scope and Depth of Christology*, edited by Niels Henrik Gregersen. Minneapolis: Fortress Press, 2015.
Jones, Ernst. *Sigmund Freud: Life and Works.* 3 vols. London: Hogarth Press, 1953-1957.
Josephson-Storm, Jason Ā. *The Myth of Disenchantment: Magic, Modernity, and the Birth of the Human Sciences.* Chicago: University of Chicago Press, 2017.
Julian of Norwich. *Revelations of Divine Love.* Translated by E. Spearing. London: Penguin, 1998.
Kant, Immanuel. *Critique of Judgement.* Translated by P. Guyer and E. Matthews. Cambridge: Cambridge University Press, 2000.
Kearney, Richard. *Anatheism: Returning to God after God.* New York: Columbia University Press, 2010.
Keller, Catherine. "The Entangled Cosmos: An Experiment in Physical Theopoetics." *Journal of Cosmology* 20 (September 2012): 8648–66. http://journalofcosmology.com/JOC20/Keller_rev1.pdf.
Keller, Catherine. *Face of the Deep: A Theology of Becoming.* London: Routledge, 2007.

Keller, Catherine. "'She Talks Too Much': Magdalene Meditations." In *Theology of the Eros: Transfiguring Passion at the Limits of Discipline*, edited by V. Burrus and C. Keller, 234–54. New York: Fordham University Press, 2007.

Keller, Catherine. "Tingles of Matter, Tangles of Theology." In *Entangled Worlds: Religion, Science, and New Materialism*, edited by C. Keller and Mary-Jane Rubenstein, 111–35. New York: Fordham University Press, 2017.

Keller, Catherine, and Mary-Jane Rubenstein, eds. *Entangled Worlds: Religion, Science, and New Materialisms*. New York: Fordham University Press, 2017.

Kirk, G. S., J. E. Raven, and M. Schofield. *The Presocratic Philosophers*. Cambridge: Cambridge University Press, 1999.

Klapwijk, Jakob. *Purpose in the Living World? Creation and Emergent Revolution*. Edited and translated by Harry Cook. Cambridge: Cambridge University Press, 2008.

Kosovel, Srečko. "'Cosmic Life." In *Open: Selected Poems and Thoughts / Srečko Kosovel*, edited by Mateja Kralj and translated by Ana Jelnikar and Barbara Siegel Carlson. Sežana: Društvo Konstruktivist, 2018.

Kropf, Andrea. *Philosophie und Parapscyhologie: Zur Rezeptionsgeschichte parapsychologischer Phänomene am Beispiel Kants, Schopenhauers und C.G. Jungs*. Munster: LIT Verlag, 2000.

Levy, Robert I., and Kedar Rāj Rājopādhyāya. *Mesocosm: Hinduism and the Organization of a Traditional Newar City of Nepal*. Berkeley: University of California Press, 1990.

Ley, Hermann. *Studie zur Geschichte des Materialismus im Mittelalter*. Berlin: VEB Deutscher Verlag der Wissenschaften, 1957.

Louth, A. *Maximus the Confessor*. New York: Routledge, 1996.

Man, R. *Jung on Synchronicity and the Paranormal*. London: Routledge, 1997.

Marder, Elisa. "Mourning, Magic and Telepathy." *Oxford Literary Review* 30, no. 2 (2008): 191–200.

Marion, Jean-Luc. *Givenness and Revelation*. Translated by Stephen E. Lewis. Oxford: Oxford University Press, 2016.

Marion, Jean-Luc. *L'Idole et la distance: Cinq études*. Paris: Bernard Grasset, 1977.

Marion, Jean-Luc. *The Idol and Distance: Five Studies*. Translated by Thomas A. Carlson. New York: Fordham University Press, 2001.

Marx, Karl. "Theses on Feuerbach." In *The Marx-Engels Reader*, edited by Robert C. Tucker. 2nd ed. New York: W.W. Norton, 1978.

Mason, Herbert W. *Al-Hallaj*. London: Routledge, 2007.

McFague, Sally. *The Body of God: An Ecological Theology*. Minneapolis: Fortress Press, 1993.

Medvešček-Klančar, Pavel. *Iz nevidne strani neba: Razkrite skrivnosti staroverstva*. Ljubljana: ZRS SAZU, 2015.

Merleau-Ponty, Maurice. *In Praise of Philosophy and Other Essays*. Translated by John Wild and James Edie John. Evanston, IL: Northwestern University Press, 1988.

Merleau-Ponty, Maurice. *Nature: Course Notes from the Collège de France*. Translated by Robert Vallier. Evanston, IL: Northwestern University Press, 1995,

Merleau-Ponty, Maurice. *Phenomenology of Perception*. Translated by David A. Landes. London: Routledge, 2012.

Merleau-Ponty, Maurice. *Sense and Non-Sense*. Translated by Hubert L. Dreyfus and Patricia Allen Dreyfus. Evanston, IL: Northwestern University Press, 1964.

Merleau-Ponty, Maurice. *Themes from the Lectures at the Collège de France (1952–1960)*. Translated by John O'Neill. In *In Praise of Philosophy and Other Essays*, translated by John Wild and James Edie John (Evanston, IL: Northwestern University Press, 1988).

Merleau-Ponty, Maurice. *The Visible and the Invisible*. Translated by Alphonso Lingis. Evanston, IL: Northwestern University Press, 1968.

Mikhailov, Nikolai. *Zgodovina slovanske mitologije v XX. stoletju*. Ljubljana: ZRC SAZU, 2021.

Miller, Adam S. *Badiou, Marion, and St. Paul: Immanent Grace*. London: Bloomsbury, 2008.

Miller, Adam S. *Future Mormon: Essays in Mormon Theology*. Salt Lake City: Greg Kofford Books, 2016.

Murnane, Kevin. "Science and Tech in Syfy's 'The Expanse': The Spectacular Launch of the 'Nauvoo.'" *Forbes*, March 1, 2017. https://www.forbes.com/sites/kevinmurnane/2017/03/01/science-and-tech-in-syfys-the-expanse-the-spectacular-launch-of-the-nauvoo/.

The Nag Hammadi Library. Edited by James M. Robinson. San Francisco: Harper & Row, 1977.

Nietzsche, Friedrich. *Thus Spoke Zarathustra*. Edited by A. Del Caro and R. Pippin, translated by A. Del Caro. Cambridge: Cambridge University Press, 2006.

O'Donnell, John. "The Trinitarian Panentheism of Sergej Bulgakov." *Gregorianum* 76, no. 1 (1995).

O'Leary, De Lacy. "Al-Hallaj." *Philosophy of East and West* 1, no. 1 (1951): 56-62.

Olivelle, Patrick. *Upaniṣads*. Oxford: Oxford University Press, 1996.

Orenstein, A. "Religion and Paranormal Belief." *Journal for the Scientific Study of Religion* 41, no. 2 (2002).

Oruka, Henry Odera. "Four Trends in Current African Philosophy." In *The African Philosophy Reader*, edited by P. H. Coetzee and A. P. J. Roux, 120-24. Routledge: London, 2003.

Oruka, Henry Odera. *Sage Philosophy: Indigenous Thinkers and Modern Debate on African Philosophy*. Leiden: Brill, 1990.

Paulsen, David L., and Martin Pulido. "'A Mother There': A Survey of Historical Teachings about Mother in Heaven." *BYU Studies* 50, no. 1 (2011): 71-97.

Peacocke, Arthur. *All That Is: A Naturalist Faith for the Twenty-First Century*. Minneapolis: Fortress Press, 2007.

Peters, John Durham. "Reflections on Mormon Materialism." *Sunstone* (March 1993): 47–52.

Peters, John Durham. *Speaking into the Air*. Chicago: University of Chicago Press, 1999.

Peters, Ted. *God—The World's Future*. Minneapolis: Fortress Press, 2017.

Petrey, Taylor G. "Rethinking Mormonism's Heavenly Mother." *Harvard Theological Review* 109, no. 3 (2016): 315–41.

Pile, Steve. "Distant Feeling: Telepathy and the Problem of Affect Transfer over Distance." *Transactions of the Institute of British Geographers*, n.s., 37, no. 1 (2012).

Pleshoyano, Alexandra. "Etty Hillesum: For God and with God." *The Way* 44, no. 1 (January 2005). https://www.theway.org.uk/back/441Pleshoyano.pdf.

Pleterski, Andrei. *Kulturni genom: Prostor in njegovi ideogrami mitične zgodbe*. Ljubljana: ZRC SAZU, 2014.

Pleterski, Andrej. "Verovanje host v sklopu staroverstva na Slovenskem in verovanja starih Slovanov." In *Staroverstvo v Sloveniji med religijo in znanostjo*, edited by S. Babič and M. Belak, 109–43. Studia mythologica Slavica, Supplementum 17. Ljubljana: Založba ZRC, 2022.

Pogačnik, Marko. *Christ's Power and Earth's Wisdom: Searching for the Fifth Gospel*. W. Sussex: Clairview, 2019.

Pogačnik, Marko. *Vesolje človeškega telesa*. Ljubljana: Beletrina; Ljubljana: Društvo za sožitje človeka, narave in prostora Vitaa, 2016.

Pramuk, Christopher. *At Play in Creation: Merton's Awakening to the Feminine Divine*. Collegeville, MI: Liturgical Press, 2015.

Propp, Vladimir Yakovlevich. *Zgodovinske korenine čarobne pravljice*. Ljubljana: ZRC SAZU, Inštitut za slovensko narodopisje, 2013.

Pryor, Adam. *Living with Tiny Aliens: The Image of God in the Anthropocene*. New York: Fordham University Press, 2020.

"Psi phenomena." *Merriam-Webster*. https://www.merriam-webster.com/dictionary/psi%20phenomena.

Randolph, Richard, and Christopher P. McKay. "Protecting and Expanding the Richness and Diversity of Life, an Ethic for Astrobiology Research and Space Exploration." *International Journal of Astrobiology* 13, no. 1 (2014): 28–34.

Reeves, Marjorie. "The Originality and Influence of Joachim of Fiore." *Traditio* 36 (1980): 269–316.

Riedl, Matthias. "A Collective Messiah: Joachim of Fiore's Constitution of Future Society." *Mirabilia* 14 (January–June 2012): 57–80.

Rice, T. W. "Believe It or Not: Religious and Other Paranormal Beliefs in the United States." *Journal for the Scientific Study of Religion* 42, no. 1 (2003): 95–106.

Rivera, Mayra. "Ethical Desires: Toward a Theology of Relational Transcendence." In *Theology of the Eros: Transfiguring Passion at the Limits of Discipline*, edited by Virginia Burrus and Catherine Keller. New York: Fordham University Press, 2007.

Robbins, Jeffrey W. "Necessity as Virtue: On Religious Materialism from Feuerbach to Žižek." In *The Future of Continental Philosophy of Religion*, edited by Clayton B. Crockett, B. Keith Putt, and Jeffrey W. Robbins, 229–41. Bloomington: Indiana University Press, 2014.
Rorty, Richard. *An Ethics for Today: Finding Common Ground between Philosophy and Religion*. New York: Columbia University Press, 2011.
Rorty, Richard. *Philosophy and Social Hope*. London: Penguin, 1999.
Rorty, Richard. *Philosophy as Cultural Politics*. Cambridge: Cambridge University Press, 2007.
Rorty, Richard, and Gianni Vattimo. *The Future of Religion*. Edited by Santiago Zabala. New York: Columbia University Press, 2011.
Rosa, Hartmut. *Resonance: A Sociology of Our Relationship to the World*. Translated by James C. Wagner. Cambridge: Polity Press, 2019.
Rowland, Ingrid D. *Giordano Bruno: Philosopher / Heretic*. Chicago: University of Chicago Press, 2009.
Rubenstein, Mary-Jane. "The Fire Each Time: Dark Energy and the Breath of Creation." In *Cosmology, Ecology, and the Energy of God*, edited by C. Crockett, 26–41. New York: Fordham University Press, 2012.
Ruyer, Raymond. "The Status of the Future and the Invisible World." Translated by R. Scott Walker. *Diogenes* 36 (1980).
Sawicki, Diethard. *Leben mit den Toten: Geisterglauben und die Entstehung des Spiritismus in Deutschland 1770–1900*. Paderborn: Ferdinand Schöningh, 2002.
Schelling, Friedrich Wilhelm Joseph. *Briefe und Dokumente, Bd. 3*. Bonn: Bouvier u. Co., 1975.
Schelling, Friedrich Wilhelm Joseph. *Bruno, or On the Natural and the Divine Principle of Things*. Translated by Michael G. Vater. New York: State University of New York Press, 1984.
Schelling, Friedrich Wilhelm Joseph. *Clara, or, On Nature's Connection to the Spirit World*. Translated by Fiona Steinkamp. New York: State University of New York Press, 2002.
Schelling, Friedrich Wilhelm Joseph. *Philosophical Inquiries into the Nature of Human Freedom*. Translated by J. Gutman. La Salle, IL: Open Court, 1989.
Schmidt, Wilhelm. *The Origin and Growth of Religion: Facts and Theories*. Translated by H. J. Rose. London: Methuen & Co., 1935; repr., Proctorville, OH: Wythe-North Publishing, 2014.
Schneider, Laurel C. *Beyond Monotheism: A Theology of Multiplicity*. London: Routledge, 2008.
Schopenhauer, Arthur. *On the Will in Nature*. Translated by Madame Karl Hillenbrand. London: G Bell and Sons, 1903.
Schopenhauer, Arthur. "Versuch über das Geistersehn." In *Parerga und Paralipomena I—Kleinere philosophische Schriften. Sämtliche Werke, Bd. IV*, ed. von Wolfgang Frhr. von Löhneysen, 273–372. Frankfurt am Main: Suhrkamp, 1986.

Schopenhauer, Arthur. *The World as Will and Representation, Vol. 1*. Translated by E. F. J. Payne. New York: Dover, 1958.

Sherwood, Y., and K. Hart. *Derrida and Religion: Other Testaments*. New York: Routledge, 2005.

Simmer-Brown, Judith. *Dakini's Warm Breath: The Feminine Principle in Tibetan Buddhism*. Boulder: Shambala, 2002.

Simmons, Ernest L. *The Entangled Trinity: Quantum Physics and Theology*. New York: Fortress Press, 2014.

Simpson, Christopher Ben. *Merleau-Ponty and Theology*. London: Bloomsbury, 2014.

Škof, Lenart. *Antigone's Sisters: On the Matrix of Love*. Albany: State University of New York Press, 2021.

Škof, Lenart. *Breath of Proximity: Intersubjectivity, Ethics and Peace*. Dordrecht: Springer, 2015.

Škof, Lenart. "Do Rta dobrega upanja in nazaj: Tri vprašanja o afriški filozofiji." *Filozofski vestnik* 26, no. 3 (2005): 171–85.

Škof, Lenart. "Food in Ancient Indian Philosophy." In *Encyclopaedia of Food and Agricultural Ethics*, edited by Paul B. Thompson and David M. Kaplan. Dordrecht: Springer, 2014. https://doi.org/10.1007/978-94-007-6167-4_491-1.

Škof, Lenart. "Metaphysical Ethics Reconsidered: Schopenhauer, Compassion, and World Religions." *Schopenhauer Jahrbuch* 87 (2006).

Sloterdijk, Peter. *You Must Change Your Life: On Anthropocentrics*. Translated by W. Hoban. Cambridge: Polity, 2013.

Smith, Joseph. "The King Follet Discourse." *Times and Seasons* 5 (1844): 612–17. http://mldb.byu.edu/follett.htm.

Smith, Wilfred Cantwell. *Wilfred Cantwell Smith: A Reader*. Edited by Kenneth Cracknell. Oxford: Oneworld, 2001.

Smith, Yancy Warren. "Hippolytus' Commentary on the Song of Songs in Social and Critical Context." PhD diss., Texas Christian University, 2009.

Snow, Eliza R. *Biography and Family Record of Lorenzo Snow*. Salt Lake City: Deseret News Co., 1884.

Spreckelmeyer, Hermann. *Die philosophische Deutung des Sundenfalls bei Franz Baader*. Translated by Robert Faas. Würzburg: C. J. Becker Universitäts Druckerei, 1938.

Staal, Frits. "Is There Philosophy in Asia?" In *Interpreting across Boundaries: New Essays in Comparative Philosophy*, edited by G. J. Larson and E. Deutsch, 203–29. Princeton: Princeton University Press, 1988.

Stewart, Georgina Tuari. *Maori Philosophy*. London: Bloomsbury, 2021.

Tattvārtha-Sūtra. Edited by Vijay K. Jain. Dehradun: Vikalp Printers, 2018.

Thijssen, J. M. M. H. "Master Amalric and the Amalricians: Inquisitional Procedure and the Suppression of Heresy at the University of Paris." *Speculum* 71 (1996).

Thorne, Kip. *The Science of Interstellar*. New York: W.W. Norton, 2014.

Teilhard de Chardin, Pierre. "The Eternal Feminine." In *Writings in Time of War*, translated by René Hague. New York: Harper and Row, 1968.

Teilhard de Chardin, Pierre. *The Future of Man*. Translated by Norman Denny. New York: Image Books, 1964.
Teilhard de Chardin, Pierre. *Hymn of the Universe*. New York: Harper & Row, 1961.
Teilhard de Chardin, Pierre. *The Phenomenon of Man*. Translated by Bernard Wall. New York: HarperCollins, 2008.
Toplak, Cirila. "Tales in Social Practices of Nature Worshippers of Western Slovenia." *Acta histriae* 30, no. 3 (2022): 627–54.
Trinick, John. *The Fire-Tried Stone*. Cornwall: Wordens of Cornwall, 1967.
Tuari Stewart, Georgina. *Maori Philosophy*. London: Bloomsbury, 2021.
Unger, Roberto M. *The Religion of the Future*. Cambridge: Harvard University Press, 2014.
Upaniṣads. Translated and edited by Valerie J. Roebuck. London: Penguin Books, 2000.
Vattimo, Giani. *After Christianity*. Translated by Luca D'Isanto. New York: Columbia University Press, 2002.
Wallace, Mark I. *When God Was a Bird: Christianity, Animism, and the Re-Enchantment of the World*. New York: Fordham University Press, 2019.
Webb, Stephen H. *Mormon Christianity*. Oxford: Oxford University Press, 2013.
Weeks, M., K. P. Weeks, and M. R. Daniel. "The Implicit Relationship between Religious and Paranormal Constructs." *Journal for the Scientific Study of Religion* 47, no. 4 (2008): 599–611.
Welch, Rosalynde. "The New Mormon Theology of Matter." *Mormon Studies Review* 4, no. 1 (2017).
Whalen, B. E. *Dominion of God: Christendom and Apocalypse in the Middle Ages*. Cambridge: Harvard University Press, 2009.
"What Is Telepathy?" *Scientific American* 148, no. 4 (April 1933): 214–15.
Whitehead, Alfred North. *Essays in Science and Philosophy*. New York: Philosophical Library, 1948.
Wiley, Kristi L. "Extrasensory Perception and Knowledge in Jainism." In *Essays in Jaina Philosophy and Religion*, edited by Piotr Balcerowicz. Delhi: Motilal Banarsidass, 2003.
Wirth, Jason. *The Conspiracy of Life: Meditations on Schelling and His Time*. Albany: State University of New York Press, 2003.
Witzel, Michael. *Kaṭha Āraṇyaka: Critical Edition with a Translation into German and an Introduction*. Cambridge: Harvard University Press, 2004.
Witzel, Michael. "Macrocosm, Mesocosm, and Microcosm: The Persistent Nature of 'Hindu' Beliefs and Symbolic Forms." *International Journal of Hindu Studies* 1, no. 3 (December 1997): 501–39.
Wunn, Ina. "Beginning of Religion." *Numen* 47, no. 4 (2000): 417–52.
Zohar, Danah, and Ian Marshall. *SQ: Connecting with Our Spiritual Intelligence*. London: Bloomsbury, 2000.

Index

Abram, David, 1, 32
abyss, 8, 10–15, 17, 22–23, 61–63, 65, 67, 72
acausality, 105
Adam, 139, 143, 157, 183n40
Adamic-Being, 157
Ādi Buddha, 23, 155
African philosophy, 177n10
Agamben, Giorgio, 46, 89, 139, 144, 147
agape, 121, 135–37
age of spirit/age of breath, 9, 172n5
Age of the Holy Spirit, 139
Akhenaton, 35
al-'Arabī, Ibn, 210n34
Albert, Karl, 148, 212n46
Albigensians, 144–45, 209n24
al-Hallāj, 146–47, 210n34
aliens/extra-terrestrials, 58
alienation, 25
al-Junaid, 146
All-Good Female, 153, 155
Alterman, Peter, 57
Amalric of Bène, 3, 9–10, 46, 87–89, 122, 141, 144, 147, 208n9
Amalricians, 4, 9, 46, 122, 140, 144–49, 151, 208n7, 211n42, 212n46–n47
American Indians/Native Americans, 37, 39–40

anarchy, 119, 129, 199
ancestors/ancestry, 2, 32, 45, 57, 59, 176n7, 181n29
Anderson, Douglas R., 133
androgyny, 39, 154, 156–157, 181n30, 214–15n12, 215n18
animal magnetism, 87, 91, 94–97
animism, 34, 37, 98
aññā, 107
annihilation, 4, 22, 77, 88–89, 124, 14–45
anthropocentrism, 184n4
anthropogenic catastrophe, 8
anthropology of religion, 36
anthropotechnics, 141, 150
anticlericalism, 78
Antigone, 18
antimatter, 191–192n52
antinomianism, 147
antisacramentalism/antisacramental, 147, 149
apophatic entanglement, 175–76n4
apotheosis, 120
appropriation, 75–76, 78, 144
Aquinas, Thomas, 209n23, 211n37
archaeology, 36
archetypes, 104, 106
Aristotle/Aristotelianism, 88, 122–23, 145–46, 209n23
ascesis, 93

Asmus (Matthias Claudius), 92
Assmann, Jan, 34–35, 38, 179n18
astrobiology, 136, 206–207n86
astrology, 115
astrophysics, 127
astrotheology, 135–36
Athanasius, 49–50, 94
atheism, 99, 115
ātman, 60, 124, 172n9, 214–15n12
atmosphere, 20, 58, 76, 101, 135, 151, 210n34
Auschwitz, 7
autoaffection, 117, 201n15
avadhi, 108–109
avadhijñāna, 108, 110
Averroës, 88, 122–24, 145–46
Avicebron, 209n23

Baader, Franz von, 3, 154–58, 161, 171n3, 214–15n12, 215n21
Babja jama, 43–44
Babylonian Talmud, 8, 140
Bachelard, Gaston, 151
Bacon, Francis, 88, 196–97n33
Badaliya, 147, 210–11n36
Badiou, Alain, 69, 193n63
Balcerowicz, Piotr, 108
bandhu, 10, 124, 203n45
baptism, 55
Barad, Karen, 99, 197n38
Battlestar Galactica, 205–206n76
Bauckham, Richard, 56, 58
Bell's theorem, 161
Benedict of Nursia, 143
Benjamin, Walter, 198n40
Bentor, Yael, 155, 214n11
Benz, Ernst, 103
Bergson, Henri, 40
Berndtson, Petri, 62, 82
Bevk, France, 29
Bible, 34, 83, 190n40
Binswanger, Ludwig, 154, 163

biosphere, 29, 64
Blake, William, 81, 160
Bloch, Ernst, 146, 208n7, 209n23
blood, 42, 45, 59–60, 69, 187n37
bodhisattva(s), 155, 206
Böhme, Jakob, 3, 52, 54, 66, 87, 154–57, 161, 185n15, 215n14
Bohr, Niels, 105
bond/*vinculum*, 4, 10, 45–46, 51, 63–64, 66, 91, 106, 115, 117, 121–24, 127–32, 135–36, 153–54, 156, 159–60, 163, 165, 168
Bonaventure, 56
bone, 80
Bosco, John, 103
Brahman, 60, 124, 172n9, 179n20
Brautmystik, 157
breath of love, 15, 24–25, 61, 101, 127, 154, 168, 185n15
breathing-together, 158
breath-kiss, 4, 155, 157–61, 165, 169
breathy eschatology, 12, 22, 24–25
Brereton, Joel P., 10
Bṛhadāraṇyaka Upaniṣad, 187n44, 214–15n12
bride, 161
Bruno, Giordano, 3–4, 87–88, 90–91, 106, 117, 122–24, 127–29, 131, 135–36, 148, 209n23
Buddha, 23–24, 107, 155–57, 160, 213n8
buddhahood, 155
Buddhism, 22–24, 107–108, 155, 157, 178n17, 213n8
Bulgakov, Sergei, 22
bulk, 130, 132–35, 167, 205n73
bulk beings, 132, 134, 206n77
Burke, Patrick, 16–17, 19

Caputo, John D., 3, 7, 30, 46–47, 55, 65, 102–103, 118–19, 129, 133, 172n2, 183n41, 199n49

cardiology, 154–55
carnality, 160, 163
Cartesianism, 181–82n33
Cartwright, David E., 96–98, 196n33
Cathars, 209
Catholicism/Catholic Church, 36, 147, 176n5, 182n36, 204n57
Celan, Paul, 192
cell division, 23
chalice, 15, 19, 25, 173n22, 194n13
chaos, 11–12, 18, 30, 119, 121, 126, 140
charity, 69, 77, 142
children, 42–43, 72–73, 149, 182n36, 190n37, 204–205n72
Christian mysticism, 161
Christ-Matrix, 61, 65
Christogenesis, 61, 64
Christ-Omega, 61, 64
Church Fathers, 51, 186n25
cinema, 130
clairvoyance, 95, 98, 100, 104–105, 108–10, 198
Claudel, Paul, 62, 192n54
climate change, 50
codependency, 87, 91
Čok, Boris, 31, 33–34
collective unconscious, 104
colonization, 32
compassion, 4, 8, 39, 53, 90–93, 96, 97, 100–102, 109, 147, 156, 166
complementarity, 88, 199n47
computers, 115, 117
Comte, August, 34, 125
conspiracy of love, 160
conspiracy/conspiration, 12, 17, 22, 25, 154, 159, 160, 163
conspiratio (co-breathing), 155, 199n44
contemplation, 51, 156
Cooper (Interstellar), 130–31, 134–35
co-ordination, 91, 128

Copenhagen interpretation of quantum physics, 88
corporal punishment, 182n36
correspondence, 29, 34, 88, 90–93, 97, 101–103, 124, 168, 172n9, 199n47
cosmic Child, 21
cosmic Christ, 50–51, 54–56, 58, 61, 63–65, 125, 128–129
cosmic economy, 64
cosmic egg, 15
cosmic Golden Rule, 206–207n86
cosmic nihilism, 172n2
cosmic uterus, 18, 25
cosmic vibration of love, 128
cosmic wetnurse, 194n13
cosmic wind (*vāyu*), 124, 172n9
cosmopoetics, 61
cosmotheism, 34, 38
cosmotheology, 31
couple, 153–57, 160, 162–63, 167–68, 171
creatio ex materia, 6
creatio ex nihilo, 1, 11, 22, 80, 82, 99, 121
cultural anthropology, 141
cybernetics, 115

d'Espagnat, Bernard, 40–41, 106
Dajbog, 38–39
Ḍākinī, 22–24, 175n45
Dalai Lama, 214n11
dancing, 101
Daoism, 178–79n17
dark energy, 16, 173n23, 191–92n52
dark love, 168
dark matter, 128, 168, 191–92n52
darkness, 10–11, 14, 71, 137
Dasein, 77–78, 154
daughters, 134
David of Dinant, 122–23, 144, 146, 209n23

Davies, Douglas J., 120
De Beauvoir, Simone, 193n62
De Chardin, Teilhard, 21, 51, 59
De Clairvaux, Bernard, 215n21
death, 10, 14, 42, 45, 50, 81, 94, 105, 135, 142, 147, 181n29, 182–83n38, 191n49, 197–98n39, 208n13
deathlessness, 10
decadence, 35
deconstruction, 16, 78, 84, 160
deification, 120, 147, 210n33
deists, 35
Deleuze, Gilles, 115
delirium, 71
Deloria, Vine, 29, 39–40, 43
Demeter, 21
demons, 29, 127–28, 131
Denisovans, 57, 183–84n3
Denz, Jacob, 18–19
depth psychology, 106
Derrida, Jacques, 74, 98, 100–101, 118, 192n54, 193n62
Descartes, Rene, 88, 192n54, 196–97n33
desert, 34, 119, 183n41
desire (*kāma/tapas*), 15, 154, 157, 161–62, 173n20, 213n56
determinism, 88, 115
Dewey, John, 52, 113–16, 119, 136, 201n9, 207n92
dharma, 60
dharma-body, 155, 213n8
dharmatā, 24
différance, 13, 74
Dionysius the Areopagite, 70, 141
Diotime, 18
discontinuity, 37
divine breath, 9, 140, 143, 159–60, 188–89n5
divine ear (*dibba-sota-dhātu*), 107

divine eye (*dibba-cakkhu/ catūpapatañāṇa*), 107
divinization, 2, 25, 121, 136, 141, 208n13
domination, 1
doves, 119
Downing, Barry H., 205
dragon, 44, 182n37
dreams, 94–95, 103–104, 176n7, 197–98n39
dualis, 153–54, 162–64, 166, 169, 213n5
dukkaṭa, 107
Dust Bowl, 130, 204–205n72
dwelling, 2, 4, 8, 30, 38, 40, 44–45, 75–76, 83–84, 132, 157, 205–206n76

ecclesiology, 148
economics, 31, 178n14
ecotheology, 58
Eden, 210–11n36
Edwards, Denis, 58, 114
Egan, Timothy, 129
egoism/egotistic, 98
Egypt (ancient), 35
Einstein, Albert, 105–106, 115, 133, 217n56
Eckhart, Meister, 62
electricity, 157, 204–205n72
Elijah, 140
Elohim, 11, 13–14, 80, 202n31
embodied spirit, 25, 147
embryogenesis, 117
Emerson, Ralph W., 113, 211n37
emptiness, 10, 14–15, 156, 213n8
Engels, Friedrich, 184n6
entanglement, 2, 30–31, 37, 47, 101–102, 137, 161, 168, 174–75n4
entropy, 30
environmental crisis, 1, 7, 25, 30, 50, 131

environmental ethics, 29, 42–43
epistemology, 29, 96, 108, 184n6, 185–86n24
Ereignis, 74–78
Eros, 159, 173n20, 214–15n12
erotic/eroticism, 157, 161, 164, 214n12
eschatology, 8, 12, 22–25, 69, 171n3
Eschenmeyer, K.A., 122
esotericism, 55, 121, 123, 203n45
ether, 76, 80, 82, 101, 202n31
ethnography, 37, 176n8, 177n10
ethnology, 33, 36, 179–80n22
ethnophilosophy, 31, 177n10
Ettinger, Bracha, 90, 98, 101
eucharist, 193n68
Evans-Pritchard, E.E., 125
evil, 7, 19, 119, 144, 174n42, 182n37
evolution/evolutionism, 35, 61, 64–65, 121
evolutionary biology, 117
excitation, 102, 126, 168
exhalation, 199n44
exorcism, 204n57
Expanse (TV series), 205–207n76
experimental metaphysics, 91, 197n38
extinction, 50, 172n2
extrasensory perception, 95, 105, 194n5

Faas, Robert, 214n12
fatalism, 115
fate, 30, 100
father-mother-in-union, 155
fear, 19, 163
feminist theology, 178–79n17
Ferguson, Kennan, 57
fetishism, 98
Feuerbach, Ludwig, 3–4, 50–55, 58–61, 63–65, 72, 141, 156–57, 164–66, 184n6, n8, 185n15, n21, 185–86n24, 192n54, 193n62, 211n37, 215n13, n16, 217n48
Fichte, J.G., 98, 122, 202–203n36, 217n48
finitude/finiteness, 174n36, 114
fire, 10, 16, 30, 38, 42, 44–45, 47, 51–52, 60, 65, 76, 82, 148, 157, 179n20, 181n29, 182n37
flesh, 16, 21, 51–53, 55, 58–59, 64–66, 80, 83, 164, 166, 191n42, 216n46
Florschütz, Gottlieb, 196n31
flourishing, 32, 69, 99, 139
folklore, 40
force, 2–3, 30, 37–43, 45, 50, 57, 89, 90–91, 106, 109, 114, 118, 127–28, 131, 144, 146, 158, 161, 167, 180n23, 181n33
forgiveness, 69, 77
fountain-spirit, 52–53, 58, 65, 67
Fourfold, 38, 76
Fourth Lateran Council, 148
fragrance(s), 168
Freud, Sigmund, 52, 98, 100–101, 195n21, 197–98n39
fungi, 64

Gaia (goddess), 18
galaxy, 137, 183n42, 216n30
Gebara, Ivone, 11, 22
Gehenna, 210–11n36
genealogical love, 74
Genesis, 11, 14, 188–89n5
genetics, 56–57
Gentiles, 143
geocentrism, 136
German Idealism, 52, 123
gesture/gesturing, 1, 3, 16, 38, 70–73, 77–78, 84, 122–23, 129, 150–51, 159–61, 163–64, 166, 179–80n22
gift, 73–75, 77, 83, 156, 210n33

gnosis, 153, 155
God the Creator, 11
God the Father, 79–80, 202n31
God-Being, 78, 84
God-Man, 185n21
Golding, William, 57
Golgotha, 30
Gospel of John, 58, 159
Gospel of Mark, 183n41
Gospel of Philip, 159
Gothic, 212n50
Gourgouris, Stathis, 179n21
grace, 46, 55, 64, 66, 78, 92–93, 120, 142, 147, 207n91, 210n33, 212n55
gradualism, 84
Grafenauer, Niko, 7, 162–63
gravity, 89, 109, 115, 122–23, 132–33, 135, 167–68
Gray, Charles, 206n81
Great Tantra of the Lion's Perfected Display-Energy, 153–54, 156
Greece/Greek people, 20, 34–35, 40, 79, 148
Greene, Brian, 199n49
Green, Michael B., 133
Gregersen, Niels Henrik, 56, 58, 183n40
Gregory the Great, 56
Grim, John, 31
Grosz, Elizabeth, 117–18
ground, 3, 12, 17, 19–20, 22–23, 25, 53, 61, 63–64, 66, 95, 101–102, 109–10, 123, 125–26, 144, 154, 181n29, 183n40, 199n44, 217n57
grounding of love, 13
groundlessness, 12–13, 62
guilt (*Urschuld*), 156, 210–11n36

Hadewijch, 162
Haeckel, Ernst, 181–82n34
Haggadah, 210–211n36
Hanafi, Hasan, 208n15

harmony, 2, 157, 182–83n38
Harvey, Van A., 185n21
heart of the matter, 51, 53, 64, 66
heart-region/breast-region, 158
heat, 10, 12, 14–15, 154, 179n20
heaven, 10, 12, 16, 20, 22, 25, 50, 53, 95, 120, 191n47
Hegel, G.W.F., 9, 52, 88, 98, 122, 143, 148–50, 165–66
Heidegger, Martin, 20, 30, 71, 74–78, 82–83, 174n36
Heraclitus, 16–17
heresy, 89, 148, 211n38
Hermann, Ley, 156
Hertha, 18
heteronormativity, 161, 216n46
heterosexuality, 161
Higgs field/boson, 103–104, 132–33, 175n48, 191–92n52, 217n56
Hillesum, Etty, 7
Hippolytus, 158
Hölderlin, Friedrich, 17–20, 82, 174n34
Hollywood, Amy, 161–62
Holy Breath, 3–4, 22, 158–59, 192n57
Holy Spirit, 3–4, 55, 82–83, 139, 142–43, 148–49, 151, 158–60, 192n55, 210n33
homo faber, 141
homo religiosus, 141
homosexuality, 161
honey, 60
hope, 2, 69–70, 73, 79, 98, 119, 134, 142, 151, 210n33
Hopkins, Gerard Manley, 17, 20–21
horizontal transcendence, 42, 45, 164
human nature, 53–54, 185n21, 217n51
humility, 32, 46
hyperspace, 133, 206n77, n83
hypersphere/hyperspherical, 132, 167

hypostasis of things, 128

Iamblichus, 204n55
iconography, 155
iddhi, 107
idolatry, 73, 78, 179n21
Imhullu, 182n37
immaterialism, 80, 84
immortality, 185n21
indeterminism, 88
indigenous people and religions, 2–3, 30–34, 38–41, 46, 54, 88, 175n1, 177n9
indigenousness, 185n21
Indra, 44
infinite/infinity, 20–21, 47, 61, 84, 88, 114, 123, 127, 131, 135, 137, 161, 163–66, 178n15
inhalation, 199n44
Innocent III, 148
intelligence, 80–81, 91, 121, 128, 132–33, 126, 206–207n86
intersexuality, 39
Interstellar (film), 116, 129–32, 135–36, 167, 205n74, 206–207n86
intersubjectivity, 4, 166, 169, 184n8, 217n28
intimacy, 4, 20 74, 137, 163, 165–66, 168
intuition, 47, 50, 134, 146, 176n7
invisibility, 31, 33, 36, 45–46, 65, 83, 107, 113, 115, 118, 123, 128, 161, 169
invisible world, 113, 115, 118
Irigaray, Luce, 3, 9–10, 47, 50, 70, 73, 134, 140–41, 143, 148, 150–51, 163–65, 168, 184–85n12, 188–89n5, 193n62, n68, 208n9, 209n27, 214–15n12, 216n46
Islam, 208n15, 210n31, 210–11n26
Islamic studies, 179–80n22

Jacob's ladder, 141
Jacobsen, Knut A., 107
Jaina epistemology, 108
Jainism, 107–110
James, William, 95, 113–14, 125, 197n36
Jamison, Stephanie, 10
Jehovah, 80, 202n31
Jesus Christ, 2–3, 8, 23, 39, 45–47, 50, 55–58, 61, 64, 67, 79–80, 82–83, 120, 147, 150, 159–60, 166–67, 183n41, 185n21, 188–89n5, 202n31, 205–206n76, 212n55, 222n40
Joachim of Fiore, 9, 25, 139–43, 149–50, 208n7, n9
Johnson, Elizabeth, 56, 58–59, 186n27, 187n39
Jones, Ernst, 197–98n39
Josephson-Storm, Jason Ā., 196–97n33
Josiah, 179n21
Judeo-Christianity, 3, 11, 22, 44, 139, 149, 178–79n17, 188–89n5
Judeo-paganism, 46, 212n55
Jung, Carl G., 3, 88, 95, 98, 100, 103–108, 195n21, 199n52, 200n55
justice, 11, 118–19

Kačarji, 44
kāma, 15, 154, 173n20
Kant, Immanuel, 18–20, 52, 122, 166, 195n23
karma, 108–110
Kearney, Richard, 173n22
Keller, Catherine, 3, 11–14, 17, 22–23, 40, 47, 88, 98, 102, 106, 137, 159–61, 175–76n4, 199n49
kenosis, 64
kevala/kevalin, 108
kevalajñāna, 108
khora, 15, 19, 22–23, 25, 30, 119, 173n22, 194n13

Kierkegaard, Søren, 52
King Follett, 81–82
kinship, 18, 31
Kircher, Athanasius, 94
kiss/kissing, 4, 24, 152, 155, 157–63, 165, 169
Klapwijk, Jakob, 56
koinonos, 159
Kolob, 205–206n76
Kosovel, Srečko, 49, 183n1
Kres, 38, 181n29
Kropf, Andrea, 106

lama(s), 24
Larson, Glen A., 205–206n76
laughter, 72–73, 78, 149
leaf/leaves, 4, 29, 63–64, 129
Leviathan, 44
Lévinas, Emmanuel, 191n51
liberation theology, 12, 208n15
lineage, 23–24, 50, 192n54
linearity, 14, 41
listening, 34, 164
Llull, Ramon, 127
logos, 16–17, 19, 25, 49
Lopez, Donald S., 214n9
lungs, 7, 9, 69, 82, 191n51

machines, 117
macrocosm, 1, 10, 42, 50, 60, 96–97, 124, 135, 137, 206n81
Madonna, 18–19
magical thinking, 126, 193–94n4
Mahāyāna, 155, 214n11
Mahdī, 147
Malli, 110
manaḥ-paryāya/manaḥ-paryaya, 108
manaḥparyayajñāna, 108, 110
manas, 173n20
Maori people and philosophy, 176n7
Marder, Elisa, 101
Marduk, 182n37

Marrett, R.R., 36
Marshall, Ian, 132
martyrdom, 147
Marx, Karl, 51–52, 149, 184n6
Marxism, 212n46
Mary, 17–23, 95, 156, 173n22, 174n40, 188–89n5, 194n13
Mary Magdalene, 159–60
masculinity, 162
Massignon, Louis, 210–11n36
materialism/new materialism, 9, 30–31, 50, 70, 80, 84, 87, 89, 98–99, 145, 148, 184n4, 191–92n52, 202n32
materiaphobia, 99
maternal, 18, 20, 104
mathematics, 127
matijñāna, 108
matrix, 3, 7, 12, 14–17, 19–25, 33, 38, 40, 66, 110, 133, 156, 168, 175n48, 191–92n52, 194n13
Matrix (film), 120
matrix of spirit, 59
matrixiality, 15–17, 19
Maximus the Confessor, 63, 210n33
māyā, 200n76
Mechtild of Magdeburg, 161
meditation, 16, 107, 163
Medvešček-Klančar, Pavel, 31, 176–77n8
membrane (brane), 131–33, 135, 167, 205n73
memory/memories, 45, 117–18, 127, 143, 163, 216n46
mental illness, 71
Merleau-Ponty, Maurice, 3–4, 8, 16–17, 19, 51, 62–66, 117, 129, 191n51, 192n54
Merton, Thomas, 22
Mesmer, Franz Anton, 94–95, 196n26
mesocosm, 10, 124, 135, 185–86n24, 203n45, 206n81
Messiah (Judaism), 140

messianic age/messianism, 9, 140, 143
metal of truth, 123
metal(s), 30, 45, 52, 126
metamorphoses, 72
microbes, 206–207n86
microcosm, 1, 10, 60, 78, 96–97, 124, 135, 137, 206n81
microorganisms, 50
Middle Ages, 9, 33, 140, 149, 157, 161
midwife, 18
migration, 141–42
Mikhailov, Nikolai, 33
Miller, Adam S., 69, 131
mindfulness, 168
mineral(s), 2, 30, 40, 46, 49, 51–52, 54–55, 64, 90–91, 121, 128, 148, 181–82n34, 183n40
miracles, 2, 95–96, 98, 106, 121, 133, 167
mnemic theme, 3, 116–18
monarchy/monarchical, 11, 38, 42, 44
monotheism, 34–35, 37–39, 179n21
moon/moons, 33–34, 44, 60, 76, 172n9, 177n9, 181n29, 203n45
Mora, 181n29
More, Henry, 179
Mormon cosmology, 79–80, 212n45
Mormonism, 3, 69–71, 78, 80–82, 84, 119–21, 125–26, 136, 202n31, 204n54, 205–206n76
mortals, 75–76, 164, 200n76
mother, 16, 18–19, 21, 23–24, 39, 41–42, 80, 104, 140, 153, 191n47, 197–98n39, 202n31
Mother Buddha, 23
mountains, 41–43, 54
mourning, 195n23, 203n38
mtDNA, 57
Muir, John, 50
Müller, Max, 35
Murphy (Interstellar), 130, 134

mystery, 8–11, 17, 31, 53, 64, 73, 79, 92, 151, 154, 156, 158, 160, 165, 172n2, 199n46
mystical theology, 25, 62, 70, 141
mysticism, 97

Nāginis (goddesses), 156
Nāsadāsīya, 9, 13
natality, 15
natural eschatology, 8, 25, 171n3
Naturvolken, 36
Nauvoo, 205–206n76
Neanderthals, 57–58
Neo-Platonism, 88, 123
Neptune/neptunism, 52
netherworld, 43–45
New Testament, 9, 56, 58, 140, 206n15
Newar religion, 203n45
Newton, Isaac, 88
nexus, 4, 63–64, 90, 92, 94, 98, 101, 115, 124, 129, 168, 203n45
nexus metaphysicus, 96, 100, 103, 109
nibbana, 107
Nicodemus, 82
Nicolas of Cusa, 88, 123
Nietzsche, Friedrich, 52, 71–74, 78, 114, 117, 141, 149
nihilism, 74, 77–78
Nikrmana, 39, 41, 44
nirvāṇa, 155, 206n77
Noble Savage, 57
Nolan, Christopher, 88, 116, 122–24, 126–30, 132, 134–35, 206–207n86
nonbeing, 13, 16–18, 24–25, 173n19
nonlocality, 88, 106
noogenesis, 61, 64
nursing, 15, 21

O'Donnell, John, 22
occult/occultism, 95, 98, 100, 195n24, 197–98n39, 198n41

Old Testament, 4, 9, 59, 140
Olivelle, Patrick, 124
omniscience, 108, 110
onto-theological gap, 74
ontotheology, 74, 88
oral tradition, 31–32, 176–77n8
organ(s) (body), 4, 117, 165–66, 169, 191n51
Oruka, Henry Odera, 177n10
ousia, 22

Padence, 43
paganism, 32–33, 42, 46, 125
paleology, 88, 124, 193–94n4, 203n43
Pāli, 155
panentheism, 101–102
panpathy, 4, 100, 109–10
pantheism, 147–48, 210n34
Papua New Guinea, 179–80n22
paranormal, 89, 91, 93, 95–98, 103–104, 106, 196n28, 196–97n33, 197–98n39, 206n83
parapsychology, 98–99, 106
Paris, 144–45, 147
Parmenides, 38
parokṣa, 108
particles, 46, 106, 109, 133, 137, 161, 167, 217n56
Patañjali, 108
patriarch/patriarchy, 12, 38, 140
Pauli, Wolfgang, 88, 103, 105
Peacocke, Arthur, 56, 187n9
Peirce, Charles S., 113
perichoresis, 101, 173n22
Persia, 3, 34, 122, 146, 149, 210n34
Perun, 180n25
Peters, John Durham, 80, 101, 212n45
Peters, Ted, 135–36, 207n91
phenomenology, 51, 149
philosophical theology, 3, 8, 18, 29, 32, 38, 40, 43, 47, 69, 71, 78, 88–89, 93, 97, 98, 136, 156

philosophy of biology, 115
philosophy of religion, 29, 32, 52, 113, 115, 164, 184n6
philosophy of sensibility, 165
photosynthesis, 56
Pile, Steve, 198n41
plane of immanence, 106, 132
plants, 30, 32, 42, 44–46, 52, 54–56, 64, 76, 84, 121, 184–85n12
plasticity, 4, 54, 58, 64, 66
Plato, 46, 88
Platonism, 88, 123, 181n33
Pleterski, Andrej, 33, 38–39, 44, 175n1, 177n9, 178n13, n15
pluralism, 37
pneuma, 12, 17, 55, 82–83, 143, 155, 157–60, 183n41, 199n44, 209n19, 215n16
pneumatic water therapy, 55, 165
poetry, 10, 20
Pogačnik, Marko, 50
polar bear, 50
polytheism, 34–35, 39, 114, 179n21
positivism, 52
postanthropocentrism, 50
postapocalyptic/postapocalypticism, 129–30, 134, 205–206n76
post-Christianity, 3–4, 22, 25, 46–47, 51, 79, 113, 147, 149, 171n2, n3
post-Enlightenment, 208n13
posthumanism, 50, 205–206n76
prajñāpāramitā, 23
prana/*prāṇa*, 24, 95, 124, 155–56, 160, 179n20
Pratt, Orson, 80
pratyakṣa, 108
prayer, 2, 82, 95, 104
pre-being, 17
precognition, 95, 98, 105
predestination, 90
pregnancy, 17, 19
premonition, 115

pre-Socratic, 3, 52, 55, 65, 78, 122, 148
Price, Robert, 159
primordial soup, 207n86
primordiality, 19, 61, 65
procreation, 13, 44
prophecy, 143, 145
Propp, Vladimir Yakovlevich, 182n37
proto-consciousness, 133, 217n56
proximity, 3–4, 8, 24, 74–75, 78, 84, 93, 101, 106, 147, 150, 162, 168, 183n41
psi phenomena, 89, 94–95, 97–99, 104–105, 194n5, 195n24, 199n52, 206n83
psyche, 101–102, 104–105, 125, 160, 168, 181–82n34, 209n19
psychoanalysis, 16, 141, 197n39
psychoanalysis of nature, 141
psychokinesis, 105, 194n5
psychology, 95, 97–99, 106
pulsation of religion, 141–42, 150
purity (*viśuddhi*), 108, 110, 146

quantum moment, 47, 118
quantum nonlocality (nonlocal correlation), 106
quantum physics, 40, 43, 88, 99, 101, 106, 117, 129–30, 132–33, 167, 191–92n52, 199n47
quantum superposition, 56
quantum theology, 3, 30, 87, 101, 108, 132, 135
quantum vacuum, 126, 132–33, 168, 217n56
queer, 161
Qur'ān, 146

radiation, 155, 196n26
radical/radicalism, 1, 22, 46, 54, 56, 72–73, 77, 81, 89, 93, 102, 116, 119, 121, 126, 166

recollection of past lives (*pubbenivāsānussatiñāṇa*), 107
redemption, 130, 140, 188–89n5, 209n27
regeneration, 92–93, 117
reincarnation/rebirth, 107
Relativity theory, 99, 105, 115
religion of nature, 54
religious beliefs/religiosity, 95, 114, 196n28
religious studies, 3, 34–36, 127, 179n21, 179–80n22, 180n25
Renaissance, 146
reservoir, 3, 113, 116, 118
resonance, 170, 196n26
respiration, 68, 160, 192n54
resurrection, 95, 104, 159–60
Ruether, Rosemary, 12, 17, 23
revelation, 22–23, 25, 34–36, 55, 61, 69, 83–84, 92, 120–21, 136–37, 143, 150, 164–65, 182–83n38
Ṛgvedic creation hymn, 9, 13, 15, 154
Rhine, J.B., 105
rituals, 125, 151, 204n55
Rivera, Mayra, 164, 216n46
Ṛksaṃhitā, 12
Rnying-ma practice (Nyingma sect), 214n9
Robbins, Jeffrey W., 52
robotics, 115
Rorty, Mary, 78
Rorty, Richard, 70, 78–80, 114, 151
Rosa, Hartmut, 196n26
Royle, Nicolas, 101
Ruah Elohim, 13
Rublev, Andrei, 173n22, 194n13
Russian Sophiology, 174n40
Ruyer, Raymond, 3, 113, 115–21, 126, 133, 136

Sabbath age, 139–40, 143
sacredness, 3, 51, 54, 72

sacredness of breath, 3
sacrifice, 53, 125, 182–83n38
Saint George, 44
saliva, 24
salvation, 46, 70, 71, 81, 93, 132, 141–42, 147–50, 172n4, 208n13, 212n50
Samantabhadrī, 23, 155–56
saṃsāra, 155
sarx, 59
saturated phenomena, 83
Saturn, 131
scar(s), 169, 216n46
Schelling, F.W.J., 8–9, 12–13, 15–16, 35, 52, 61–63, 65–66, 98, 122–23, 150, 154, 156–57, 185n15, 192n54, 199n44, 202–203n36, 213n6, 215n13
Schleiermacher, Friedrich, 52, 54
Schmidt, Wilhelm, 34–37, 179–78n22, 180n25
Schneider, Laurel, 38–39
Schopenhauer, Arthur, 3, 87–98, 100–110, 117, 168, 194n12, 195n21, n23
Scotus Eriugena, 145
secret of creation, 16, 166
secularism, 70
seer, 10, 60, 65, 124
self-affection, 2, 70, 73, 150–51, 213n56
semen, 15, 60
semideath (*demi-mort*), 72
semigod (*demi-dieu*), 71
sensibility, 8–9, 51, 66, 165, 184n4, 185–86n24
sensuous contemplation, 51
sex/sexuality, 39, 157, 161, 165, 214–15n12
sexual abuse, 182n36
sexual difference, 1, 145, 154–55, 193n62, 214–15n12

sexuate theology, 156, 214–15n12
sickness/fever, 12
silence, 62, 154, 163, 187–88n49, 193n68
Silesius, Angelus, 87
Simmer-Brown, Judith, 23
Simmons, Ernest L., 101, 199n46, n47
Simpson, Christopher Ben, 63, 129
Singer, Wolf, 206n81
singularity/singularities, 73, 205n73, 206n77, 213n56
Sioux people, 39
skin, 164–67, 197–98n39, 216n46
sky, 24, 31, 33, 41, 44, 49, 75–76, 164, 181n29
slavery, 142
Slavic monotheism, 179n21
Slovenian language, 154, 213n5
Smith, Joseph, 79–82, 120–21, 191n49, 202n31
Smith, Wilfred Cantwell, 35–36, 179–80n22, 180n24, 182n38
snake, 41–44
sociology of religion, 141
Solar System, 205–206n76, 206–207n86
solipsism, 88
solitude, 166, 213n56
Sloterdijk, Peter, 141–42, 150, 192n54
Song of Songs, 158
Sophia, 22–23, 156–57, 178–79
sophiology, 21, 23
spacetime, 7, 97, 104, 109, 130, 154, 176n7
speculation, 125, 166
spells, 125
Spinoza, Baruch, 148
spirit world, 81
Spiritual Church, 9, 140
spiritual materiality, 40
Spreckelmeyer, Hermann, 156–57

Index | 245

śrutajñāna, 108
Staal, Frits, 203n44
standing reserve, 30
stardust, 46, 126
Staroverstvo, 31–34, 42–44, 175n1, 176n5, 178n14
stars, 7, 76, 128, 136
starvation, 50, 130
stigmata, 102
stillness, 62, 162–63, 168
stomach, 90, 132, 165, 167–69
stones, 2, 28, 30, 40–42, 45–46, 51–52, 56, 90, 127–28, 181–82n34, 183n40
sublime, 155–56, 162
subterranean connection, 96, 100, 102, 195n21
suffering, 45, 53, 93, 100, 147, 194n12, 199n48
Sufis/Sufism, 146
sun, 7, 16, 47, 60, 76, 172n9, 203n45
supernatural, 57, 98–99, 104, 107–108, 110–11, 113–14, 119, 196n28, 198n41
superstring theory, 133, 205n73, 206n84
Supreme Being, 4, 30, 36–38, 57, 124, 180n23, 206n77
Sūrya, 16
Sutra, 107–108, 110
Svetovid, 38
symbolism, 25, 33, 125, 153, 155, 215n15
sympathy, 92–93, 96, 100
synchronicity, 3, 14, 76, 87–88, 91, 98, 101, 103, 105, 107, 131, 168, 195n21, 199n47

tad ekam, 13–14, 154
Talmud, 8, 140, 210–11n36
Tantric bond, 153
Tantrism, 178–79n17

Tao/Dao, 115, 126, 201n10
Tao-God, 115, 201n10
tapas, 15, 154
Tattvārtha-Sūtra, 108, 110
Tau Ceti, 205–206n76
tears, 79
Tehom, 11, 14, 102, 217n57
tehomic alterity, 11
telepathic coupling, 47, 106, 168
telepathic knowledge (dibba-sota-dhātu/ paracittañāṇa), 107
telepathy/mindreading, 4, 58, 87, 90, 94–95, 97–101, 104–105, 107–10, 167–68, 175n48, 195n21, 197n36, 197–98n39, 198n40, n41
temporality, 9, 11, 13, 106, 115–16, 118–19, 121, 130, 133, 136, 153, 167, 195n23
terror, 25, 45, 142–43
tesseract, 130–33, 135, 206n77
theology of religion, 35–36, 179–80n22
theopoetics, 47
theosis, 120, 210n33
theotechnics, 141
thing-in-itself, 92
Third Testament, 9, 140, 150
Third Way, 11, 13
Thoreau, Henry D., 113–14
Thorne, Kip, 206n77, n83
Tibetan Tantras, 161
time travel, 115–16, 129, 134
timelessness, 41, 45
Tīrthaṅkara, 110
Torah, 8, 140
totemism, 34
transubstantiation, 193n68
tree of life, 118
trees, 29, 41, 54, 126, 184–85n12
triad/tradic/tročan, 42–43, 45, 79
Triglav, 29, 33, 38, 42
Trinick, John, 160

trinitarianism, 22, 80, 101, 140, 159, 199n44, 202n31
Trinity, 38, 42, 83, 101–102, 140, 143, 173n22, 194n13, 199n44, n46
twoness, 154–55, 162–63

uncertainty, 88
unconscious, 54, 72, 104–105, 197–98n39
uncreated intelligence, 80
uncreation, 7
Unger, Roberto M., 147, 211n37
Unground, 17, 19
Ungrund, 12, 62
unitarianism, 179n21
unity of space, 37
unity of time, 37
unknown God, 115–16, 118
Upanishads, 187n44, 203n44
Urkultur, 36
Ur-Monotheismus, 35
Uroffenbarung, 36
uterus/uterine, 18, 25, 119

vacuum, 40, 103, 126, 132–33, 168, 217n56
vacuum state of energy, 103
Vajrayāna, 155–56, 214n10, 215n15
Valdesians, 209n24
vanity, 77, 80–81, 83
Vattimo, Gianni, 142–43, 150, 208n15
Vedas, 44, 154, 200n76
Vedic Sāṃhitās, 154
vegetables/vegetative, 56, 184–85n12
veil, 71, 109–10, 200n76
Velika Baba, 39
Vilež, 38, 181n29
vision, 4–5, 58–60, 103, 113, 149, 207n91
vitalism, 46, 50, 145, 184n4
Vulcan/Vulcanism, 52

vulnerability, 81, 102
vulva, 161

Waldenfels, Hans, 179–80n22
warmth, 14–16, 154
water, 3, 10–11, 29–30, 38, 41–45, 47, 51–52, 54–55, 60, 65, 75–76, 83, 118, 129, 138, 148, 165–66, 179n20, 182n37, 185–86n24, 215n16
Webb, Stephen, 84, 103–105, 125–26, 191–92n52
West/Western, 1–2, 4, 8, 18, 23, 34, 38–40, 51, 53, 88–89, 103, 108, 141, 145–46, 149, 156, 160, 176n5, 176–77n8, 177n10, 179–80n22, 192n54, 193n62, 195n24, 196–97n33, 208n15
Whitehead, Alfred North, 40, 88, 99, 113, 160, 166, 197n35
will to power, 117
wind, 10–11, 13–14, 16, 20, 24, 45, 47, 60, 76–78, 80–83, 124, 142, 151, 172n9, 182n37, 203n45
Wirheit, 154
Wirth, Jason M., 12
Witzel, Michael, 124, 203n45
womb, 15–23, 25, 90, 119, 154, 168, 173n22, 185–86n24, 194n13, 209n23
womb of creation, 19, 209n23
womb-heart, 17, 22–23, 173n22, 194n13
woods, 41
Word of God, 61
World War I, 176–77n8, 178n14
worm(s), 89, 109, 144
wormhole, 131
wound(s), 102, 161, 169
Wunn, Ina, 57

Yeshua, 55

Yoga, 107, 214n11
Yosemite Valley, 50
Yup'ik people, 32

Zarathustra, 79, 149

Zduhci, 45
Živa, 181n29
Zohar, Danah, 132
zoology, 119, 181–82n34
Zoroaster/Zoroastrianism, 210n34

About the Author

Lenart Škof is Head of the Institute for Philosophical and Religious Studies at the Science and Research Centre (Koper, Slovenia) and Dean of Alma Mater Europaea University—Faculty ISH (Ljubljana, Slovenia). He is a member of the European Academy of Sciences and Arts in Salzburg and president of the Slovenian Society for Comparative Religion. He coedited *Shame, Gender Violence, and Ethics: Terrors of Injustice* (2021), *Atmospheres of Breathing* (2018), *The Poesis of Peace* (2017), and *Breathing with Luce Irigaray* (2013). Škof is the author of several books, among them *Antigone's Sisters: On the Matrix of Love* (2021) and *Breath of Proximity: Intersubjectivity, Ethics and Peace* (2015). He is editor-in-chief of the Routledge Critical Perspectives on Breath and Breathing series (with Magdalena Górska), and his main research interests are in respiratory philosophy, new elemental philosophy, and philosophical theology.

Homepage: https://zrs-kp.academia.edu/LenartŠkof.

www.ingramcontent.com/pod-product-compliance
Lightning Source LLC
Chambersburg PA
CBHW030617230426
43661CB00053B/2033